Where Am I And Who's Winning?

ndrew Baker read English at Cambridge University
efore joining the staff of *Vogue*. He has subsequently
ritten for *Harper's & Queen, Esquire, GQ*, the *Evening
andard* and the *Observer*, among many other publica-
ons. In 1993 he joined the *Independent on Sunday* as
 sports writer, and since 1997 has been a sports feature
writer for the *Daily Telegraph*. Andrew lives in London
with his wife and two daughters, and would like to
spend less time at Heathrow airport.

WHERE AM I
AND WHO'S WINNING?

Travelling the World of Sport

Andrew Baker

YELLOW JERSEY PRESS
LONDON

Published by Yellow Jersey Press 2004

2 4 6 8 10 9 7 5 3

First published in Great Britain in 2004 by
Yellow Jersey Press

Yellow Jersey Press
Random House, 20 Vauxhall Bridge Road,
London SW1V 2SA

Random House Australia (Pty) Limited
20 Alfred Street, Milsons Point, Sydney,
New South Wales 2061, Australia

Random House New Zealand Limited
18 Poland Road, Glenfield,
Auckland 10, New Zealand

Random House (Pty) Limited
Endulini, 5A Jubilee Road, Parktown 2193,
South Africa

The Random House Group Limited Reg. No. 954009
www.randomhouse.co.uk

A CIP catalogue record for this book
is available from the British Library

ISBN 0–224–07273–0

Papers used by Random House are natural, recyclable products
made from wood grown in sustainable forests. The manufacturing
processes conform to the environmental regulations of the country of origin

Typeset by Palimpsest Book Production Limited,
Polmont, Stirlingshire

Printed and bound in Great Britain by
Mackays of Chatham plc, Chatham, Kent

For Ingrid, Lucy and Emily,
without whom this book would not have been possible.
Or necessary.

Where Am I And Who's Winning?

Foreword

I'm a sports writer. I watch all sorts of sports in all sorts of countries, then write reports and feature articles about them which are published in a newspaper. This is a fine and privileged occupation, and one to be disclosed with tact. People who do respectable, important jobs don't like to hear about it. They get grumpy, or vindictive. Sports writing is categorised alongside beer-tasting and aphrodisiac-evaluation. People say: 'More of a hobby than a job, isn't it?'

This is the reality. The Sports Editor issues a memo from his lair at Canary Wharf. It pops up in my inbox, headed: 'Andrew Baker. Schedule.' I'm looking at one now. It tells me that my next job is to locate and interview a parallel snowboarder (whatever that is), that in two weeks' time I am to fly to Italy for a Formula One race, that I am due to visit a yachtsman in Florida (date to be confirmed) and that the month of August will be spent preparing for and attending the Olympics in Athens. It all sounds fairly predictable, doesn't it?

But experience suggests that the parallel snowboarder will be available for interview only at the top of a mountain in Carpathia next Tuesday fortnight, which will also turn out to be the only date that the Floridian yachtsman can manage. Meanwhile, all the hotel rooms in Bologna will have been booked and I will have to secure accommodation in a flop-house above a trattoria, and my wife will have reminded me that she had already earmarked August for family holidays, and what do the International Olympic Committee propose to do about that?

When I get home from my current trip, a fax will be waiting for me: a press release, in all likelihood, announcing that Ellen MacArthur will be available for interview at the launch of her new trimaran at a remote fishing port in Brittany at nine a.m. the next day. There will be a note scribbled at the top in the Sports Editor's firm hand, command dressed up as request: 'AB: pls attend.'

I keep my passport in my jacket pocket, a toothbrush and a change of underwear in my laptop case, and my wife in a state of permanent insecurity. 'I have to leave for Brittany in three and a half minutes,' I'll call downstairs. 'I'll write you a list of the important household jobs that I haven't done. I'll be back in three days. Or five. It depends on the tides.'

Most of the large-scale trips are planned months in advance: we know when the Olympics are going to happen, even if there is occasionally some doubt about where. But within the framework of a major competition there is ample scope for hectic travel, as I found soon after I joined my current employers.

'Football. World Cup. France.' That's what the schedule said. But there was nothing simple about the project. Weeks before leaving I had to get used to watching football, and if that sounds like the most ludicrous excuse for freeloading you have ever heard in your life I can only say that there was, unfortunately, more to it than flopping down in front of *Match of the Day* with a can of lager. I had to learn the technique of match reporting, sending half my copy at half-time, a little more with twenty minutes remaining and an introduction and conclusion as the final whistle blew. I can hear the chorus building: 'What's so difficult about that?'

Football writers need to develop a third eye, an organ which allows them to tap away at a laptop while remaining aware of what is happening on the field, telling them exactly when to look up in order to see a crucial tackle or deftly worked goal. My third eye seemed constantly on the blink. As I schlepped around the country contributing modest reports about modest matches, I found I was developing, instead of a third eye, a condition that might be described as midfield myopia. I'd scan the field for the incipient lull which would allow me to craft a sentence or two, convince myself that the game had gone dead, and drop my eyes to the screen only to hear a roar as a striker tumbled writhing to the ground in the penalty area, or looped in the winner from the centre circle.

I spent half my time sneaking sideways glances at the notebooks of the reporters packed sardine-tight with me into the press box. They used shorthand. I didn't. The other half of my time was expended on formations: every report had to conclude with the teams, including the substitutes and the times at which they took the field and, worst of all, the tactical line-ups they employed.

The thing that finished my brief and inglorious career as a match reporter was semi-colons. When a team lines up in the four-four-two formation, you write the goalkeeper's name, then a semi-colon; then you identify the four starting defenders; midfielders; and two strikers.

I know, I know: you could do it in an instant. So could your kid sister. You have probably read in the paper about dogs who bark tactical advice at *Match of the Day*. Mrs Bradshaw behind the fish counter at my local supermarket, who has difficulty distinguishing salmon from herring, can tell a wing-back from a stopper. I couldn't, and I had no commentary team to confirm that my version was the right one. Why wouldn't the players stand still for a minute?

I pored over my sketched diagrams and annotated my match programmes. Is that a back three with a sweeper? Is he a winger, or an optimistic full-back? Is that guy anchoring the midfield, or a lazy striker? Two up front and one in the hole: fashionable forward strategy or pornographic scenario?

Thus unprepared, off to France I went, clutching my laptop and huge suitcase containing far too many clothes and *The Bluffer's Guide to Football Formations*.

I had a kind of glorified Inter-Rail card, a £700 *grand billet* that allowed me to hop on and off any train I fancied in order to get from city to city, match to match. Come the end of the tournament, my knowledge of football had increased hardly at all, but the three-chord phrase that announces the arrival of a train into a French station was waking me in the night like an hourly alarm call.

Any delusions of grandeur were dissipated in the chilly evening air of the Stade de Mosson in Montpellier, where I watched Paraguay and Bulgaria contest – if that is not too strong a word – a goalless draw. This was not a glamour tie. I was not going to watch any glamour ties. Nor was I going to watch any England matches, a point that had eluded the friends who had been bemoaning my good fortune before I left home.

From Montpellier I travelled by mighty high-speed TGV up to Lens in the north, to watch Chile vs. Austria. When England played their opening match against Tunisia, I was on my way to Lyons to write about the Iranian team. My brother phoned me on the train with score flashes. He sounded very happy. I went to Paris, where I solved an accreditation glitch in the magnificent Stade de France, but was not required to watch a match there. I lugged my bags back down to Lyons, then back up to Paris (to the shabby Parc des Princes) and on to the gastronomic powerhouse of Bordeaux, where I spent the night throwing up the remnants of a rancid prawn. The next afternoon I was woken by a kindly waiter in the press restaurant at the stadium. I had fallen asleep with my head on the table, narrowly missing a jam croissant, and was dimly aware that the match had started.

'Where am I?' I asked the solicitous *garçon*. 'And who's winning?'

My missions became increasingly bizarre. Match-reporting assignments mysteriously dwindled. I was sent to stake out the Argentine squad ahead of their quarter-final. They were based in a deliberately obscure location (a one-horse town, until the locals had eaten it) and I couldn't get within a quarter-mile of their training session.

But the Sports Editor didn't seem to mind: perhaps the further that I was kept from matters technical the better. So I was sent back to Lyons, and told to look for Australian Croatians.

I complained. 'This is ridiculous. Find the Argentine team? Fine. Find the Croatian team? That I can handle. I could probably manage to find some Croatia fans. But Croatia fans who come from Australia? It's impossible. Why not Belgium supporters from the Ukraine? Or Chile-crazed Scotsmen?'

'Andrew,' said the Sports Editor. 'Just get on with it.'

They were everywhere, of course: as Mrs Bradshaw behind the fish counter could probably have told me, Australian soccer is founded on a bedrock of Balkan emigrants. The Aussies are Croatia crazy.

I left my only smart jacket in a Lyons hotel wardrobe, went back to find it (too late) and missed my TGV to Marseilles. When my later train finally drew into that great and seedy southern city, I had twenty-three minutes to get to the ground before kick-off.

It is perfectly acceptable to be late for a party. It is quite all right (if you are the bride) to be late for your wedding. It is tolerable, though unpopular, to be late for a movie or a meal. But for certain occasions one really must be on time: the birth of a child, for example; a relative's funeral; a university final examination; a World Cup football match.

Dragging my suitcase behind me like a dead body, I stumped the unfriendly back streets of Marseilles looking for the stadium. I asked directions in a *tabac*, causing a fierce argument to break out. That way. No, that way. No, *that* way . . .

Like Tony Blair, I chose the third way, swiped the arm carrying my laptop across my brow, wiped away a pint of sweat and tugged back the sleeve of my jacket with my teeth to look at my watch: twelve minutes to kick-off. I didn't have the breath to curse. I picked up my pace, to the amusement of local youths too busy giggling even to think about an easy mugging.

I made it to the stadium with seven minutes to spare: minutes that were spent fruitlessly trying to force my suitcase into a locker in the press room. I approached the volunteers at the help desk. Would they mind my bag while I watched the game?

Mais non. Non non non. What if it was a bomb?

Weepily, I opened the suitcase and displayed my collection of punch-drunk boxer shorts and *vieux fromage* socks. The volunteers were horrified into submission, and locked the bag in a toilet cleaner's cupboard. I took my seat as the referee put his whistle to his lips.

That night, I slumped, trying to doze, on my whiffy suitcase aboard an overfull sleeper to Paris. Enough World Cup now, thank you.

I was not alone in my exhaustion. On the day of the final, all soccered out, I dragged myself on to the Eurostar at the Gare du Nord to go home. The world's greatest footballer had also found the tournament a strain. While I snoozed and twitched under the Channel, Ronaldo had a flip-out and his Brazilian team-mates were too stunned to respond. France had won the World Cup, as my wife told me when I arrived home ten minutes after the final whistle.

Missing the climax summed up my France '98 experience. I had specialised in cultural, sporting and geographical confusion, failed to see any match I had wanted to see, and discovered how little I knew about the art of getting from one place to another in a foreign land.

A lot more of that would follow, as I explored the wide borders of the sporting world and tested the extremes of the Sports Editor's patience. The job hasn't changed. Nor has my level of competence. But the scenery keeps moving. I write these words in a hotel in the capital of a tiny, dusty Middle Eastern state. The hotel opened three days ago. Next door to my room, a workman with a big drill is putting a few finishing touches to the decor. A loud Arabic argument is taking place outside my door, and the corridor is a bedlam of bed linen. The shower doesn't work, the mini-bar is Islamically empty, and the television shows only commentary on the Koran, pictures of the King and belly-dancing pop videos. According to the Foreign Office, this is not a good place for Westerners to be.

Last night I dreamed I was stuck in a feature film, a high-speed-chase epic, an amalgam of transport disasters. I occupied careering taxis, doomed buses, derailed trains, hopping from one to another without incurring a scratch. David Beckham was in there somewhere, with sensible hair, a dinner jacket and a gun; so was Tim Henman, in an Arabic dish-dash, and Michael Schumacher riding a camel. A very fast, red camel.

I woke pouring with sweat, in cold and clammy sheets, and heard the call to prayer from the mosque on the far side of the tatty car park behind the hotel. It was four o'clock in the morning. If this is more of a hobby than a job, I thought, perhaps I could switch to basket-weaving.

I have to go. I have a bus to catch, then a plane, then another plane.

Where am I? Manama. Who's winning? The man with the drill.

I hope you enjoy the book.

Chapter One

Sodomy and
Synchronised Swimming

*Objectives: Attend and report on the Commonwealth Games
in Kuala Lumpur, Malaysia, paying particular attention to
synchronised swimming, ten-pin bowling and Scottish cricket.
Also rioting. Try to avoid tropical storms, death by bus and
arrest. Time allocated: three weeks.*

I woke with that sense of disorientation and time-slip that
always accompanies long-haul travel. Morning or night?
Morning. Morning in Kuala Lumpur, three days before the
start of the 1998 Commonwealth Games. What a strange
place to be. What a strange reason for being here. But this
is what I do, now. For three years, working for a fine but
underfinanced Sunday newspaper, I travelled around
Britain learning to be a sports writer. I went on one or two
long train journeys, occasionally stayed a night in a cheap
hotel. I flew once, to the Isle of Man. Then I joined a daily
newspaper with a bigger budget and things got a lot more
complicated.

I looked at my schedule one day not long after the World
Cup in France. It had sprouted, unfanfared, a new assignment: 'Commonwealth Games, Malaysia'. I rang my wife
and said: 'I seem to be going to Malaysia for three weeks.
Is that OK?'

She said: 'It will have to be, won't it?'

I felt elated, nervous, mean. Ingrid was pregnant with our second child. The first, Lucy, was fifteen months old. Very mean.

I packed, in the chilly English autumn, T-shirts, shorts, sun-tan lotion. Ingrid loves sunbathing. This simply wasn't fair. I promised presents all round, which made Lucy very happy, and strode off to the Tube trying to look more confident than I felt.

Now here I was: time to go to work. Time to get accredited.

The majority of the foreign press covering the Games were accommodated in the Mint Hotel, a giant glazed cube not far from the National Sports Complex where many of the events were to be held. I vaguely recalled driving past the Mint during my taxi ride from the airport the previous night, and driving on much, much further to reach the Quality Hotel (City Centre) which was my billet.

Among the pre-Games bumph I'd waded through on the flight, I recalled something about shuttle buses running from the city centre to the press-accreditation office at the Mint. In the lobby of my hotel half a dozen yellow-T-shirted Games volunteers scuttled around pretending to be busy, while two more sat behind a desk signposted 'Enquiries'.

I chose the less unattractive of the two young women. 'Can you tell me anything about buses to the media centre?'

'You want a bus?' She was incredulous, delighted: jumped to her feet and called something in Malay to a male colleague, who immediately started jabbering into a walkie-talkie as he headed for the hotel entrance. Action.

'Bus will be one moment,' the not-quite-so-ugly sister said.

Her sibling (you could tell they were related by the design of their chins, which should probably have been sent back to the drawing-board) gathered various pamphlets from the desk and shoved them under my nose. 'You must have some information,' she said.

I looked at brochures for shopping centres and folk museums for ten minutes, while the Chin Twins sat in tense silence, grimly resisting the impulse to tell me that the bus would be here in one moment.

Their friend with the walkie-talkie zoomed back into the lobby. 'Bus will be here very shortly. Bad traffic!' he cried, and burst into peals of laughter. 'Very bad traffic!' He scuttled out again.

Ten minutes later, the uglier sister topped up my pile of leaflets. 'Very bad traffic,' she murmured.

Thirty-two minutes after I had first asked about this form of transport, a battered red bus, looking like it had earned an honourable retirement after a lifetime ferrying school children, wheezed on to the hotel forecourt. The walkie-talkie man was beside himself with excitement. He escorted me to the bus door, accompanied me aboard, made sure I had the comfiest seat.

'Mint Hotel, right?' I reminded him.

'Min' Hotel, sure, sure,' he said, and scuttled forwards to enter into a deep discussion with the driver. This went on for some time. Other volunteers stepped aboard to chip in, then left again; walkie-talkie man pressed buttons and yelled into his device. Eventually he elected to stay aboard, and the doors closed. He and I were the only passengers. We passed at alarming speed down a multi-lane highway flanked with recent skyscrapers, walls of windows flashing in the sun. The bus had no air conditioning, and humidity and fumes rendered the air on board a toxic soup. Two patches of sweat radiated from my T-shirt's armpits, looking to rendezvous at my navel and head south.

The driver, who seemed to think he was in charge of a taxi, or even a moped, suddenly swerved across two lanes of traffic and dived down a curving approach road on to an American-scale highway: five lanes each side, crammed with speeding, weaving vehicles. At this, the walkie-talkie man gave a terrible cry, and leapt out of his seat to berate the driver. I could make out the word 'Min' occurring frequently in what became an intense discussion, conducted while the driver looked over his shoulder at his interlocutor and let the bus get on with steering itself. I yelped quietly at every near miss.

Eventually the pair came to some conclusion, and the bus mercifully slowed and pulled on to the hard shoulder. That was the good news.

The bad news was that it then began to reverse.

Walkie-talkie man strolled down the aisle grinning at me. 'We go right way now,' he proudly announced, before kneeling on the back seat to yell instructions to his pal at the wheel.

Inspired with fresh confidence in his colleague, the driver put his foot down, and the bus shot back up the hard shoulder almost as fast as it had come down the motorway. Incredulous motorists honked, flashed and gesticulated as we weaved towards the blind curve of the access ramp and then, speed barely diminished, back up it.

I will truly never know how the driver of the cement truck managed to miss us, because as his monstrous cab and horrified face loomed in the coach's rear window I finally managed to shut my eyes, something I had been trying to achieve ever since the bus had first set off. I shrunk into my seat, and tried to assemble my limbs into the bracing posture recommended on in-flight safety cards.

Some considerable time later, I felt a prod on my shoulder. Walkie-talkie man grinned at me. 'Min' Hotel, sir,' he said.

Accreditation was a lengthy bureaucratic struggle, but I was too numb from the bus ride to complain. I was issued with a laminated press pass and a plethora of less useful kit: glossy folders on stadium construction and catering logistics, a T-shirt, a baseball cap, an enamel pin badge, a soft-toy orang-utan (the Games mascot, Wira) and a backpack in which to carry it all to the nearest bin.

I could now gain free access to any of the magnificent arenas constructed for the Games. Just across the highway from the hotel, the National Sports Complex at Bukit Jalil baked its white bulk in the sunshine. I could hop on a shuttle bus and go and watch the preparations for the opening ceremony.

Or I could have a lunchtime beer.

It should have been no contest, but something very peculiar was happening in the Mint Hotel bar. It was full of journalists, as any bar should be, but few of them were drinking.

'What's going on?' I asked a pink-faced Australian.

'We're on strike,' he said.

'You mean you're refusing to write?'

'Nah, mate. We're refusing to drink. Know what these bastards have done? Doubled the beer prices to welcome the Commonwealth media. It's a rort.'

Rort – the Australian term for an outrageous swindle – is an evocative word, and a number of the man's colleagues grumbled their agreement. One or two local television crews were starting to take an interest, and the strikers produced little placards identifying their organisation as PINT, the Press Institute for Non-Teetotallers.

I had no wish to be labelled a scab, or televised in the act of strike-breaking. So I bought a mineral water and took it over to a corner of the airline-lounge-style bar where I had spotted a gaggle of British journalists.

Dave, a tabloid man of traditional tastes, was not on strike. He was drinking a beer and holding forth. 'It's disgusting,' he was saying as I walked up.

'What is?' I asked. 'The beer or the prices?'

'Nah,' Dave said. 'The beer's OK, and the price doesn't matter if you stick it on expenses, does it?' He looked at me – not for the first time – as if I was someone pretending to be a sports journalist. Which is how I sometimes felt.

'It's the tarts,' Dave said.

'The . . . tarts?'

'Slappers. Professional ladies. There aren't any. I am told,' he lowered his voice to a conspiratorial level, 'that this place is normally one huge knocking shop. But where's the action now? Nowhere to be seen. It's disgusting.'

Dave's expertise in these areas is a matter of legend among the British sporting media. He it was whose (now ex-) wife had thrown his laptop off a high-rise hotel balcony, having discovered him in flagrante with a chambermaid. He it was who had marched up to a startled female receptionist at a hotel in Stockholm to complain that the pay-TV pornography in his room was insufficiently hardcore.

Dave had a theory, confirmed, or so he claimed, by a number of knowledgeable local taxi drivers, that prior to the Games the Malaysian Government had rounded up Kuala Lumpur's prostitute population and bused them out of town to some kind of camp, where they were being held under guard for the duration of the Games.

'It's a fantastic story, isn't it?' Dave said, wistfully. 'If I can get a break from all this sports stuff, I'm going to find that camp. And I tell you what, when I get there, I'm not going to make my excuses and leave.'

That evening the King of Malaysia, His Majesty the Yang Dipertuan Agong, declared the Commonwealth Games open in a ceremony even longer than his name.

I am an anti-connoisseur of these events – I hate everything about them – but not even the most strenuous wriggling could relieve me of my duty to attend. The time difference back to the UK meant, as the Sports Editor oh so reasonably pointed out, that I could sit through the entire performance and still have plenty of time to write about it.

It was purgatory. Six hours of marching bands, traditional dancers and those clever-clever 'human pictures' made by thousands of students holding up coloured cards. A Malaysian pop duo, Wah Idris and Ella, a sort of south-east-Asian Sonny and Cher, sang a specially commissioned song called 'Standing in the Eyes of the World', while I hummed a ditty of my own composition entitled 'Sitting in a Pool of My Sweat'.

I don't want to sound too bitter about this, since I was probably the only one of the 100,000 people in the stadium who wasn't enjoying it. The arena itself, it should also be said, was magnificent. A triple-tiered bowl that somehow managed to be vast, elegant, and ever so slightly Islamic, it made a loud statement about the country in which it stood. It said: 'Can we have the Olympics, now, please?'

Malaysia is the only country in the Commonwealth to have its own monarch, though I am not sure how the constitutional lawyers square this with having Queen Elizabeth as nominal head of state. Anyhow, Elizabeth's son Edward, who pretty much exists to be wheeled out for these events, was keeping a tactfully low profile that evening, as the Yang Thingumajig was driven slowly around the athletics track in a monstrous Mercedes, waving in a proprietorial manner.

Next it was the turn of the Prime Minister, Datuk Seri Dr Mahathir Mohamad (the Datuk Seri bit equates to our 'Right Honourable'). He was driven around the stadium waving modestly from the back of a Land-Rover – he's so humble, you see – before making a speech that was anything but.

Unusually for him, Dr Mohamad avoided the topic of the worldwide Jewish conspiracy that prevents his country from thriving. His theme was '*malaysia boleh*' – Malaysia can – and this slogan was flashed up on the giant screen as

7

fireworks arced into the sky to mark the end of the beginning of the Games.

I stood in the crowd waiting for a monorail train to take
me back to the hotel at the end of a long day with a long
article still to write, thinking, I am ashamed to admit,
Malaysia boleh? Malaysia bollocks.

The Light Railway was an instant cynicism cure: it was clean,
fast and efficient, attributes that were all the more startling
since (a) it had only recently been commissioned especially
for the Games, and (b) it had been built by a British
company. A project of a similar pedigree and age in London
would still have been at the Hey-Bill-pass-me-that-hammer
stage. What is more, unlike the shuttle-bus drivers, it knew
where it was going. The clincher was that as long as I was
wearing my Commonwealth Games accreditation, I rode
for free.

So I rode a lot, breaking the hearts of the Chin Twins
and walkie-talkie man. The stations had such wonderful
names, announced by the taped voice on the public-
address system with great dramatic emphasis. The ride
from the Bukit Jalil sports complex to the station outside
my hotel sounded like an episode from the *Arabian Nights*,
with a new character announced at each stop. Bandar
Tun Razak, Titiwangsa, Cheras, Pudu, Bandaraya, Sultan
Ismail . . . such romance! I had to get off at Sultan Ismail,
but I was always tempted to ride on to the end of the
line, where the trains hit the buffers at a station called
Klang.

Another unexpected attraction of Kuala Lumpur was the
daily riot. I'd be sitting in my room in the Quality Hotel
(City Centre), reading or writing up some notes, counting
the minutes until it was time to phone home, when the
thud of helicopter blades overhead would announce trouble

on the streets. I would skip down to the hotel foyer and head for the glass lift.

I had tried to join in the first Malaysian riot I had seen. I was walking back to the hotel from Sultan Ismail station when a scuffle broke out on the pavement in front of me: half a dozen young people facing up to half a dozen policemen. Half of me said 'Run'. The other half said: 'Get in there and find out what's going on.' Unfortunately, the would-be foreign-correspondent half won the argument. I found out what was going on: Dr Mohamad had slung his deputy Anwar Ibrahim in jail, on lurid accusations of sodomy. Anwar's numerous supporters were protesting against the PM. I also found out what tear gas does to you.

It stings. No, that's not good enough. It stung like someone had removed my eyes and replaced them having lined the sockets with sand. Blundering around my room, I tipped some ice cubes into the basin, filled it with water and spent the best part of an hour submerged and blinking. When I sat down for dinner that night, I had to ask the waiter to read me the menu.

So I had formulated a safer way of keeping tabs on local unrest. The Quality Hotel (City Centre) had very little to recommend itself, apart from its location, accurately delineated in those brackets. But Kuala Lumpur in the late nineties was a place of seething architectural innovation, and the management had felt they had to keep up. So they had installed a glass-walled elevator that ran up the outside of the building. Aesthetically, this did little for the hotel's appeal, since the view, even from the top floor, was dominated by the air-conditioning system of the shopping centre over the road. But the lift was a perfect place from which to watch a riot.

Whenever a helicopter called, I would head for the lift and sail up and down at the whim of other hotel guests, watching through the pollution-grimed glass a repetitive,

9

seemingly inevitable, series of events. First, a little knot of young people wearing headscarves would gather on the pavement in the shade of the overhead railway. They would spend a few minutes stoking their righteous indignation, then produce home-made banners, some of which said 'Free Anwar' and some of which said presumably similar things in Malay, and wave them at drivers on the adjacent three-lane highway, Jalan Raja Laut. Within ten minutes an unmarked bus would draw up at the roadside and disgorge a score of policemen. Each wore a scarlet helmet with visor and neck shield and carried in his left hand a large rectangular riot shield, and in his right a hefty truncheon. Gas masks in green bags hung from their belts.

They would start arresting protesters, which would attract more protesters. Hotel guests would enter my lift, ascend to their floor, have a cup of tea and re-enter the lift to find the strange European man still glued to the glass wall.

When the original police force were clearly outnumbered and it looked like the protesters had them on the run, two more busloads of police would show up, together with an armoured car and a sort of fire truck with plenty of hoses but no ladder. As the new arrivals stormed into the ruck with truncheons flying, a water cannon on the roof of the fire truck would open up and wash protesters off their feet and into the commodious gutters.

Finally, if the water cannon had run dry without dispersing the crowd, a word would go around the police ranks. Gas masks would be donned and a couple of steaming canisters fired into the air. That always did the trick. As rebels and onlookers scattered with streaming eyes and stinging throats, the police mopped up the ringleaders they wanted and shoved them into the back of the armoured car.

I liked the chaotic choreography of it all, felt sorry for the protestors and mildly outraged by the police tactics.

Besides, daytime television in Kuala Lumpur is appalling.

Move along now, ladies and gents. Nothing more to see here.

Time to go and watch some synchronised swimming.

As usual, the Chin Twins in the hotel lobby tried to persuade me to get on one of their courtesy buses, but I wasn't having any of that. I hailed a tatty Malaysian-made Proton taxi instead.

'Bukit Jalil. Swimming pool.'

'Swimming poo? OK.'

That Malaysian tic of swallowing the final consonant took a bit of getting used to, as did their style of driving. This guy was typical, switching lane on impulse, turning around to ask what I thought of the Prime Minister while in the process of overtaking a bus on the wrong side, jumping lights, hooting randomly. It's difficult to relax in a Kuala Lumpur taxi.

'Dr Mahathir Mohamad. Grey man, yes?' he prompted, beadily.

Great? Egocentric despot, to be frank. Which I wasn't. 'His achievements are remarkable.'

'No lie Anwar. He a gayboy.'

'That certainly seems to be the impression we are being given.'

'You lie him? You mus be gayboy too. Hahaha!'

'Haha indeed. I'll tell you what. You just concentrate on not crashing the car, and I'll read my newspaper.'

Brief, grumpy silence.

'You English?'

'Yes.'

'You wan be my penfriend?'

'No.'

'Humph.'

Sometimes – one taxi in ten – the conversation went the

11

other way, and the driver worked his way round to admitting that, actually, he had a doubt or two about Dr Mohamad's qualifications for sainthood. The tricky thing was trying to guess your driver's location on the political spectrum before you made an incorrect remark and got ejected on to the hard shoulder of the Jin Kutching expressway.

Bukit Jalil, the sprawling sports complex built especially for the Games in a suburb of Kuala Lumpur, was heaving with people as usual. But, puzzlingly, more seemed to be making their way away from the aquatic centre than into it. Why this should be became clear when I walked into the empty press box to see the scoreboard displaying the final results of the synchronized-swimming competition I had come to see. Valerie Hould-Marshand, of Canada, had won the gold medal, while I had been amusing myself with a little light rioting.

In deepest Leicestershire, eight hours behind Kuala Lumpur time, the Sports Editor was munching his breakfast toast and contemplating the day's schedule. 'Baker on synchronised swimming, eh? Wonder what he'll make of that . . .'

Wonder what I'll make of unemployment, I thought, as I scoured the echoing corridors of the aquatic complex in search of volunteers. Wherever you didn't want them – cluttering up your hotel lobby, for instance – the volunteers were ubiquitous. When you desperately needed one – for example, to locate a synchronised swimmer – they vanished quicker than tear-gassed rioters.

Finally I came to a door marked 'Press Only'. I looked through the glass panel: there, bountiful providence, was a teenage girl wearing a tracksuit and what looked like most of her mother's cosmetics cabinet, talking to half a dozen journalists.

'Will there be any more questions?' the Malaysian moderator asked as I sat down.

Thank goodness, a local journalist asked something about artistic inspiration. Miss Hould-Marshand's routine had, it transpired, been an interpretation of the tragic history of Shakespeare's Juliet. Blocking out the notion that Ophelia might have been more appropriate, I scribbled down the quotes. 'I can't say that I have lived through Juliet's experience,' Valerie conceded. 'I'm still alive, for one thing. But I tried to imagine what it would be like to have your heart broken into a million pieces.' Especially while swimming upside down and waving your legs in the air.

Then Valerie was getting up to go . . .

'Just one more, question, please,' I blurted, realising that I didn't have a clue what to ask. 'Er . . . your hair looks lovely. Any problems on that front today?'

Bless her, Valerie sat down again. 'What with the heat from the television lights, and of course the water, hair can be tricky,' she said, with professional sincerity. 'At one stage today I thought I was going to have a meltdown situation out there, but it all held together.' Then, with a grin that spoke volumes for modern Canadian dentistry, she was gone.

Like Valerie's hair, my piece just about held together, once I had blagged a videotape of her performance and a copy of the results. Ethically iffy, I know. But if I had not seen the competition live, I had at least watched the tape and taken the trouble to question the winner, albeit on matters of coiffure. To be honest, the sense of relief overwhelmed any stabs of guilt.

But one thing still troubled me. Delightful though Valerie H-M had been, there was only one of her. Surely the point of synchronised swimming was that you had other people to synchronise with. Had her colleagues all drowned?

I had a feeling – an all too familiar feeling – of dangerous ignorance. Writing about sport, any sport, anywhere, is mostly delightful. But everywhere I go I am accompanied by a gaping void where expert knowledge should be, and a resultant compulsion to ask stupid questions.

I found a middle-aged lady in a tracksuit standing outside the pool building. Valerie Hould-Marshand's mum, for all I knew. Nothing ventured . . .

'I do beg your pardon,' I said, 'but you look like an expert. Would you mind confirming something for me?'

'Of course,' the lady said. She was wearing a lot of make-up, a reassuring sign in this context.

'In solo synchronised swimming, what exactly are the swimmers synchronising with?'

'The music, of course,' she said, her smile fading. 'Weren't you watching this morning?'

I felt I would be on safer ground with the Commonwealth Games cricket tournament, which was getting underway at a number of picturesque venues around Kuala Lumpur. Although the sport was new to the Games, a strong line-up of teams had travelled to Malaysia, including near-Test strength squads from Australia, New Zealand and South Africa.

The only absentees among the Test-playing nations were England, and a variety of excuses were doing the rounds. Giving the players a rest at the end of a long county season was quite plausible; another suggestion was conflicts of loyalty among the large proportion of the England team not qualified by birth to play for England. Personally, I reckon some old buffer at the English Cricket Board had mislaid the invitation and then forgotten all about it.

Whatever the reason, Scotland were the team most likely to be of interest to newspaper readers back home, so I decided to go and watch their game against Pakistan, who had selected a team of youngsters hungry to prove their credentials for Test cricket.

The cricket pitch was in the grounds of a grand colonial-era building called the Victoria Institution. The scene viewed from the first floor of the pavilion might have been an English pastoral idyll; white figures dashing across a swath of lush greenery to the thwack of leather on willow.

The almost total absence of any spectators only increased the resemblance to an English county championship match. The similarity ended at the edge of the ground, however, for the pitch was surrounded not by dreary suburbs but by yet more of Kuala Lumpur's aggressively modern office blocks.

The world's press (me and two gentlemen from Lahore) were accommodated – well, to be honest, we weren't accommodated at all. We just wandered around. Need an opinion on the Pakistani batting order? Stroll up to the coach, the military chap in the deck-chair over there, and ask him. Want to check the score? Look over the scorer's shoulder. Want to plug in your laptop? Hard luck.

Still, the cricket was good to watch. The Scots bowled with pace and accuracy, and at one stage reduced the Pakistanis to 95 for 5. But then the Pakistani coach – a former Test player and star of my childhood table-cricket team – climbed out of his deck-chair and bristled on the boundary, after which his batsmen played with spines of steel. At the end of their allotted 55 overs, they had accumulated 201 runs.

I spent the luncheon interval scanning the horizon for the van marked 'Beer and sandwiches for journalists,' but it never showed. I was reduced to raiding the dressing room for the players' leftovers, which had quickly curled and soggified in the stifling humidity.

As the Scottish openers sauntered out to the middle I cornered their coach, a former Yorkshire stalwart called Jim Love. I was hoping for easy laughs, of course, but a Scottish Yorkshireman is not going to give anything away cheaply, and Love faced all my sneaky lines with a straight bat. His team had beaten county opposition in the NatWest Trophy, he pointed out, defeated Bangladesh, who were just about to be granted Test status, and qualified for the World Cup. Not bad for a nation whose instinctive response to being handed a wooden implement is to toss it.

As we spoke, though, Love's comments were frequently interrupted by the sound of splintering timber and Gaelic oaths. His batsmen were finding it hard to cope with the Pakistani fast bowlers, in particular one slight, floppy-haired teenager who started his run-up in an adjacent suburb. 'He's nippy, that fellow, that's for sure,' Love grudgingly admitted.

I asked one of the Pakistani journalists who the young bowler was.

'We call him the Rawalpindi Express,' he said. 'I'll write his name down for you.'

Shoaib Akhtar, he wrote. 'One for the future, I believe,' said the man from Lahore. He was right. These days, when the Rawalpindi Express steams in, he's the fastest, nastiest bowler in the world.

Fortunately for the Scots, the match was interrupted, and then terminated, by Kuala Lumpur's regular afternoon thunderstorm. When I first encountered this meteorological quirk I wondered how the Games would survive. Surely such deluges would wreck every schedule? Far from it. Most of the sports were either indoor or waterproof: hockey players love rain, as do rugby players, though their slides over the try-line here could carry them almost to the border with Singapore. Sure, the athletics might be threatened, but, as a volunteer at the main stadium had told me: 'In Malaysia we build very big drains.'

For cricket, though, rain is fatal, and surely there cannot have been more water on a field since the animals followed on in their fixture with Noah. The Scotland vs. Pakistan match was abandoned at teatime, to the ill-concealed relief of the few Scotsmen yet to wield a bat.

The Pakistani players (and their two journalists) sloshed on to one coach, the Scots on to another, the officials into a minibus, leaving me, quite suddenly, alone on the open-sided first floor of the pavilion, gazing at an outfield that was rapidly becoming more suitable for deep-sea fishing than deep fine leg. In theory, a bus should have turned up to ferry members of the press back to the Mint Hotel. But I had already seen enough of the shuttle system in action not to expect such a miracle. I would have phoned for a taxi, if I had thought to bring along the number, or bothered to memorise that of Malaysian directory enquiries.

Thunder rumbled and lightning flashed as the storm settled down and made itself comfortable over the city. I could do the same: arrange the five plastic chairs and the litter into a cosy shelter and doze off until ... hmm, until arrested for vagrancy by Dr Mohamad's tidy-minded policemen. In any case, I had a story to write, and my laptop was in my room at the Quality Hotel (City Centre), so I would jolly well have to walk back there. When did a spot of rain ever prevent an Englishman from doing his duty?

That kind of pompous self-deception sustained me for the first hundred yards or so of the journey. Then I began to feel uncomfortable. I was wearing my standard cater-for-any-eventuality Malaysian uniform: rope-soled espadrilles, baggy shorts (and, under them, baggy boxer shorts) and a T-shirt. On top of this I had pulled my lightweight, hooded rain-jacket, my secret weapon against the worst of the KL climate.

The secret weapon backfired. One of the many annoying things about Malaysia's equatorial downpours is that they do very little to alleviate local heat or humidity. So, while the plastic rain-jacket did a splendid job in keeping the rain off my T-shirt, the T-shirt rapidly became soaked in perspiration. It was feasible, I thought, that I could become the first man to die of dehydration in a rainstorm.

I took the jacket off and stuffed it back into my holdall, where it efficiently smudged all my notes from the day's cricket. I trudged on, constantly scanning the horizon for taxis. But it seems to be a global commonplace that at the first hint of rain the cabbies go home for tea, and Kuala Lumpur's Proton-jockeys were no exception.

Condensation and raindrops had rendered my spectacles practically opaque, but I could make out the misty bulk of substantial residences beside the road: embassies, perhaps, or the homes of the city's wealthiest merchants. That would explain the high walls and gated entrance-ways, the peering video cameras and the general impression that this was not the sort of household which would happily supply itinerant journalists with a spare umbrella.

So I trudged on. The volume of rain was such that there was a constant inch or so of water on the pavement surface, and my shoes resembled small black boats struggling in a choppy sea. I conducted a careful study of the city's guttering, recalling that the only practical use I had hitherto seen for it was as a receptacle for water-cannoned dissidents. Kuala Lumpur's gutters are both wide and deep: a substantial stride across (not a stride that you would want to miss) and dropping as much as a foot from the surface of the road. These concrete canyons had become torrents foaming with urban detritus: cans, newspapers, and cigarette packets overtook me in their headlong rush to the cavernous drains. At any moment I expected them to be followed by dustbins, lamp-posts and defunct domestic animals.

To my right the long march of mansions continued. To my left the road was now flanked by a wide, muddy river, frothing like maddened cappuccino between its man-made banks. If I was lucky, this would be the Gombak, which flowed past my hotel. I contemplated throwing myself in and floating back to base: it wouldn't have made me any wetter.

But there was another clue to my location. In the far

18

distance I could dimly detect the H shape of the Petronas Towers, decapitated by cloud not far above the platform that linked the two tallest buildings in the world. Somewhere between me and them lay my hotel, so I had a bearing that would remain visible so long as the cloud did not descend to street level.

Things were looking up, until I looked down. My water-logged shoes were starting to disintegrate: snakes of rope from the soles were whipping out with every step and biting my ankles. There was more trouble in the trouser depart-ment. Two elements of my intimate anatomy had been rubbing against sopping cloth to create 'Marathon Groin', a condition which long-distance runners protect against by slathering on Vaseline. The only way, however, I could imagine knocking on the door of a Kuala Lumpur mansion with a successful request for Vaseline was if some miracle brought me straight to the home of the former Deputy Prime Minister; and when I remembered that he was, in any case, incarcerated, I gave up even this distant hope. Instead I altered my gait in an attempt to alleviate both ankle-whip and appendage-chafe and thus hobbled, eventually, into the foyer of the Quality Hotel (City Centre) like a small, soggy John Wayne.

As I waited in a rapidly accumulating puddle of water and sweat for the lift to arrive, the Chin Twins sat with their shoulders heaving, valiantly suppressing their laughter. Walkie-talkie man was more forthright.

'Oh, Mr Englishman,' he spluttered. 'You should have taken a shuttle bus.'

I decided, as I applied towels, tissues, ointments and a hairdryer to the appropriate areas, that I deserved a night out. So far I had virtuously avoided the fleshpots and bars in order to remain *compos mentis* for the late-night check call to the newspaper to find out if my contribution for the day was fit to print. There would be little point if, when asked to make a couple of changes, you were unable to distinguish your laptop from the bedside lamp. So I had got into a dull routine of small beers and indifferent meals in the hotel's Chinese restaurant, and had quickly exhausted my book supply, a crucial element in my overseas sanity rations.

There must be something more to this place, I thought, setting out into the sweltering dusk on a comforting tide of Nivea. Over the main road from the hotel was a large and chaotic shopping centre that specialised in luxury knock-offs: Rolix watches and Cucci belts, Rolf Lauren shirts and Badidas trainers. The noodle bars there were busy at lunchtime but were near deserted now, and the thought of spiced-up leftover soup turned my stomach.

I left the centre and struck out towards the blinking peaks of the Petronas Towers. The afternoon's deluge might never have happened: the heat had simply hoovered up the water and stored it to drop on our heads again tomorrow. But the pavements were scattered with bleached and dried wreckage, like a concrete beach after a high tide.

I picked my way through faded lumps that had once been newsprint, washed-out burger wrappers and dehydrated kebab entrails, noting that with my unerring traveller's instinct I had chosen a route that was entirely devoid of any kind of life. Never mind: persist.

I should explain here that I have certain principles when exploring abroad, the most important of which is a stubborn refusal to ask for advice or directions. I like to walk, and see what I find, and if I don't find anything I like, I will walk some more. Taxis, I high-handedly believe, are the enemies of discovery, and in any case KL's taxis were all driven by politically unreliable homicidal maniacs.

Some might have given up after half an hour of unrelieved office blocks and niche retailers. But, I reminded myself, that is not the Way of Baker. It is the Way of Baker to enjoy whatever the walk brings, such as, well, look here: a shop specialising in receipt books for the catering trade. A retailer of reconditioned computer equipment. A closed branch of Marks and Spencer . . .

And Dave bellowing at me from the doorway of an Irish bar.

I blinked twice, checking against heat-induced hallucination, but the bar, which was called Finnegan's Irish Restoran, was really there, and Dave was really calling my name, and adding one or two choice epithets. 'Get in here, yer poof!' he yelled. 'They've got real beer.'

So they had. I had a pint of Old Speckled Hen. Dave was at work on what, from the evidence of the empties, was his fifth pint of Guinness. 'That,' he belched, 'is the authentic taste of Dublin. Not like the crap they make around here. It's the water, you see, the water from the Liffey. Makes all the difference.'

Dave is in his mid-fifties, tall, stout-bellied and somewhat scarlet around the edges. He writes a lot about football but there is no sport that he has not covered: Dave is an expert. An expert on everything. He knows everyone, and has influenced in some way every significant sporting happening of the last quarter century. According to Dave, Dave had a hand in the early grooming of (among others) Pete Sampras, Michael Schumacher, Nick Faldo and Shane Warne. Dave pointed out the young Ryan Giggs to Alex Ferguson, and spotted Frank Bruno in a boys' club gym. Dave would also admit – if pushed, for he is a modest man – that he once gave a couple of crucial tips to Cassius Clay.

It is always difficult to tell with Dave where the fantasy and the reality joins. Over the years he has convinced himself that all of his preposterous anecdotes are grounded in truth. Unquestionably, he has met all the celebrities to whom he refers. Equally unquestionably, very few of them, were they now to push open the door of Finnegan's Irish Restoran, would have recognised their eminent former adviser.

Dave wanted to know what I had been up to, so I told him all about the afternoon's wet walk and the evening's trudge. Only once did he raise an eyebrow, as I described one of the dreary retail premises I had passed on my way to Finnegan's. Dave's day, naturally, had been considerably more glamorous. In the morning, he had dropped in on the Australian swimming squad with a couple of tweaks for their leading freestyler. 'He's a good kid, but he needs polishing. Big feet. Name of Thorpe.' Over lunch at the Palace of the Golden Horses, he had advised a Malaysian Cabinet minister ('can't tell you which one, mate. Hush hush') on the security situation, and received in turn a steer on his disappearing-prostitutes story ('which I can't share with you, for obvious reasons'). A 'gorgeous' Canadian masseuse had begged his company for dinner, but Dave had declined 'because I wanted a man's night out. Know what I mean?'

I did. And I didn't want to join him. I listened politely while Dave described conditions at the Mint Hotel, where ladies of the night who had escaped the Government clampdown were apparently patrolling the lounge, and where the management had given in to the strikers and reduced the price of beer.

'All in all,' Dave concluded, 'Things are shaping up pretty well. Have another?'

Reckoning that an evening with Dave would end in certain inebriation and probable police custody, I muttered something feeble about deadlines and left him to it. But I had a brief word with the evidently ex-pat barman on my way out.

'Is it true that the Guinness is imported from Ireland?' I asked.

'Nah, mate,' he replied in broadest Aussie. 'They brew it at Sungei Wei, just down the road.'

So my night on the town was a washout, as the afternoon had been. But there was an unexpected dividend. The next evening I found a bottle of champagne waiting in my room, with a note from Dave: 'Baker, you're a genius. The place that sells receipt books is a gift from the gods. The expenses department won't know what's hit them. Best wishes, Dave. PS. You missed one hell of a night.'

The Sports Editor had wisely deployed his most experienced journalists at the Commonwealth Games on the coverage of sensible sports such as athletics, swimming and hockey, leaving the inexperienced on the lunatic fringe. So no sooner were my shorts dry than I was sent to cover ten-pin bowling, a sport never previously included in a major international Games, and one never likely to be so honoured again. It is a sport of which the Malaysians are inordinately fond. I cannot say why this should be, but their expertise no doubt derives from ample opportunities to practise. Ten-pin bowling alleys are ideally sited in shopping centres, and in Kuala Lumpur there are shopping centres all over the city. It's all mall.

The Commonwealth Games bowling competition was taking place in the daddy of all KL retail conglomerations, the Sunway Pyramid. So large is this temple of capitalism that it was difficult to locate the major sporting event going on among all the frantic shoppers. Up this escalator? Nope, that's a ten-screen cineplex. Around this corner . . . ah, a skating rink. And over here? A supermarket.

'Sunway Pyramid', a sign announced, 'is an irresistible world where every visit becomes a memorable treat for the senses.' Yes, yes. But where have they hidden the bloody bowling alley? I decided to ask a policeman, which was suddenly easy because the atrium where I stood, marooned, had filled up with them. None of them paid me any attention, however, because at that moment Dr Mahathir Mohamad entered the shopping centre, accompanied by His Royal Baldness, the Prince Edward. Reasoning that the Prime Minister was unlikely to be here to stock up on breakfast cereal, I attached myself to their retinue and thus swept into the bowling alley with the ease that only a massed and heavily armed police escort can bring.

It was an extraordinary sight: lane upon lane of shiny laminated wood stretching almost as far as the eye could see. Forty-eight of them, a proud official was explaining, each equipped with the latest in scoring and pin-retrieval technology. His spiel was interrupted by cries of *Malaysia boleh!* from the temporary grandstand erected along one wall of the building. I squeezed into a seat and studied the flickering red digits on a distant scoreboard. It seemed that the local heroes, Kenny Ang and Ben Heng, were heading for victory in the men's doubles competition, which would bring Malaysia's first gold medal of the Games. Hence the presence of Dr M, who must have had some very bowling-savvy advisers.

Luckily for those advisers – who would probably have found themselves on the wrong end of sodomy charges had the boys mucked up – Ang and Heng were on tremendous form. Ang looked like a bank manager: neat, tidy, middle-aged. Heng, younger, crew-cut, sensible, looked like a trainee bank manager. Both were about to become, briefly, the biggest stars in their country.

They could do no wrong, obliterating the pins time after time for strike after strike. I took to analysing their techniques. Ang was the more restrained, daintily cocking his right leg behind his left knee as he released the ball. Heng, with the suppleness of youth, followed through with more enthusiasm, finishing up with his right heel approximately adjacent to his left ear.

It worked, though, and as the last pin rolled over in submission to the might of the host nation, the crowd went noisily bonkers. Ang and Heng embraced, illuminated by a thousand exploding flashguns: every paper in the country would carry this image tomorrow. Dr Mohamad looked pleased; his advisers relieved.

I grabbed a few words with Ang and Heng's coach, a globe-trotting Canadian called Sid. 'It's a huge thrill for all the people here,' he yelled above the hubbub. 'The crowd were worth a lot of pins to us, and I'm sure that they made a difference to our competitors. These guys are tremend-ous athletes.' I nodded in sycophantic, hypocritical agree-ment. 'Which paper are you from?' Sid asked. I told him. 'Good for you,' he said. 'I'm a Luton Town fan. Watch out for the Hatters when you get home.'

The best evenings in Kuala Lumpur started with a phone call: joyously banal domestic discussions (disputes with neighbours, a lost watch, soap-opera plot updates), and my regular fix of enthusiastic gobbledegook from Lucy, whose sibling-to-be was due in two months' time. They continued with another phone call, this time to the sports desk, to confirm that my copy for the day had arrived, been read and checked by a sub-editor, and deemed adequate, or at least literate. Then glorious freedom, frittered away on chow mein and a bad thriller in the hotel restaurant, or ranks of beers with colleagues in a noisy bar near the Mint Hotel.

There were bad evenings, too: missed phone calls home, busy sub-editors requesting facts checked at midnight, a room-service cheeseburger while channel-surfing through a miasma of architectural documentaries, Malaysian histor-ical dramas and paeans to Datuk Seri Dr Mahathir Mohamad.

The morning after a night like this I would be welded to my bed with misery, prised out of the room only by the increasingly desperate encouragement of the hotel's cleaning staff. It was no more than a combination of delayed jet lag and pointless self-pity, but in Malaysia I didn't recognise the symptoms. I was still learning about travel, about separation.

And about sport. Rhythmic gymnastics, for example, was not a pastime that I had previously committed to prose, nor, had I prevailed, would it have been added to my repertoire in Kuala Lumpur. 'Look,' I whinged to the Sports Editor, 'there's real stuff going on out here. People are breaking world records in the swimming pool. Triple jumpers are hopping, skipping and leaping into history. Australians are playing West Indians at cricket. Why do I have to go and watch bloody rhythmic gymnastics?'

'Because that's what I want you to do,' said the Sports Editor, not for the first or last time.

Thirty-five minutes' unstinting praise of Dr Mohamad later, my taxi driver dropped me at the National Sports Complex. The Putra stadium crouched next door to the main athletics arena, and as I was early I sat down on a low wall in some welcome shade to make some notes.

After a minute I could feel that I was being stared at, and looked up to see a young man eyeballing the press pass around my neck. 'Ah,' he said. 'You are from England.' He held out his hand. Reluctantly, I put down my notebook and pen and shook it.

This he took as an invitation to sit down next to me on the wall. 'My name is Chang,' he said. He was in his early twenties, his inky hair was cut short, and he wore spectacles and a Planet Hollywood T-shirt. 'These new sports stadiums are very impressive, I think.' He nodded agreement with himself. 'Very impressive for a young nation to build such things so quickly.'

He was waiting for me to agree.

'Very impressive,' I conceded. 'I hope that you will find

some use for them after the Games are finished.' As prisons, perhaps, I thought. Or shopping malls.

'The Olympics will come here,' Chang said with conviction. 'You will see. Dr Mohamad will arrange it. Then you can come back again to write about our country.'

I said that if the Olympics came to Malaysia I would be happy to return.

'That will be good.' Chang changed his tone suddenly, from triumphalism to supplication in a breath. 'I would like to come to your country as well,' he said. 'Could you . . . would you give me your address?'

Oh, gawd . . . This was the fifth or sixth time I had been asked for my details, always by young Malaysian men who loved their country so much that they couldn't wait to leave it. 'I'm sorry,' I said, standing up, feeling mean. 'I really don't think so.'

'But we could be penfriends . . .' I was already on my way.

Inside the Putra stadium, a cuboid arena with giant television screens suspended over the gymnasts' floor space, I reflected on my conduct. Narrow-minded, patronising, selfish. All of these might apply. But rather that than Chang on my doorstep with a sleeping bag and a cheery grin.

It was a relief to concentrate on the gymnastics, which was, to my surprise, extremely well attended. Then I looked down the entry list and saw the name of Carolyn Au-Yong, the local girl whose face had been all over the newspapers in the preceding week. She was Malaysian. She was pretty. She might win a medal. The Putra stadium was a sell-out.

The Malaysians, I discovered, had won the team competition the previous day, so Au-Yong had some form. No wonder their fans were working themselves into a state of patriotic delirium. *Malaysia boleh*! Malaysia can win! At rhythmic gymnastics as well as ten-pin bowling!

The stadium announcer caught the mood: 'Ladies and gentlemen, boys and girls, and you wonderful, wonderful people out there,' he began. Was the Prime Minister in the house, by any chance?

The announcer's voice oozed the kind of bogus sincerity that was shortly to be found on the faces of the competitors, cosmetically enhanced masks of beaming contentment with vivacious grins that remained intact even when things had gone horribly wrong.

As they so frequently did.

In straightforward (non-rhythmic?) gymnastics, the opportunities for embarrassing failure are plentiful, and generally involve landings on bottoms rather than feet. But in rhythmic gymnastics the competitor is further burdened with compulsory props, any of which can ruin her routine if they fail to behave. The gymnast must cavort with four props in four separate routines: a rope, a hoop, a pair of juggler's clubs and a long ribbon on the end of a sort of wand. The better gymnasts can get these inanimate objects to perform in pretty and sometimes spectacular ways; for the not so good girls the props behave like recalcitrant pets, refusing to do what they are told and nipping their mistresses when they least expect it.

A ribbon on a stick is a fine thing when it is describing fluttery coils in the air while its wielder somersaults and lands with hand extended to grasp the wand in its dying parabola. But it is a funnier thing, at least to a Malaysian audience, when it wraps itself around the knees of a teenager from Singapore and brings her down with a bump on her pretty little nose. Miss your hoop in mid-routine and it will be over the floral arrangements and lassooing a judge before you can say 'whoops'. Then there was the rhythm thing: some girls just don't have it. I am not going to name names here, but let us say that the field from which Namibia selected their squad cannot have been over-large. And what music! How can coaches allow such acts of self-sabotage? And where does the stuff come from? Is there an unscrupulous mail-order firm peddling CDs called *Now That's What I Call Music for Rhythmic Gymnastics 4*?

The routines of Malaysian competitors were treated by the crowd with veneration followed by hysteria. Every time Carolyn Au-Yong caught her clubs or rolled her hoop in a pretty circle, the crowd gasped in admiration, and the performer presented throughout the happy smile and joyful countenance of one who has just sewn up a lucrative contract for toothpaste endorsement.

But a white grin and a local address were not quite enough to sway the judges, and as it became clear that their girl was not going to win, the Malaysians, so recently converted to rhythmic gymnastics, suddenly decided that they didn't like it after all, and deserted the arena in droves. A Canadian girl won in the end, but there weren't many spectators left to applaud her.

I wrapped up my piece and, keeping a wary eye open for would-be penfriends, snared a taxi. It was my birthday, and in the absence of friends or family I had decided to treat myself to a sightseeing trip.

'Petronas Towers, please,' I asked the driver.

'Petro Towels, OK,' he said, revving up the Proton. 'What you think of Dr Mohamad?'

The Petronas Towers were at the time – and for all I know may still be – the tallest buildings on the planet. It is somehow typical of Malaysia at the end of the twentieth century that they should seek to build not only one record-breaking building but two of them: statements of national self-confidence do not come much louder. This was acknowledged in typically sensitive style by Dr Mohamad when he declared the towers open. 'When one is short,' he explained, 'one should stand on a box to get a better view. The twin towers are to our ego what the box is to the shorty.'

Being a bit of a shorty myself, I could sympathise with the scale of the ego problem that must have prompted the

Petronas Towers. Here was national insecurity paraded for the world to see: 'You think you've got a big one?' Malaysia was crowing, 'I've got two, and they're both bigger than yours. Impressive, or what?'

Impressive, I reluctantly conceded, standing at the foot of the towers. They soared, tapering, towards their crenellated peaks, joined at nipple-level by a bridge, the whole forming a monumental H, for 'Hey, over here, look at us!'

I wondered what the view would be like from the top.

'I would like to go to the top of the towers,' I told the lady at the reception desk. I fingered the press ID I had purposefully hung around my neck. 'As you can see,' I said, self-importantly, 'I am here for the Commonwealth Games.'

'I'm sorry,' the receptionist said. 'That pass will not get you into the towers. You need to have special permission. I could give you the address . . .'

'No, no,' I said. 'Please don't worry. I'm going home tomorrow.' I toyed briefly with the idea of telling her that it was my birthday, then remembered how old I was going to be: too old to be begging favours from grown-ups.

Instead of viewing south-east Asia from one hundred stories high, I wandered the basement shopping centre, trying to cheer myself up by adding to my already considerable store of trinkets for Lucy, and attempting without success to locate a gift for Ingrid that would compensate for three weeks of night duty.

I had a tremendous birthday treat that evening: the closing ceremony, which I was on a three-line whip to attend and describe. Somehow it did not seem quite as painful as the opening performance: perhaps it was shorter, perhaps I was demob-happy. It ended with the athletes dancing all over the infield as the Irish band The Corrs performed on a temporary stage at one end of the stadium. They were great; or at least they were not Wah Idris and Ella.

I left while the band played on, and on the train back

to the hotel a little old Malaysian lady wearing a volunteer's headscarf came and sat down beside me and pulled out a wallet of photographs: herself, with athletes. 'That's Annika Reeder,' I said, recognising the British gymnast. 'She just took part in the closing ceremony. She was on the stage.' The woman grinned at me, nodding, understanding not a word. She showed me a dozen more pictures, featuring that grin and athletes I could not recognise. Then she put the wallet carefully away and, making sure that I was watching, made a broad sweeping gesture with her right hand, through as close as she could get to 360 degrees. All of this, I understood: the Games, our city, our people. I nodded.

'Good?' she said.

I nodded again. 'Good,' I said.

It seemed the simplest, least offensive response, and it seemed to make the old lady very happy.

But it would have been more honest, if more linguistically challenging, to have said: 'To be honest, I've no idea. Ask me in four years' time. Ask me when I've seen another one. Ask me when I know what I'm doing.'

Conclusion: Should probably have been nicer to would-be pen-pals.

Chapter Two

Going Downhill Fast

Objective: Ride the Olympic bobsled course at Lillehammer in Norway. Stay alive. Time allocated: one minute and seven seconds.

The Major inclined his head towards the top of the mountain.

'Come with me for a moment,' he said.

We walked uphill on crunchy snow. Behind the bobsled shed was the British team's lorry. The Major leapt athletically into the rear of the vehicle and began rootling around in piles of equipment. He paused, examined my hairline for a moment, carried on rootling. 'Just trying to work out what size head you've got,' he explained, then straightened up. 'Here,' he threw me a scarred, visorless, full-face helmet. 'Try that on.'

I did. Bit of a fiddle to get it over my glasses, but there was no denying it fitted. Damn. I had rather been hoping . . .

The Major finished adjusting the strap under my chin. 'Good,' he said, stepping back, looking me in the eyes. 'You'll do.' He swivelled and marched back down towards the sled shed.

Damn.

I had a few surprises when I returned from Kuala Lumpur,

not all of them good. I found out, for example, the truth behind a peculiar telephone conversation I had had with Ingrid while I was away.

The lost watch she had told me about had not been lost at all: it had been cut from her wrist by a mugger who didn't draw the line at assaulting pregnant women. She was fine, she said, fingering the abrasion on her wrist. There had not been much point in worrying me, Ingrid continued, with habitual common sense. What was I going to do, catch the next plane home and the mugger?

Another, less traumatic surprise was the discovery that I was expected by the Sports Editor to go to the Winter Olympics in Salt Lake City in 2002, and that in the meantime I should acquaint myself with as many of the disciplines as possible.

And then a surprise that was big and small at once: a second daughter, born five weeks early, very tiny and very loud, swiftly named Emily and installed at home. Any plans to take up cross-country skiing or figure skating would have to be put on hold while I brushed up once more on my nappy-changing skills. I reckoned a week was about enough paternity leave (Ingrid thought I might reasonably have doubled, or even tripled the stint) and started to make some exploratory calls into the world of winter sport.

Philip Pope, of the British Olympic Association, was keen to introduce me to what he called 'sliding sports'. Not sports about to slip out of existence, but sports that were all about going downhill. Fast. One of them, bobsled, I had even heard of. I dimly recalled that in the days when winter sports were the exclusive preserve of the chap, two British chaps named Nash and Dixon had won Olympic gold in a bob.

But there were other sliding disciplines encompassed by Pope's enthusiasm: luge and skeleton.

'I haven't the first idea what you're talking about,' I told him.

'No problem,' Pope said. 'You'll have to come and see for yourself.'

The original plan had sounded pretty innocuous. Travel to Lillehammer in Norway and watch some of the British Olympic sliders in action. Interview one or two of them, and fly home again. What could be simpler?

It was on the flight out to Oslo that Pope, who had kindly volunteered to accompany me, started to drop unpleasant hints.

'Can't make any promises,' he said, between mouthfuls of British Airways cheesecake, 'but once we've done the chats it might be possible to get you a run.'

'A run?'

'A run down the mountain.' Pope was grinning.

'Why would I want to run down a mountain? I gave up running years ago.'

'I mean,' Pope said, and he knew that I knew what he meant, 'a run in a bobsled.'

'Oh,' I said. I took a slug of Château Heathrow.

'Be tremendous fun,' Pope said.

'Tremendous,' I said. 'Look, Philip, can we just, sort of, see how things go when we get there? I might be horribly tired from, from interviewing and so on.'

'Of course,' Pope said.

'I mean, it's not as if I'm young, free and single any more,' I went on.

'What on earth has that got to do with anything?' Pope asked, not unreasonably.

'Well, I have responsibilities. Two of them. Three, rather, their mother included. I'm nearly forty.'

'Andrew . . .'

'I can't just go throwing myself off the top of a mountain for the hell of it. And what about insurance?'

'Andrew, calm down.' Pope was loving this. 'Take a deep breath. Relax. Nobody is going to force you to jump off the top of a mountain. You might get a ride in a bobsled. That's all. And even that might not be possible.'

'No,' I said. 'There's always that.' I turned away, looked out of the window, tried to think placid thoughts. I seemed to hear – though it might just have been something in the engine note – the sound of clucking.

At Oslo airport we caught a train to Lillehammer. The train was slow, and crowded, and stopped frequently. Pope slept. I didn't. Night fell, and then snow, and still we plodded past fjords and wound up increasingly remote valleys. I stared out of the window, hoping to catch sight of a Moomintroll. No such luck. At about ten o'clock we reached Lillehammer, and clambered off into the icy darkness to be met by . . . more icy darkness.

'I don't understand it,' Pope said. 'They knew which train we were coming on.'

The waiting room was closed. The temperature was ten below freezing. Look on the bright side, I thought: if you die of exposure you won't have to ride in a bobsled.

After half an hour or so of foot-stamping, hand-whacking and general pointless cursing, a minibus came hurtling out of the darkness and screeched to a halt beside us. 'Sorry, boys,' the driver said, 'one or two things to catch up with.' This was Mark Armstrong, who was running a training camp on behalf of the British Bobsled Association. He was an army man – most British bobsledders are forces types – so I wittily christened him the Major. 'There should still be some grub left,' he said, crashing through the gears.

There was. It was reindeer stew, and it had been on the table for too long. The Major – evidently used to worse in the way of rations – tucked in. He said that the camp had two purposes: to train the nation's best bobsledders – and here he looked meaningfully at me – oh, and also to allow total novices to try their hands at the different sliding disciplines and work out which, if any, they fancied.

I said that what I fancied most of all was a lift back to the station, and the Major gave me a thin grin and strode off to harry some of his charges up to bed. A jolly-looking young man in a Team GB sweatshirt sat down next to me.

'Mark Hatton,' he introduced himself. 'I'm a luger.'

'You are . . . a German handgun, popular with officers in both the First and Second World Wars?'

'No, no. It's a soft 'g'. I ride a luge – a sort of high-speed sledge. I design them, too. See, what you need to do is . . .'

He talked, I chewed pieces of Santa's helpers. I enjoyed the conversation more than the stew, and by the time my plate was removed I had a thorough grounding in how sliders did what they did, if not why. Lugers, I now knew, went down the run feet first, skeleton bobsledders head first. Mark offered to lend me his luge the next morning. I made my excuses and tried to leave, but Pope slid into the space that Hatton had vacated.

'I'm on for a skeleton.'

Thanks to Hatton, I knew that he was not talking about some kind of Norwegian cocktail. 'You're going to ride a skeleton bobsled?'

'Yup.' Pope looked tremendously pleased with himself.

I thought he was a maniac. 'You do realise,' I said, flush with fresh knowledge, 'that the skeleton is a one-man operation? That you won't have a driver?'

'Yup.' He looked positively eager.

'That you will be riding head-first down a chute of ice, and steering, if I have understood this correctly, by minuscule movements of your shoulders and ankles?'

'Yup. Though I'm not so sure that you're right about the ankles.'

Head case. The man was a head case. His job was to promote skeleton bobsledders, not emulate them.

36

'Hey . . .' Pope gripped my wrist. Whispered intently. 'Over there. Sitting in reception. Know who that is?'

I saw a handsome black man in a yellow tracksuit. 'I haven't a clue,' I said. 'Is Lennox Lewis switching sports?'

Pope was unimpressed. 'Haven't you heard of *Cool Runnings*?' he asked. 'The most famous bobsled movie of all time?'

That's the winner in a pretty small field, I thought, but I had heard of the film in question, had even watched most of it one night when I was up late waiting for the next nappy-change. It was the story – mostly uplifting, often amusing – of the Jamaican bobsled squad who were determined to qualify for the 1988 Winter Olympics. They trained on giant skateboards on the hilly roads around Kingston, snow being in short supply in the Caribbean, and 'lived the dream': they made it to the Games, without either killing themselves or ever looking likely to win a medal. A great story, which became a hit movie.

'That guy was one of the team,' Pope said.

'You're kidding.' I was suitably awed. 'But that was ten years ago. What's he doing here now?'

'Trying to qualify for the skeleton competition at Salt Lake City. Some of our guys are helping him out.'

I couldn't cope with this. 'Is anyone in this hotel right in the head?' I asked, getting up from the table.

'Odds against,' said Pope. 'Sleep well.'

The room was spartan, the bed comfortable and cosy, the cold intense. All of which made me very reluctant to get up when Pope came hammering on my door soon after dawn the next morning.

For breakfast there was more in the way of reindeer (dried and thinly sliced, if you want to know; I didn't). Instead I glugged orange juice and forced down about an eighth of a small brown roll. The Major bounced in like a military Tigger, keen to get us moving.

'All set?' he asked. 'How are you feeling? Raring to go?'

'Raring to go,' I said, mentally adding: home.

We scrambled into the minibus and set off up the mountain, with the Major conducting a brisk briefing on the Lillehammer track as he drove. 'You're looking at the only artificially refrigerated bob and luge track in northern Europe,' he said. 'Built, of course, for the 1994 Winter Olympics. It's 1,365 metres long, and there's a 114-metre vertical difference between the start line and the finish line. There are 16 curves, and a good four-man bob should be doing about 90 miles an hour by the end of a run. Anything else you need to know?'

'Are the British the only team using the track?' I asked.

'Well, we are now,' the Major said. 'The Swedes were here until yesterday, when their best two-man driver had a crash and bust his arm, poor fella. So we've got it all to ourselves this morning, which is good news, eh?'

I was too preoccupied to answer.

At the top of the track was a group of pine buildings. A control tower, a changing room cluttered with helmets and reeking of Deep Heat, and a sort of open-sided shed crowded with bobsleds, skeleton bobsleds like giant tea trays, and luges, which resembled miniature, streamlined versions of Father Christmas's sleigh.

Every couple of minutes the public-address system burped into life and the track announcer would say in heavily accented English: 'The track is clear. The track is clear for so-and-so,' and once the driver, or luger, or skeletoneer or whatever they are called, had heard his or her name they were free to head off down the track.

Some – the novices, I guessed – went downhill at an initially gentle pace, while others hurled themselves off the top of the run like Lycra-clad lemmings. I wandered around smoking and asking people Prince Charles-style questions: 'What's your name? Where are you from? And how long have you been sliding head-first down mountains?' My hands were shaking so much that I couldn't write down their answers. Cold, I told myself. Just cold.

It was around now that the Major started sizing me up like an undertaker.

'Now you've got the helmet on,' he said, as we walked back towards the shed, 'don't take it off again. When it's your turn you'll have to move pretty quick. This here is going to be your bob . . .'

It was white, smoothly streamlined and rather beautiful, if you liked that kind of thing.

'You're going to sit here,' the Major said, indicating the second rudimentary seat from the front. 'That way you'll have two people behind you to stop you falling out. When the time comes to get in, climb aboard quickly and put your legs either side of the driver. There is a little grab-handle on either side of the cockpit for you to hold on to. I strongly advise you not to let go of them. If the bob crashes, keep your head down and hang on. It is much safer to be inside the bob, even upside down, than it is to be outside it. You'll hit the snowbank at the bottom either way, but you don't want the bob hitting you. That's it. Any questions?'

'Where's the loo?' I asked.

'Behind the changing room. No hiding.'

You don't actually need to piss, I told myself as I shivered, not pissing, in the little cubicle. You just feel like you want to do a piss because you're scared, and you don't want to wet yourself in the bobsled. Oh, well, thanks for that, I told myself, and tucked everything away. Then I thought, why am I talking to myself? A man could go mad in here.

Back outside, the Major had a line of people for me to meet. 'This is Dai Palmer,' he said, introducing a smiling young Welshman. 'Dai's in the top dozen in the world junior rankings for the two-man bob. He's going to drive you today. Neil Armstrong, here, and Martin Wright are there to make sure you don't fall out.'

'Or run away,' Armstrong added.

'The very idea,' I said.

The three of them heaved the bob over to the head of the run.

'Andrew's going to be number two,' the Major explained, 'and we'll put him and Dai in first and then just walk it off the top of the run. You won't need a flying start today.'

I was enjoying a momentary sense of relief when the PA crackled.

'The track is clear. The track is clear for Palmer, Baker, Armstrong and Wright. Four-man bob.'

Palmer climbed quickly aboard and settled himself at the controls. I followed, plonked my bottom on to the vestigial seat, positioned one leg either side of Palmer's thighs – cosy, this – and established a death-grip on the grab-handles. Out of the corner of my eye I saw a grinning Pope wielding a throwaway camera.

The bob began to trundle forwards at walking pace, and Armstrong's legs arrived either side of mine. He gave me a friendly tap on the helmet, then reached for his grab-handles. His job was to make sure I did nothing stupid. Palmer's job was to steer the bob, while Wright was entrusted with hitting the brakes at the bottom.

I was entrusted with not getting in anyone's way.

The hill steepened, and our speed started to pick up. We were still heading straight ahead, and I was looking around from side to side, determined to take in as much as I could, thinking, oh, ice, nice; hmm, snow, very good; still no Moomintrolls, ho hum, when suddenly I was canted sideways through ninety degrees and an invisible hand whacked me on the back of the head.

That was gravity's way of saying hello.

We've all heard of G-forces, but we rarely meet them in everyday life. We rock and sway on a Tube train, or are pressed back into our seats when an airliner accelerates on take-off, but it is another order of experience altogether to find suddenly that your head is three times heavier than usual and is stubbornly refusing to rise from between your legs.

The bob thumped down from the banked turn and straightened out. I was keen to keep track of where we were on the course: one curve down, I thought, so now . . .

This time we were whipped the other way, and my head thumped into the driver's spine. The bob shot up the banking, and for a moment we were at a lot more than ninety degrees to the track, held to a roof of ice only by gravity's glue. We thumped down again, and the knuckles of my right hand scraped against the bob's shell. Another straight, another chance to heave my head off Palmer's back.

When you watch a bobsled descent on television, everything seems very smooth: the craft swoops and glides down the mountain, and all is achieved with high-speed grace. Inside the bob is not a graceful space. The ice below has been heavily rutted by previous competitors, and the runners are steel: the vibration knocks your teeth together, the noise numbs the mind. But it is the G-forces that boggle. Halfway down the course now, and a switchback threw us from side to side like a pinball, then a longer left-hander forced my head so far down that I listened for a crack. I was desperately concerned not to whack the driver in the back with my helmet – God knows, I didn't want to distract him – but the tendons in my neck were starting to scream.

I had lost track of the track, lost count of the corners, and was hanging on to the grab-handles for dear life when the bob flipped once more with vicious suddenness and we flew along the roof of a left-hand turn. I thought: this is it. The bob is going to tip, my fingers are going to be torn from their sockets and my face is going to be smeared all over the ice like jam on Sunblest Sliced White.

But then the bob crashed down once more and speared, with stomach-turning novelty, uphill.

I was just trying to work that one out when gravity grabbed us again, via Martin Wright's brake handles, and the bob skittered and slithered to a halt just short of a huge pile of loose snow. I put my head up slowly – just checking it was still attached – and patted Dai Palmer on the helmet. We hopped out, and Palmer took his helmet off, flush-faced, smiling.

'Not so bad, was it?' he said, and the funny thing was that it already seemed that way, posterity applying instant balm to ragged memory.

'It was fantastic,' I heard myself saying. 'Thank you so much. But you must have done it a million times.'

'Christ, no,' the young Welshman said. 'That's only the third time I've driven a four-man bob. Heavy bugger on the steering. Cheers, then.'

And he walked off with the other two to supervise the lifting of the bob on to a flat-bed truck. I wrestled my helmet off, dropped my glasses in the snow, wiped them clean, all the while thinking: That was his *third* time in a four-man bobsled, was it?

I wanted a word with the Major.

But as I puffed back up the path that ran alongside the track, endorphins were skittering around happily in my cerebellum, and I couldn't stop grinning. I had gone down the Lillehammer Olympic course in a four-man bobsled. This was good. With a novice driver. This was – retrospectively, of course – even better.

I will try to be honest about this. There is a difference between wanting to do something and wanting to have done it. The word games with Pope on the plane, the evasive banter with the Major, the urge to flush myself down the

42

changing-room loo: this was the Baker who wanted to have been a bobsledder at war with the Baker who didn't want to be a bobsledder. It's all a question of tenses.

It is also, I considered, as the happy chemicals faded back into the bloodstream, a question of responsibility, and I had just been very irresponsible indeed. Worse still, I now had to write about it.

There was, at least, a family precedent. When my brother James was a reporter for a children's television programme soon after he left school, he managed to wangle a drive in a race for single-seater Formula Ford cars at Brands Hatch. He did a brilliant job, qualifying in midfield and managing to finish a race run in pouring rain. But he had not told our mother about his escapade, and since the whole adventure was about to appear on the small screen – and she always watched his show – he had a difficult phone call to make.

As I did now. Once the newspaper found out what I had done – and Pope would make sure they did – I would have to write it up, and my dear wife would no doubt read it, and be extremely unimpressed. But before my own difficult phone call, I made an easy one. I called my brother – who these days has a proper grown-up job – had him hauled out of a meeting and, because he is my brother, because this is what brothers do, said: 'Ner ner ne ner ner, I've been down an Olympic bobsled run and you haven't.'

'You bastard,' James said. 'You absolute bastard.'

'You bastard,' I said to the Major. 'You absolute bastard. You knew that Dai had barely sat in a four-man bob, and yet you sent me down a mountain with him. You ratbag.'

'Seemed to me like a very good idea,' the Major said with a grin. 'Dai's one of the best two-man drivers we've got, but he's got to learn the four-man. What better way than a demonstration run with a very gentle push from the top? It *was* a very gentle push from the top, wasn't it?'

'Very,' I said, knowing when I'd been beaten.

'I wonder,' said Pope, who was getting ready to jump aboard a skeleton bob, 'how gentle it will be by the time it gets into print?'

I wandered off out of earshot to make that tricky phone call.

'Don't tell me,' Ingrid said. 'You went down a mountain in a bobsled.'

'How did you know?' I asked.

'It was perfectly obvious that that was what you were going to do, even if you were pretending you wouldn't dream of such a thing. Was it fun?'

'Fantastic,' I said.

'Well, don't do it again.'

'OK, OK. I promise. Is Lucy there?'

'Yup, hold on . . .'

'Daddy?'

'Hi, Lucy.'

'Daddy?'

'Yes, Lucy?'

'Daddy. Mummy says you're an iddy. Iddy.' Ingrid prompted her. 'An idiot. What's that?'

'Ask her, Lucy,' I said. 'She's right.'

And here was another one: but Pope looked disappointed.

'They're not going to let me go from the top,' he said through his helmet. 'Too many of the novices have been coming off.'

I would have been dancing a jig if the prohibition had been applied to me, but sympathy was in order here. 'You mean, they're only going to let you throw yourself down half a mountain?' I asked.

'Yeah,' sighed Pope.

44

'The heartless bastards,' I said. 'Never mind. Fork over the camera and I'll record the moment for posterity.'

He handed me the cardboard-and-plastic item with which he had snapped the early stages of my descent, and took his place, head-first on an overgrown tea tray.

'Wooo-ooooo!' said Pope.

That evening there was a lot of joshing over the reindeer stew. Everyone recalled their first bobsled runs and, remarkably, no one had been scared beforehand. Equally remarkably, by this time nor had I.

Nonetheless, I felt the need of something a little stronger than the water and fruit juice on offer around the bobbers, and since I wouldn't be doing anything more athletic than catching a plane the next day, I excused myself and headed for the hotel bar.

I asked the barman for a large vodka, and received a dribble, a mere suggestion of liquid, as if a gnat with a watery eye had shaken his head over the glass.

I said: 'This is *large*?'

The barman sighed. 'I cannot serve you a large drink,' he said. 'It is against the law.'

'OK then,' I said. 'Give me another small one.'

'I can't,' he said. 'Not until you have finished that one.' He sighed again. This was not the first time that he had had this conversation. 'It is the law.'

My God, what a country. First it makes you cold and miserable, then it denies you the antidote.

I finished the first one, and took my time – about two and a half seconds – over the second. The bar was starting to fill up with bobbers and lugers and coaches by now, and I had no wish to make a spectacle of myself by the serial ordering and consumption of vodkas, so I slunk miserably and soberly up to my room.

Needless to say, there was no mini-bar.

45

I turned on the television: the weather, in Norwegian. It was going to be cold for the forseeable future, as far as I could make out. No surprises there, then. Flick. The news, in Norwegian. Couldn't make head nor tail of that. Flick. A Norwegian football match. Flick. A blonde unbuttoning her blouse. Flick. Hold on . . .

This was a bit more like it.

I am as indifferent to pornography as the next man, which is not very indifferent at all, and since the trip had so far offered rather more in terms of fear than fun, I didn't see anything wrong with a few minutes' not so innocent entertainment. The Scandinavians, after all, have always been notorious for cinematic hanky-panky.

The blonde had been joined by a blond bloke without a shirt, who started to pay detailed attention to the fixings of his companion's brassiere. As the straps sprang loose, she reached for the button of his jeans, then eased down the zip, and . . .

Ninety-eight per cent of the screen was obscured by an opaque, royal-blue rectangle.

How utterly Norwegian. You can have a drink but you can't have a large one. You can watch a naughty movie, but you can't see anything naughty.

I stayed with it for a few minutes, hoping, I suppose, that the rectangle would shrink or disappear altogether. But it remained relentlessly present, accompanied by a sound-track of gasps and slurps. An occasional gland would appear momentarily in the narrow strip between rectangle and screen edge, which made the whole thing even more ludicrous, as if to say, yes, you can see the private parts, and glimpses of what they are up to, but we will make sure you don't enjoy it.

Any sociologist with the time and the inclination could construct a thesis defining national culture through pornography. The Germans are keen on what are known as water

46

sports, and they don't mean synchronised swimming. The Italians are obsessed with the tradesman's entrance, presumably a result of the need to preserve maidenhood in a good Catholic country. Ditto the Spanish. The Japanese like to dress their women as schoolgirls and then beat them up. Americans like their women artificially pneumatic and intimately depilated, ideals that are spreading as fast as more mainstream American cultural fads. Brazilians like their porn nicked from other countries and cheaply recycled. And so on.

Please don't run away with the idea that I have spent much time conducting such sociological research myself. Oh, no. Pornography is demeaning, both for those who produce it and for those who consume it. It is also incredibly boring. Every now and then, though, when marooned in a second-rate hotel miles from anywhere and far from home, I might briefly check that it is still boring and demeaning. Always is. Never changes.

The Norwegian version, more blue square than blue movie, was another one for the file, though more boring and less demeaning than most. I switched it off.

The next morning I shovelled down the reindeer prosciutto in keen anticipation of another run down the mountain. This time, the Major had said, I could ride shotgun behind Palmer in a two-man bob, with a proper running shove from the top. I could hardly wait. Bobsled, I had decided, was just like riding a bike: it looked impossible to the novice, but once you had got the hang of it, there was nothing to it . . .

Nonsense, nonsense, all nonsense, I am afraid, except for my new-found appetite. The Major had indeed mooted a run in a two-man bob, but I had insisted that my brief but glorious bobsledding career was over.

'Are you sure?' he had asked.

'I have never been more sure about anything in my entire life.'

That was why I tucked into breakfast with such gusto: because I had ensured that I would not have to set foot in a bobsled ever again. I was quite happy to watch other people, though, and Pope and I spent a happy hour at the top of the run watching athletes trying not to look sick. Then we had to set off for the long plod back to Oslo airport.

The Major drove us to the station. 'Pity you're off so soon,' he said. 'I'm sure with a little more persuasion I could have got you into a two-man bob.'

I reiterated my conviction that the sport was not for me.

'Shame,' The Major said, pulling into the station car park. 'I thought you really had something. As a dead weight, you showed great promise.'

Conclusion: Norway is a very boring country.

Chapter Three

Dances With Lawnmowers

Objectives: Accompany the Sports Minister around Australia's Gold Coast; attend the Sydney Olympics, paying particular attention to obscure and/or remote venues; look for Thomas the Tank Engine and his lesser-known Friends; avoid samba-dancers, and try not to fall in the harbour. Time allocated: one month.

'My colleague, Mr Baker, is a journalist of international standing,' said Mihir Bose. 'He is without question deserving of the preferential treatment which you are about to afford myself. This treatment is no doubt detailed in the letter you will have from your managing director, with whom I have been corresponding.'

I like travelling with Mihir. He is my newspaper's investigative sports reporter, an award-winning journalist with more contacts than a rugby-league match, a man used to mixing in elevated circles, a man who regards anything less than a first-class seat on an aeroplane as a personal affront.

Mihir is a meticulous traveller. We were standing at the Emirates airline desk at Dubai airport, a stopover en route from London to the Olympic Games in Sydney. Mihir had expended his usual efforts to ensure that he would be travelling in the style to which he had become accustomed, and he had kindly offered to have me elevated with him.

We had flown the nine hours from London in business class on the Emirates 777, reduced circumstances which Mihir had borne with stoical good grace. Our mildly bizarre ticketing arrangements now decreed that we should spend the remaining two-thirds of the journey, to Sydney via Singapore, in economy class, a category of travel which has no place in Mihir's world-view.

He had, accordingly, conducted a polite correspondence over several weeks with Emirates' senior executive in London, informing the gentleman of the signal honour that his airline would enjoy in conveying Mr Bose to Sydney, and of the manner in which Mr Bose expected to travel. Mysteriously, no trace of this correspondence had filtered down to the transfer desk in Dubai, where the Emirates official, while suitably impressed by Mihir's imperious manner, was still politely refusing to move him up to the sharp end of the aircraft.

'This is quite unacceptable,' Mihir declared. 'Careful arrangements have been made. If you were to send an email to London they would be confirmed in moments.'

Undoubtedly so, the Emirates man concurred. However, the time in London was approaching three o'clock in the morning, and by the time there was anyone in the office to respond to the email, our plane would be in south-east-Asian skies.

Mihir was undaunted. Contact must immediately be made with the airline's head office here in Dubai, where the status of Mr Bose would be instantly confirmed and his upgrade authorised. 'And while you are about it,' Mihir said, 'you will kindly ensure that the same courtesies are extended to my eminent colleague, Mr Baker.'

Mihir led me away for a consoling drink, tutting over the ineptitude of the airline staff. 'It is really quite unaccept-able,' he said. 'I do apologise for the trouble.'

I was starting to regret my involvement in the escapade.

Mihir – as is his way – had made the process sound so simple as we tucked into our champagne and canapés outbound from Heathrow. He had the whole thing sewn up, he had assured me, and he was as confident of his own entitlement as he had seemed of mine. But I don't have an upgradable face, or an upgradable manner. There is something about me that screams 'economy class' loud enough for all airline staff to hear: in fact I am constantly surprised that when checking in I am not lifted on to the conveyor belt with the baggage and consigned to the cargo hold.

Sure enough, when the time came to re-board our aircraft, Mihir was spirited away from me by a pretty stewardess and directed down the walkway aimed at the front of the plane, while I arrived in cattle class to find that the seat which would have been his had been reassigned to an ancient Singaporean droolhound.

Mihir spent the subsequent stopover in Singapore regaling us with the splendours of his first-class bed, the beauty of the stewardesses and the many subtle pleasures of the menu. When we re-boarded once more, we were rather surprised that he was not carried aboard in a personal litter, with stewardesses strewing orchids at his feet. And Mihir was surprised that when we arrived at Sydney's Kingston Smith airport it was a humble yellow taxi, rather than a limousine, which ferried him and most of the paper's other writers to the Furama Hotel in Darling Harbour.

I wanted to go with them, to strip off my sticky continent-crossing clothing, hose myself down under a cool shower, and sleep for a couple of days. But I hadn't finished travelling yet. With Tom Knight, the paper's athletics correspondent, I had been detailed to fly on up to the Gold Coast, where most of the British athletes were fine-tuning their Olympic preparations.

Tom and I sat next to the airport taxi rank watching the others disappear towards their beds, perched on our luggage like birds on oblong nests, trying desperately to stay awake long enough to check in for our internal flight to Coolongatta.

'So this is Sydney, home of the Olympic Games,' Tom said, propping himself up on a rucksack to light a slim cigar.

'Yup,' I said, mopping Singaporean saliva from my jacket's shoulder. An empty plastic bag from the duty-free shop blew across the car park and wrapped itself around my laptop case.

'Home of the greatest festival of sport the world has ever known,' Tom said.

'Uh-hunh,' I said.

A taxi coasted to a halt in front of us. The driver, portly, grey haired, sullen, opened his door a few inches and spat copiously on the tarmac.

'Glamorous, isn't it?' said Tom, and shut his eyes.

It was not an auspicious start, but I refused to be downcast. This was the big one: the event that every sports writer on the planet dreams of covering. Everything I had learnt in France and Kuala Lumpur and almost nothing that I had learnt in Norway would be applied at my first Olympic Games. Tom didn't share my excitement – he had seen it all before – but Tom was asleep, so I did a little private jig of anticipation.

We flew up to Coolongatta on an Ansett Airlines BAE 146, one of those dinky little regional jetliners with four small engines doing the work of two big ones. I've always liked these aeroplanes, on the basis that the more engines you have hanging off your wings, the more likely you are to stay in the air should one of them conk out. The little plane banked over the centre of Sydney as it headed north towards the coast. I looked past the grizzled profile of the middle-aged Australian man in the seat next to me at a scene framed by the window like a postcard: the great arch of the Harbour Bridge, the concertinaed conch shells of the Opera House. A few moments later, Tom leant over from the seat behind and tapped me on the shoulder.

'Look,' he said, 'there's Homebush Park: there's the stadium.'

So it was. The vast, newly created Olympic site, a sprawling city of sport with Stadium Australia at its centre. 'Fantastic,' I sighed.

The man next to me hadn't looked out of the window since we took off.

'You'll be here for the Olympics, then?' he asked.

'Yes,' I said. 'It's going to be amazing. Did you see that stadium? Wonderful. It's going to be a great Games, what with this being such a sports-loving country. And the facilities are going to be out of this world. Then there are the athletes. You'll have your own heroes, I guess, Ian Thorpe in the pool, Cathy Freeman on the track, that amazing pole-vaulter. But you won't have it all your own way, you know. Don't forget our rowers, don't forget our sailors. We'll be picking up a few medals, don't you worry. But that doesn't matter so much as the Games themselves, does it? What a fantastic festival. It's going to be so good, I can hardly wait for it to get started. How about you?'

He looked at me for quite a long time. 'I'm a rugby league man, myself,' he said. 'I don't give a rat's arse for the Olympics.'

Nor did the taxi driver who collected us from Coolongatta an hour later. 'Waste of money, if you ask me,' he said. He was in his mid-thirties, wore a dirty yellow T-shirt and smelled slightly of disinfectant. 'They'd be better off spending the money on jobs for the people up here.'

'Is work hard to find, then?' Tom asked politely.

'Impossible. That's why I'm driving this bloody thing. Thing is, you see, they give all the jobs to the blacks.' He paused, assessing his audience. 'You have blacks in your country?'

'Well, yes we do,' I said, 'but . . .'

'You'll know what I'm talking about then. All you need to get a job round here is black skin. Not that they do any work once they get the bloody jobs, of course.'

'But . . .'

'They should give the jobs to the people who deserve them.' The driver had an accent of some kind, hard to place, but definitely there.

'Have you always lived in Australia?' I asked.

'No, mate,' said the driver. 'I'm from Croatia.'

'Have you ever thought of going back there?' asked Tom.

The rest of the journey was conducted in an unfriendly silence.

The Gold Coast is a city without a centre, a narrow strip of developed land twenty miles long sandwiched between the bush and the ocean, modern condominiums and hotels adjoining the broad beach, houses with pools arranged in suburban clusters with here and there a sprinkling of shops, a cinema, petrol station or themed restaurant, but no identifiable nucleus. A strange place, filled, or so it seemed to me, with oddly discontented people, who felt that life owed them more than a beach and a beer, and that they were somehow missing out.

The happiest were those who hung out at the Northcliffe Surf Life-Saving Club, an admirable institution abutting the endless beach five minutes' walk from the hotel. An SLSC is a social hub, as much a part of Australian coastal life as the surf itself. You will see them dotted all along the nation's shores, one every few miles, or every few hundred yards in coastal cities: pubs with a purpose.

Surf life-saving is not just a rescue service: it is a sport. Australia's SLSCs compete among each other, honing the skills of their life-savers and more importantly, trying to beat the arse off the opposition. The bar and restaurant area of the Northcliffe SLSC was bedecked with commemorative swimming trunks, banners and team photos. Once I had finished interviewing Simon Lessing, a British triathlete, on the beach terrace, I wandered inside in search of beer and enlightenment.

'Are you a member, mate?' the barman asked in a not entirely unfriendly manner.

'Well, yes, I think I am, actually,' I said, producing the documentation that confirmed my temporary membership, arranged as a perk by the British Olympic Association.

'So you are,' said the barman. 'Have to say you don't sound like a member. Last time we had an accent like that in here it was coming from *Brideshead* bloody *Revisited* on the TV. What'll you have?'

I ordered a lager – when in Rome, etc. – and asked the barman if he could set me right on a couple of points.

'Sure thing,' He was tall, well built, vaguely Greek in appearance. Name of Pete.

'This surf life-saving business,' I said. 'You can compete at it, is that right?'

'Sure is,' said Pete. 'That's what all this stuff is about.' He gestured at the massed memorabilia. 'This is a pretty good club.'

'So how does it go, in competition?' I asked. 'Just run me through it.'

'There's all sorts of different formats,' Pete said. 'But basically when the whistle blows you grab your board, run down the beach, paddle out to wherever, make your "rescue" then paddle back and run up the beach with your board.'

I was still a bit puzzled. 'What about the people being saved? Do they all have to be the same weight? Or do the best swimmers have to rescue the fatties? Is there some kind of handicap system?'

Pete looked at me as if I was from a different planet, which, in truth, was how I felt.

'You don't rescue people in competition, you dork,' he

said, with a broad grin. 'It's a test of swimming power, stamina and board skills.' He shook his head. 'What didja think, we'd have people tethered to buoys out there waiting to be picked up? You ever heard of sharks?' Still, shaking his head, he wandered off towards the kitchen to share this gem with the chef.

I thought I'd go and commune with something of about my intelligence level until the scarlet in my cheeks faded, so I walked into the back room of the club, which was entirely given over to fruit machines.

Hold on, though, these weren't the common or garden fruit machines of the British pub, but something altogether more complicated. Pokies, according to the flashing signs. What on earth was a pokie?

A poker machine: silicon-chipped five-card draw. I used to quite fancy myself as a poker player, in the pre-fatherhood days of surplus income, so I settled myself down with my lager and fed a few dollars into the nearest pokie.

Hopeless. Every card I changed I should have kept. Every card I kept I should have changed. Speaking of change, I soon ran out, and then became aware of Pete the barman and his mate the chef watching me around the corner of the bar.

'Don't worry, mate,' Pete called as I made for the exit. 'You could always take up life-saving.'

That night I had dinner in the revolving restaurant on the twentieth floor of the hotel with some of the other British writers on Gold Coast duty. Most of us were in terrible shape, jet lagged, tipsy, dog-tired. One of the tabloid contingent fell asleep with his head on his plate, and was dispatched to his room with a rectangle of sesame prawn toast attached to his left eyebrow like a plaster.

'What I want to know,' I said, 'is why they bothered to build a revolving restaurant on top of a hotel in the middle of nowhere.'

'What goes around, comes around,' said Duncan from the *Guardian*, waking up like the Mad Hatter's dormouse.

'It gives the locals something to be proud of,' said Vikki from the *Sun*. 'You know, "This might not be much of a town but we do have the only revolving restaurant this side of Brisbane." '

'But what's the point?' I demanded. 'Look out of the window . . .' A sprinkling of distant suburban street lights, three pairs of speeding headlights.

'Sod-all,' Duncan and Vikki said as one.

I let the conversation, such as it was, resume, and returned to playing with my sweet-and-sour chicken. The most annoying thing about jet lag for me is not fatigue: there are ways of fighting that. I can alter my sleeping pattern relatively easily with a couple of glasses of wine, but I can't con my stomach. Jet lag mucks up my appetite, rendering me ravenous at four in the morning when there is nothing to eat but a miniature packet of mini-bar cashews, and sickeningly sated at anything approximating a normal mealtime.

'Look out of the window again,' I shouted, interrupting the table talk twenty minutes and 180 degrees later. A sprinkling of suburban street lights, three pairs of speeding headlights.

'Sod-all once more,' my companions agreed.

'But you're just a cynical tourist,' said Vikki. 'A Gold Coaster could read a ton of detail in either one of those sod-alls. You just need time to get used to your surroundings.'

'But I don't want to get used to my surroundings,' I said. 'I want to go to Sydney.'

'What goes around, came around,' said Duncan the dormouse, and shut his eyes again.

Back in my room I was just dropping off into the most blissful of long-prolonged jet-lagged snoozes, one that I planned to extend well into the following morning, when my mobile rang. Curses.

'Andrew?' Woman. Ulster accent. My goodness . . . 'It's Kate Hoey.' Britain's Sports Minister. Bloody Norah.

'Bloody Norah,' I said.

'No, bloody Kate. What are you up to tomorrow?'

'Um, nothing much. Spot of reporting, you know, usual stuff.'

'I'm going round to see some of the British athletes and their training venues,' the minister said. 'Why don't you tag along?'

Bye-bye lie-in.

'Andrew? Why don't you tag along?'

'I will,' I said. 'Tremendous. Terrific.'

'Great,' she said. 'Meet me at the badminton venue at nine tomorrow morning, OK? Bye.'

Nine? Oh God. I didn't even know where the badminton players were training. I booked an alarm call and blacked out.

Another bigoted taxi driver took me to a large shed in the middle of nowhere. I lurked by the door, smoking furtively, until the minister's official car swung into the car park. Out popped Hoey and her ministry minder. She pecked me on the cheek (we had met a couple of times before), and wrinkled her nose. 'When are you going to give up?' she asked.

Hoey is a perpetual-motion machine. There is always another hand to be shaken, another view to be canvassed. She charged into the shed and turned left, discovering the nation's badminton players shuttlecocking frenziedly in front of an empty grandstand. Within ten minutes, the minister had chatted to a dozen individuals, including Simon Archer and Jo Goode, the mixed-doubles pair supposed to have a lively chance of a medal.

I stumbled around in Hoey's wake, usually asking the

same questions that she had done: Accommodation OK? Food all right? Over the jet lag? I might have been mistaken for a minor consular official, had it not been for the crumpled jeans, old training shoes and purple T-shirt.

'The judokas are down here,' Hoey called over her shoulder, charging down an anonymous corridor. Sure enough, the floor started to shake with the impact of hurled bodies. The judo fighters seemed delighted to see us, not so much for our glamour as the opportunity we offered for fifteen pain-free minutes. The head coach seemed particularly keen for the minister to meet the female middleweight on the squad. 'Kate Hoey,' he said with a smirk, 'meet Kate Howey.' How we laughed.

Back in the car and off to see the swimmers, training in a palatial fifty-metre pool nearby. There is a pool on this scale on every other block on the Gold Coast; fewer than a dozen in the whole of the United Kingdom. Aussies adore swimming, Brits tolerate it.

The minister, her minder and I headed further inland, to what looked like a village hall, but which turned out to be the Nerang Police Civic Youth Club. The civil servant checked his notes as we drew up: 'Boxing and tae kwon do,' he announced.

It was quite a carnival. These training camps were doubly beneficial: they allowed the visiting athletes to acclimatise and sharpen up before the Games, and they spread the spirit of sporting festivities far beyond the host city. This was the closest that most people in this little suburb were going to get to the five rings, and they wanted to make the most of it: this was Nerang's Olympics.

In one corner of the hall, our two tae kwon do fighters, Colin Daley and the junior world champion, Sarah Stevenson, were doing their best to kick their respective coaches into next week.

Hoey stepped in and broke them up, like a determined

referee. They started to discuss bruised feet, which are apparently the bane of a tae kwon do fighter's life. If I followed Hoey for much longer I'd be suffering them too.

I grilled assorted locals on the topic of the visiting Brits. The general consensus seemed to be that the training camp was the most exciting thing to happen in Nerang since the arrival of the first automobile. This was good to hear, because in general I found Poms to be as welcome in Australia as foot-and-mouth disease.

Over in the other corner of the hall was another fighter, at this stage in his career as little known as Daley and Stevenson: the super-heavyweight boxer Audley Harrison. I'd met him a couple of months previously, for an Olympic preview piece. He was not an easy man to forget.

'Come to West Hampstead station,' he had said. 'I'll meet you outside in my car.'

'How will I recognise you?' I'd asked.

'You'll recognise me,' he had said.

He was sitting in a smart, if very old, Ford saloon. Sitting so far from the wheel, though, that he might as well have done away with the front seat altogether and steered from the back. Sitting in the front passenger seat, I had to turn right round over my right shoulder to talk to him. Harrison is big. He drove us to a large, shabby pub near Hampstead Cemetery, parked unworriedly on a yellow line and led me into a back room. 'They know me here,' he said.

Then, over gallons of orange juice, he gave me the whole spiel.

Audley Harrison had a master plan. He also had a degree in sports marketing, a sensationally complex hairdo and a level of self-belief rarely found outside a Marvel comic. Audley, in short, was, he said, going to become the heavyweight champion of the world. First, though, it would be necessary for him to win an Olympic gold medal. Which he would do, he assured me, in Sydney.

I reminded him of this next to the improvised ring in the Nerang sports hall, where he was dispatching bloody-nosed local sparring partners at a rate of one every three minutes.

'Sure, sure,' he said. 'I'm still on target.'

While Hoey posed for photographs, her head roughly at the level of Harrison's left nipple, I noted down some of the gung-ho philosophy pinned to the wall of the warm-up room.

'Repeating the same behaviour will produce the same result,' was a mantra that might have been applied to a multitude of British teams over the past couple of decades. Another slogan might have been adopted to good effect by the politician as well as the fighter: 'If you really want to do something, you'll find a way. If you don't, you'll find an excuse.'

On second thoughts, that applied rather well to me. The next day I found an excuse to fly to Sydney: the Olympic Games were starting that evening, and I rather wanted to be there.

I checked in to the Furama Hotel at Darling Harbour, close to Chinatown and Central station, and asked at the desk if they had any special arrangements for the opening ceremony.

'There's a TV in the bar,' the receptionist shrugged. So there was: a TV and 300 people. 'Or there's a big screen in the park,' she added. The park it was.

Opening ceremonies normally give me the heebie-jeebies, but this one was different: it was funny. We watched 100 men in garish shirts and bright green sunhats dancing with lawnmowers, a tribute, the locals in the crowd told us, to suburban Australia. We watched hundreds of little children fitted with fish tails dashing around Stadium Australia pretending to be minnows. An ancient folk singer called

Slim Dusty sang 'Waltzing Matilda' and managed to make it moving; giant metal machines that might have driven straight out of *Mad Max* clanked and thundered around the arena. It was breathtaking.

Then a great waterfall appeared at one end of the stadium, and within it stood a slim, muscular female figure in a skin-tight white suit: Cathy Freeman, the aboriginal 400-metre runner, the heroine of all Australia. She held a torch which somehow burned through the deluge, and when she touched it to the cauldron the Olympic flame leapt up and a great cheer swept the park. Then the cauldron started to move up a sort of railway towards the roof of the stadium. For one terrible moment it got stuck, and every breath in the park was held, but then it moved on, up to the top of the stadium roof where it would burn throughout the Games.

All the while that the cranky cauldron struggled up to the roof, Freeman stood under the waterfall. Her pose contributed dignity to the tableau, but can't have done much for her health. Ten out of ten for style, Australia, but minus several for sporting acumen.

My first assignment continued the watery theme (I was going to have a thoroughly wet Games). I was dispatched to assess the progress through their opening heat of Britain's brightest hopes for a gold medal, the rowers of the coxless four. Steve Redgrave, Matthew Pinsent, James Cracknell and Tim Foster bore the greatest weight of expectation in the British squad and they bore it with unfailing good grace.

On the train up to the rowing venue at Penrith, about an hour from Sydney, I recalled a breakfast that the Four had hosted at the Leander Club in Henley-on-Thames just before they travelled to Australia. Over gargantuan servings of cereal, croissants, toast, eggs, fruit and pastries, Pinsent had insisted that their task was much more difficult than the public seemed to think. Redgrave pointed out that the fact that he had won four consecutive gold medals did not automatically entitle him to a fifth: it would have to be earned. The Italians, the Kiwis and the Australians, Cracknell reminded me, had just beaten the British Four at the Lucerne regatta. And would I mind passing the cornflakes?

What everyone wanted to know, of course, was whether Redgrave, who after the Atlanta Games had famously asked to be shot if ever seen near a boat again, would finally retire after this one. It seemed he might. 'I'm definitely going to stop rowing,' he dead-panned between mouthfuls. 'But who knows when?'

Pinsent stepped in before his eminent shipmate could become any more garrulous. 'One of the things we learnt in Atlanta,' he said, smirking at Redgrave, 'was not to go shooting our mouths off in the heat of the moment.' Or, in other words, not to tell the press anything too inter-esting.

OK then, Matthew. What are *your* plans?

'Right now,' said Pinsent, 'the plan is to get the gold, get incredibly drunk and then sort things out from there.'

What a curious collection of characters: Redgrave, a sporting immortal humanised by the onset of diabetes; Pinsent, the apple-cheeked Old Etonian with the chest of an ox and the manners of a diplomat; Cracknell, with his square-jawed, cartoon-character good looks and worrying plans for a feature-writing career on my newspaper; and Foster, the wild-haired wild boy with the dodgy back who, on medical if not mental grounds, should have retired long before.

Now I was going to see them in action in person for the first time, at the Penrith Olympic Rowing Lake or, to be equally accurate but less impressive, on a converted gravel pit beyond the farthest suburbs of Sydney. Few traces of the site's former incarnation remained. The course stretched into the distance like a liquid runway, the boats at the distant start line no bigger than pond-skimmers. But they raced into a funnel of noise, the grandstands already crowded even for the earliest heats, with substantial outbreaks of Union Jacks among the inflatable kangaroos.

Redgrave and Co. competed in the first heat of all, against, among others, the powerful and powerfully supported Australians. The British Four prevailed with some ease, the Aussies slacking off in a safe second place. The grandstand shook with cheers, but this was nothing more than a prelude.

Afterwards, the Four filed into a Portakabin to address the press. The trouble was, they didn't really have anything to say to us that they had not already said in Henley. There was some desultory chat about the venue (fine), the transport (fine) and the accommodation (which gave us our only angle). Redgrave was sharing his room in the Olympic Village with Pinsent; Cracknell and Foster had the room next door. 'Steve and I were just dropping off to sleep,' Pinsent said, 'when we heard a terrible crash, and then, worse than that, a terrible silence.' It transpired that Cracknell, who is roughly the size and weight of a brick-filled wardrobe, had stood on the bedside table in order to climb up to the top bunk. The table had, understandably, exploded, and Cracknell had crashed down with it. Redgrave and Pinsent had rushed in to investigate, and found that their colleague was unscathed. 'He was fine,' Pinsent said. 'Just worried about the state of his sunglasses and his Walkman.'

Exit half a dozen happy journalists. It was too early to be breaking records, but a broken table would suit us just fine.

The next day was a Saturday, a theoretical day off which I spent at Stadium Australia, the showpiece arena at the centre of the main Olympic complex at Homebush Bay. It was a glorious edifice, with vast and vertiginous grandstands arcing into the sky. I had visited the previous year, and found it impressive even when empty. Now that it was crammed with almost 100,000 excited people and crowned with the fluttering Olympic flame, I was awestruck.

I was also mothstruck: a large, dead insect landed with a soft thud right on the top of my head. Looking around, I could see hundreds of them lying in gangways and on the track surrounds, their tattered yellow wings two or three inches across. More were falling by the moment, as if the Red Baron had been reborn with an insect phobia and was prowling the skies above the stadium.

The real culprits were the arena's gigantic floodlights. Before and during the building of the Homebush Bay complex, extraordinary lengths had been gone to in order to protect the area's existing wildlife: lizards had been lovingly relocated, frogs found alternative accommodation, birds built nesting-boxes.

But no one had recalled that moths are drawn to a flame, and the illumination of four of the brightest lights on the continent had enticed a local giant, the Bogong moth, into an early migration. The subsequent mass extinction was tough on the moths, but tough, too, on the spectators at Homebush, particularly European visitors who were not used to being buzzed by insects the size of a paperback.

The tourists were freaking out, which in turn frightened the Sydney Olympic organisers. They called in a top entomologist for advice. 'The easiest way to deal with the moths,' he told them, 'is to learn to love them.'

That's easy for an entomologist to say. But it is hard to love a moth when it spirals smokily out of the sky like a stricken Sopwith Camel and spreads its internal organs all over your laptop keyboard.

I never learnt to love the Bogongs. But I learnt to ignore them sufficiently to clock Cathy Freeman's performance in her opening heat of the 400 metres. She ran the race in the manner of a high-speed royal progress, seemingly unaffected by her prolonged shower at the opening ceremony. 'The crowd was amazing,' she told the assembled press afterwards. So was she. So were the moths.

Back at the Furama I found that the bar had been invaded by a squadron of samba dancers: Brazilian fans from the volleyball arena across the road. They were fantastically happy and fantastically loud, and the only way to get a drink was to dance to the bar and dance back, in the process spilling most of your beer (Foster's of course: the samba nectar). But no one seemed to mind, and it was the most exercise I had taken in months.

So loud were the samba contingent that at first I could not make out the urgent news that the Sports Editor was trying to pass on to me.

'Rerun old metal!' he yelled into my ear as a whooping six-foot brunette trod on my left little toe. 'Queasy! Clearly! Strike-list!'

After several more attempts and a brief lull in the drumming, it became clear that Great Britain had won their first medal of the Games – a gold, no less – secured by the cyclist Jason Queally, in the one-kilometre time trial at the Dunc Gray Velodrome. Feelings of patriotism and pride were tempered by Queally having succeeded on a Saturday, the one day of the week when daily newspaper journalists cannot file copy. Instead, our friendly Sunday rivals had a fantastic splash and we would only get the trickles of second-hand information the next day. But I was delighted for Queally, and for myself. He was one of half a dozen athletes from the less glamorous reaches of the British squad whom I had interviewed before the Games: a nice, shy, brave man who had overcome terrible injuries from a racing accident to make it to Sydney.

'I'll go and see him tomorrow!' I yelled to the Sports Editor.

I interviewed Queally. And on the succeeding days I sat in the deafening echo of the aquatic centre and watched Ian Thorpe, the big-footed teenage wonder Dave had 'advised' in Kuala Lumpur, take the 400-metre freestyle gold in front of his besotted home crowd; I watched the British men lose a hockey match; I watched some baseball in some bafflement; watched Simon Archer burst into tears when he and Jo Goode won a bronze medal for badminton. In between missions I wandered the vast Main Press Centre, cosmetically converted cattle sheds on the former Sydney Showground, and Barbied My Own steak in the central grill area, declining the offer to Char My Own kangaroo fillet.

Everything was working as it should: the trains were fast and efficient, the bus drivers knew their routes, the security was non-intrusive, the venues smart. The Games were good.

One night my mobile rang just as I had dropped off to sleep.

'Daddy?'

'Yes, Lucy.'

'Daddy.'

'I'm here.'

'Daddy. Why are you doing your work in 'Stralia?'

'Because that is where the Olympic Games are being held.'

'Games? Like my games?'

'Well, not exactly . . .'

'Gameboy games?'

'No, they're . . .'

'Animal games. Are you pretending to be an animal?'

'Lucy. No. These are grown-up games. My newspaper wants me to write about them.'

'Why?'

'Lucy, it's one o'clock in the morning here.'

'What! Don't be crazy. It's tea time.'

'Yes, Lucy, I know, but in Australia it's night-time, Daddy's bed time.'

'Why? How?'

'I . . . I don't really know. It's just the way the world works. Lucy, I really have to go to sleep now, because I have to do some writing for my newspaper in the morning.'

'Why?'

'So that they will give me some money.'

'Ooo. Good. I can do writing. I can write my name, and "mum" and "dad".'

'I know. That's brilliant. Now . . .'

'If I do some writing, will you give me some money?'

Huge yawn.

'Daddy? Will you?'

'Yes, Lucy. A little bit.'

'Good. Then I can buy a dolphin.'

The line went dead. I slumped back on to the pillow, longing for sleep but tormented by visions of a delivery van parked outside a St John's Wood house, rear doors ajar to reveal a large, thrashing tail.

Every night at half past ten there was a show on Australian television which was almost as unmissable as a telephone call home. Most of the local coverage of the Games was smotheringly parochial, in that if Australia had the slightest sniff of medal hope the cameras would be there, while if they didn't the coverage was negligible. The trouble was that the Australians had so many strong competitors that it was hard to notice that anyone else was at the Games at all.

The antidote to this wall-to-wall boosterism was a wonderful late-night satirical show called *The Dream*, in which two grizzled and cynical hosts called Roy and HG ruthlessly roasted the heroes of the day and sent up the self-importance of the whole Olympic movement.

A particular target was the political correctness of the organisers, who, in their eagerness to do right by every ethnic group and interest, had produced a bewildering array of official Games mascots, each intended to represent a crucial element of Australian culture. Olly, for instance, was a kookaburra (a kind of kingfisher) who also, we were told, represented the Olympic spirit of generosity. Syd was a duck-billed platypus who personified not only the environment but the vigour and energy of the Australian people. And Milly, an echidna, embodied the information revolution of the new millennium, which is not bad going for a small, spiny marsupial.

There are Greek gods invested with less symbolic importance than Sydney's stuffed toys. Roy and HG agreed, and came up with an alternative mascot of their own, introduced on *The Dream* one night as 'Fatso the Fat-Arsed Wombat, the lovable little fella with a big arse'. I laughed so loudly my neighbour had to bang on the wall to shut me up.

Fatso took off in a big way. His inane grin and expansive posterior were soon to be seen in shop windows all over the capital, and Aussie athletes were carrying him on to the podium for their numerous medal ceremonies. This was too much for SOCOG, the Sydney Organising Committee Olympic Games. Fatso was banned from medal celebrations, and Roy and HG had the fuel for several more evenings of wombat-based satire.

Around this time another notable Olympic anti-hero was enjoying his brief spell in the international spotlight. Eric 'The Eel' Moussambani was Equatorial Guinea's man in the 100-metre freestyle, for which he had trained back home in a crocodile-infested river. Victory seemed to be out of the question: survival was his priority. But then his two rivals were both disqualified for a false start, and Eric the Eel swam, with increasing difficulty, towards the slowest heat win, and indeed the slowest time for the distance, in Olympic history.

He had, at times, seemed to be finding it hard to keep his head above water. As soon as he emerged from the water, he found it difficult to keep his feet on the ground. Eric was in demand. Speedo gave him a bodysuit, a German television crew took him around Sydney Harbour, and one of the British tabloids gave him a medal.

His time was way outside the qualification standard for the semi-finals, and Eric was disappointed to find that his Olympics were over after just 1 minute 52.72 seconds of breathless effort. 'I think they should let me back into the event,' Moussambani told us. 'I did win my heat.'

It didn't matter: even in this land dedicated to winners, Eric the Eel was Australia's favourite loser. The celebrity of Fatso and Moussambani proved that every Olympic Games develops its own culture more rapidly than a yoghurt under a sun-lamp. Talking with Mihir on the long flight down I had predicted that the biggest stars of the Games would be Ian Thorpe and Cathy Freeman, little reckoning that they would be upstaged on their own patch by an imitation marsupial and a bad swimmer.

So the greatest sporting event on the planet did not take itself too seriously: that was never going to be the way in Sydney, where men dance with lawnmowers and a merry cynicism is bred in the bone. In Kuala Lumpur, the volunteers had been desperate for approval. Here, they just wanted you to have a good time.

It's hard to have a bad time in Sydney, harder still when fed a daily, ever-changing diet of high-class sport. The schedule, though, was getting to be a grind, and the sheer variety of competition a strain on the intellect. Since the Commonwealth Games, I had become quite used to the idea of instant expertise, but gaining and employing a working knowledge of, say, target archery and dinghy-sailing on the same day could be quite a challenge.

'What now?' I asked the Sports Editor in the course of my wake-up call on the sixth day of the Games. 'Graeco-Roman wrestling? Women's softball?'

'Nice easy one for you today,' he said. 'Kayaking.'

Oh, tremendous.

I did some swotting on the bus. The sport had been borderline for inclusion in the Games, I read, but once it was confirmed the Australians had swiftly knocked up a bastard of a course: a long, concrete horseshoe down which thousands of gallons of water rushed in foaming torrents. Rapidly constructed rapids, in fact. Grandstands had been built around the outer edge of the horseshoe, and they were full: the Penrith Whitewater Stadium, unlikely though it may seem, had become a hot ticket.

I soon saw why. Simply getting down the course without capsizing or smashing your craft to pieces would have been a praiseworthy achievement. But the competitors also had to negotiate twenty-three gates, each comprising two poles a couple of feet apart, dangling above the water. Most of the gates could be taken heading downstream, but for a few the kayakers had to turn and battle against the current.

It was horrendously difficult, and the penalties for inaccuracy were severe: tap a gate and two seconds would be added to your time; miss one altogether and fifty seconds would be added on, effectively ending your chances.

So much for the swotting. But what was I doing there? Watching another British medal prospect: Paul Ratcliffe, who was competing in the final of the men's K1 event. What is more, Ratcliffe's chief rival was a German, one Thomas Schmidt.

Down the course came Ratcliffe on his first run, bobbing and weaving and heaving, at times disappearing almost entirely beneath the waves. He looked all set for a place in the top three, but when he splashed down after the final, four-foot drop, he suddenly tipped over and floated towards the finish line capsized.

This was dangerous, of course, but also (as any recently qualified kayaking expert could tell you) illegal. You may cross the line in a kayak event forwards, backwards or sideways, but not upside down. It is a way, I suspect, of avoiding a preponderance of posthumous champions.

Whatever the reason, Ratcliffe knew the rules, and with his final ounce of energy he righted his craft and swept over the line. His second run was considerably tidier, and completed without any underwater interludes, but the brief inversion had cost him dear: Schmidt, paddling with metronomic and (one has to say) Germanic efficiency, had finished five seconds clear of the field.

But Ratcliffe had the silver medal, and proved to be a charming interviewee. 'I remember thinking, "This shouldn't happen at the Olympics,"' he said. 'But I've enjoyed every minute of it – except the capsize.'

My report must have demonstrated some spurious affinity with water-based sport, for a few days later I found myself dispatched to Rushcutters' Bay, where Britain's sailors were poised to bring ashore some fabulous booty. 'I don't *like* boats,' I reminded the Sports Editor. 'I get seasick.'

'Nobody is telling you to get on a boat,' he said. 'Just go and watch them.'

This proved to be trickier than I had envisaged. Having never witnessed an Olympic sailing regatta, I had naively imagined that the competitors would be racing in a single, small, defined area clearly visible from the shore. Not so. The various fleets scattered to different corners of Sydney Harbour – which is vast – and conducted their races entirely out of sight of the press centre at the marina.

Furthermore, each class involved a different kind of boat, with various crew permutations. Even the names were confusing: Mistral, 49er, Soling, Europe, 470, Finn, Laser, Star. And as for the rules . . . the first piece of paper I examined on the press-room noticeboard was some kind of protest by the event jury against the organisers, or the other way round.

Matthew Norman, from the *Evening Standard,* walked up to me looking as perplexed as I felt.

'Have you got any idea what is going on?' he asked.

'As far as I can see,' I indicated the noticeboard, 'the entire event is illegal. With any luck we are all about to get arrested.'

The police stayed away, the jury got over their huff – I never did find out what it was all about – and Matthew decided to go and follow a race on one of the press boats. This was, of course, the proper thing to do, but I managed to convince myself that it was more sensible to stay in the press room where one could follow a number of races at once on a bank of television screens and where, what is more, one was not likely to throw up all over one's notes.

I went back to Rushcutters' Bay three days on the trot, and while I never quite got the hang of what was going on, or indeed set foot on a boat, I witnessed a great many celebrations that those out on the water missed.

I saw Shirley Robertson sailing in after winning gold in the Europe class, blonde hair blowing in the warm breeze, gloved hands punching the sky. Fellow Britons descended on her as she drew up next to the jetty, willing hands securing the ropes, then securing a grip on the sailor and 'One, two, three . . .' into the harbour she went. Ironic, really: you spend a week trying to avoid sinking in Sydney's coastal waters and at the end of it all you are submerged by your own team-mates.

The same thing happened to Ben Ainslie at the conclusion of a vicious tactical battle in the Laser class with his Brazilian rival, Robert Scheidt (cue the British press corps:

'You're Scheidt, and you know you are . . .'). Iain Percy was the other golden duckee, after victory in the Finn class, and others to make a splash were Ian Barker and Simon Hiscocks, who took silver in the 49ers, and Ian Walker and Mark Covell, who won the silver medal in the Star class.

Success for the latter pairing provoked a huge outpouring of emotion among the British squad, for the crew had been brought together in shared adversity, and raced with two ghostly accomplices: John Merricks, who had shared the silver-medal boat with Walker at the 1996 Olympics, but who had subsequently been killed in a car crash, and Glyn Charles, Covell's racing partner, who had lost his life in the Sydney to Hobart race.

I often find a lump in my throat when interviewing medal-winners, being a total softy rather than a hard-hearted hack. But talking to Walker and Covell on the jetty, I was not the only one among the journalists with a wobbling top lip.

'When Glyn died, a lot of my life was up in the air,' Covell said, taking deep breaths between sentences. 'Ian called and offered help. He understood what I was going through. He said, "Come sailing. Help me finish what I started with John." I couldn't have wished for a better person to be with than Ian. He has given me space when I needed it and supported me really well.'

Walker paid tribute to his former partner. 'A lot of what I learnt at the start of this campaign, I learnt with John,' he said. 'There is a lot of Glyn and John in this result. We dedicate this to them.' The impromptu press conference broke up, as most of those who had attended it broke down.

At the end of that day I decided to walk back to the Furama, even though it was several miles. It was a beautiful, early-autumnal evening, and as I walked past pretty cottages with beautiful gardens, past busy pubs and intriguing restaurants, I thought for the thousandth time how different my life might have been if I had found Sydney before I had started a family in London.

And that got me thinking about that family in London, and their gift requests: Thomas the Tank Engine, and as many of his friends as possible. I changed my route, and walked across the Pyrmont Bridge to the Harbourside Shopping Centre, where (the hotel receptionist had told me) there was a toy shop.

So there was. The premises had been almost entirely annexed by Olly, Syd and Milly, but in a dusty corner uncolonised by Olympic mascots I found – what joy – a treasure trove of anthropomorphic engines. Thomas was here, with his closest friends James, Gordon and Toby.

But here too, in miniature form, were some of the more obscure creations of the Rev. W. Awdry, engines who were hardly friends of Thomas at all, mere nodding acquaintances: Skarloey and Sir Handel, Donald and Douglas, Peter Sam and Dodge the Diesel. Not only was I convinced that my daughters did not already possess these paragons of talkative traction, but – far more importantly – I was certain that no other child in our neighbourhood would have them either. Playground bragging rights would be secured at least until Christmas, and I would hold my head high in the checkout queue at Gap Kids.

I selected about a dozen of the most obscure engines (the feeble Australian dollar encouraged profligacy) and strolled happily back to my hotel, chock-a-block with rolling stock. I composed a triumphant email to Ingrid, then settled down, my conscience salved, to write up the deeds of the British sailors.

Much later, curled up in front of *The Dream* with a large glass of the local Chardonnay, I was surprised to find Roy and HG starting to slip into valedictory mode. The Games were almost over, yet I had been tearing around so much that they barely seemed to have begun.

The Sports Editor had ensured that almost every waking moment had been filled and – to be fair, as the football writers put it – not just with work. He had arranged a noisy dinner at the Bayswater Brasserie in Kings Cross, at which I was startled to find myself sitting next to Lord Coe (the Olympic gold medallist formerly known as Seb) and equally startled to see the normally ebullient Mihir Bose having a little nap on an adjacent banquette.

That dinner was good. *The Dream* was good. But my Games were . . . frustrating. I suppose I had imagined an effortless progression from British triumph to British triumph, with myself as cheerleader for a battalion of national heroes. Not the case. I piped ashore the sailors, but otherwise missed out on all the headline-making golds.

I'd watched the Four in training and seen their victory in the heats. But when they hauled themselves to victory in the final I was not racing against an early-morning dead-line in the grandstand at Penrith, but alternately whooping and sock-donning in my hotel room as I prepared to go somewhere completely different. When Denise Lewis defied injury over two days to win gold in the heptathlon, I was watching hockey and baseball. When, at the end of the Games, Audley Harrison, whose car and wisdom I had shared in London, was boxing for gold, I was touring naval relics tied up near Darling Harbour. (Though this last example, I must admit, was more my fault than the Sports Editor's. I had set out to see Harrison's bout, but walked to completely the wrong harbour, got confused, got late and eventually settled for a superannuated submarine rather than a super-heavyweight champion.)

So I started to feel, just as I had in France, that I was persistently in the wrong place at the right time, or the right place at the wrong time. To others, the glory. To me, the rhythmic bloody gymnastics.

I finally got to mingle with the highest-profile winners

when I was detailed to go to the airport to see our brave boys and girls on to the plane. Courage was much in evidence at the terminal, where Britain's finest athletes were struggling to combine the processes of checking in and signing autographs while suffering the (for them) unusual symptoms of monstrous hangovers.

Simon Clegg, the leader of the team, looked about as fresh, as the locals might have put it, as a dead dingo's dong. 'We drank the place dry,' he haggardly confessed, before clocking my notebook and adding diplomatically, 'which typifies the close spirit of unity which we have had all the way through these Games.'

I ambushed Matthew Pinsent as he loaded what seemed to be several boats on to a luggage trolley. 'Since I won the medal? I've been all over the place: climbed the Harbour Bridge, sailed across the harbour, visited the gymnastics, the track and field, the volleyball. I tried to get down to the boxing on Sunday, but I couldn't get a ticket, so I watched it on telly and shouted myself hoarse for Audley.' And had he celebrated last night? 'Oh, sure, I was up most of the night. But that was mainly because I couldn't find my passport.'

I gushed at Denise Lewis, who had enjoyed 'several' parties but still looked gorgeous, and I squeezed a couple of syllables out of Steve Redgrave, who was almost submerged by a human tide of autograph hunters. The overwhelming mood in the terminal was one of joyful exhaustion. 'Everyone is up,' said Audley Harrison, who had won the gold medal he had so confidently predicted, and was signing autographs with a massively bandaged hand. 'Team GB is up.'

And so they were, as I wrote on my laptop in the Furama that evening, 'at 37,000 feet, on wings of joy'. A suitably lofty personal farewell, I thought, from the Olympian heights. Then I started packing dozens of whiffy socks.

Chapter Four

Michael Schumacher and the Brown Slug

Objectives: Attend Austrian Grand Prix; interview Jenson Button; verify existence of Arnold Schwarzenegger Museum; take a walk in the woods; eat lots of asparagus. Time allocated: three days.

Friday morning at the A1-Ring, a motor-racing track miles from anywhere in the Styrian Alps of Austria. All is rural bliss: cows and horses graze, crows flap among the fir trees, bunnies hop happily through flower-filled meadows.

But there is trouble: a human traffic jam at the entrance to the paddock gates. A dozen corporate guests, some in the leather-lapelled tweed jackets favoured by conservative Austrians, are being herded through the electronic barriers by a minder from one of the Formula One teams. The guests do not know what to do with their high-tech passes and the security guards are reluctant to tell them; the minder doesn't have enough hands.

'Bloody Norah,' mutters an English voice, whose owner wears a more substantial pass around his neck. 'It's amateur hour.'

First-timers are always flummoxed by these gates, and hours of innocent fun can be had watching corporate guests grow increasingly embarrassed at their failure to cross the final barrier into the land of silk and money. You have to pick up your pass and wave it close to a red sensor light at head height. If your pass is good, the light will flash green, the gate will emit a 'Beep-beep-boop' and the turnstile will open.

If nothing happens, your pass has been cancelled, you are a non-person, and you have no more chance of getting into the Formula One paddock than Eddie Irvine has of entering a nunnery. Worse still, if the gate makes a honking sound, you will be marched smartly to a security office where you will have to explain how you managed to leave the paddock without passing through an electronic gate.

Every time you get a beep-beep-boop, your entry or exit to or from the paddock is registered on a computer system. This means that, once in, you cannot chuck your pass over the fence to a chum so that they can also come in. Furthermore, it means that Formula One's bosses can tell whether or not people are using their credentials properly. There's another beep-beep-boop at the entrance to the press room. If you have a press pass and never go in or out of there during the weekend, the powers-that-be will assume you have been freeloading, and you will not get another Grand Prix pass.

If this all sounds a bit Big Brother, it is. The Big Brother is called Bernie Ecclestone. He is actually quite little, and he lives in a mirror-windowed grey bus in the corner of the paddock. He is watching you. He is watching everyone. He runs Formula One.

Paddock passes have to be earned, and once earned, cherished. They reflect a hierarchy among the Formula One tribe. A red permanent pass confers season-long access to the grid before the start of the race, one of the great posing opportunities in world sport. Long-serving, respectable journalists have red passes. Team bosses have red passes.

The racing drivers themselves have red passes. Even Bernie has to wear a red pass to get on to the grid.

There is no practical purpose to be served by the print journalist being on the grid, yet most of Fleet Street's finest will be there among the throng, pretending to be looking at tyre treads while actually ogling pop stars, jostling royalty, exchanging jocular insults with David Coulthard and getting in the way of ITV's cameras once a fortnight. Actually, a practical purpose has just occurred to me: by hogging the cameras the journalists can reassure their wives, watching at home, that they really are at the race and not shacked up in the hotel with a couple of Slovakian blondes, watching the Grand Prix on local television.

Green permanent pass holders are denied access to the grid (usually – it depends how dozy the local stewards are) but have the run of the paddock and (usually – see above) the pit lane, although not while the race is on. Green pass holders are looked down upon by red pass holders, but the greens in turn look down upon single-event pass holders, who possess an altogether flimsier credential issued only for one race at a time. The single-event pass still works the magic bleeping gates into the paddock, but it does not (usually) allow access to the pit lane and does not work the same charm upon race officials and (more importantly) team public-relations persons as the chunkier green or red versions.

The nature of your pass goes quite some way to defining the nature of your Grand Prix weekend. With a red pass you can go where you like and talk to whomever you please in the certain knowledge that they will talk back to you (if only to tell you to piss off).

If there is a green pass dangling from the embossed ribbon around your neck you can at least be sure of being well fed: show up at the British American Racing or McLaren motorhomes and you will be welcomed by logoed

81

lovelies keen to serve you elaborate canapés, cold beer and comforting bowls of pasta. There is also an even chance that you will be granted a few minutes' chat with a driver.

Wear only a single-event badge, though, and you must work hard for your food and your quotes. You will have to subsist on whatever scraps the organisers throw your way: a morsel of bread and cheese, a subsidised beer; a sound bite at a crowded press conference, an illicitly eavesdropped television interview.

Approach, as a stranger, any individual of status within Formula One and their eyes will instantly drop to your chest, checking out the pass. In this way Bernie Ecclestone, Michael Schumacher and all their glamorous hangers-on resemble a pack of privileged dogs, sniffing each other's bottoms.

Once the Styrian corporate jolliers (*definitely* single-event) got their beep-beep-boops, I waved my pass (green, since you ask) and headed for the press centre, which is above the pit garages. Beep-beep-boop.

The main press room at a Formula One Grand Prix is always arranged in the same way, no matter which country you are in. Desks for 600 journalists stand in rows; banks of television sets hang from the ceiling, each bank serving four rows of seats. At the far end of the room there is a little stage with seats and microphones for six. The left-hand side of the room is usually reserved for smokers, of whom there are a great many among the F1 press corps: sponsorship in action. Those who will be contributing to radio stations as well as writing tend to sit at the back, where their rants will be less disturbing.

The knack is to bag a spot fairly close to the front (away from radio reporters, close to the press-conference stage) three rows back from a bank of televisions. In this position you can read what is displayed on the various data screens without cricking your neck. Regulars know all this, so the best places are quickly nabbed.

I chose my spot, went back to the reception desk and gave the desk number to an Austrian lady. I signed the register (just like school), requested a car-park pass for the next race (as always, whether I need it or not – it's part of the ritual) and was marched back to my chosen location, which was then identified as mine with a sticker with my name and the name of my newspaper on it.

Phew. And to think that all dogs have to do to identify their territory is wee on a tree.

I trotted back down to the paddock, blagged a ham roll from the Jordan motorhome and a bottle of mineral water from BAR, nicked a couple of my favourite dinky little notebooks from Minardi, and went back up to the press room for the press conference.

This sadly failed to provide any material of significant interest (no British drivers, no petty feuds, no startling technical insights), so after a brief consultation with the sports desk – funny how much time I spend conversing with furniture – I went to have tea with Jenson Button.

This was easily arranged, because the team for whom he was then driving, Benetton, stipulated that their drivers would be available for interview on the Friday and Saturday before each Grand Prix, at 4 p.m. Reckoning that the boy Button would be of scant interest to the local media, I thought I might get him to myself.

I did. A practice session for one of the support races droned on the television in the corner, a hostess brought coffee and biscuits, every now and then a technician would slip Button a piece of paper. He was, as usual, charming, scatological, implausibly good-looking, irritatingly tactful.

His car didn't suit him. His team didn't trust him. He was having a horrible season. All of this was clear, but expressed in the universal code of Formula One: winks, raised eyebrows, avoided questions, ironic answers.

Good stuff, all the same. I scuttled back up to the press room and wrote it up, then headed through the dank concrete tunnel under the main straight and out of the circuit. You can get a shuttle bus from the paddock entrance to the car park, but experimentation has proved that it is actually as fast to walk; and the walk affords a moment's reflection at the touching little flower-strewn monument at the gates to the track.

Jochen Rindt, Formula One World Champion, 1970.

Dead before he was crowned, killed in a practice crash at Monza. That was before I knew that motor racing existed, yet every time I come here I stop and look at the bust with a lump in my throat. The only posthumous champion in Formula One history.

I had been too young to be a fan of Rindt: I attended my first Grand Prix nearly three years after he was killed. I was taken to Silverstone, in July 1973, when I was ten. There was a huge pile-up on the second lap, which terrified and thrilled me in equal measure. I remember Jackie Stewart driving his car through a hayfield, the dark blue airbox poking above the grass like a periscope. And I remember spotting the reigning world champion, the saturnine Brazilian Emerson Fittipaldi, strolling back to the pits from his abandoned Lotus, carrying his red and black helmet, his black and gold overalls sweaty, undone at the neck. As he passed below us I hopped over the fence with a scrap of paper and a pencil and asked, with best schoolboy politeness: 'Please Mr Fittipaldi, may I have your autograph?' He smiled, and signed, and I was smitten, not just with Fittipaldi, but with the sport. I lost the autograph, but I have never lost my love of Formula One motor racing. As true love should be, it is irrational, and survives tedium and tiffs, and defies explanation. I love the noise, the

84

glamour, the bravery, the severe beauty of the cars, the danger.

The danger. When I stand at the Rindt monument it always makes me think of all the other unlucky drivers, that crowded grid of those who found an early grave. My first idol in Formula One was an impossibly handsome young Frenchman named François Cevert, a blue-eyed ladykiller, a dazzlingly talented driver, a concert-level pianist. He was Jackie Stewart's team-mate on the Tyrell team in 1973, when I saw him drive at Silverstone, and was being groomed to take over from the great Scot as number one in 1974. World titles beckoned. I bought a biography of him – the first hardback book I ever purchased – and I painted my go-karting helmet in his colours.

Cevert was killed in practice for the last race of 1973, torn to pieces when his car demolished crash barriers at the primitive Watkins Glen track in the United States. I remember where I was when my mother told me: in the hallway at home, playing with my Corgi model racing cars. I wanted to cry, but I didn't.

I think Cevert's death probably consummated my love of Formula One: there is something horribly compelling about a sport that can kill your heroes. As it has continued to do. I left the monument and walked to my car, thinking of Mark Donohue, fatally injured here in Austria in 1975, of Ronnie Peterson, of Gilles Villeneuve, of Ayrton Senna and of the others, less famous, but no less brave, no less dead: Helmuth Koinigg, Ricardo Paletti, Roland Ratzenberger . . .

Gloomily, I climbed into my little rented Mercedes and within three minutes I was on the motorway towards Graz. I turned on the reliably upbeat HitRadio Drei to cheer myself up, and soon I was humming along to S Club 7. The route was ridiculously scenic: mountains with straggly streaks of snow on their peaks, like the droppings of giant birds; brooding rocky eminences crowned with tumbledown towers;

gloriously green fields of waving haygrass. The only blight on the landscape was the frequent quarries in which Austrians with colossal yellow diggers chipped rocky scars into the hill-sides. The only blight on the road were the tunnels which bored through some of the prettiest mountains.

There you are, barrelling along happily at 80 mph, when in a blur of incomprehensible signs the road is reduced from three lanes to one and you are funnelled into the side of a mountain in almost total darkness. The first time this happened to me I was completely unprepared: I didn't even know where the switch for the car's headlights was located. I spent three miles being flashed by drivers on the other side of the road, and hooted from behind, trying to steer a straight course between rock wall and passing traffic while activating everything – indicator, sun-roof, cigarette lighter, vanity-mirror light, rear wash/wiper – bar the things that would allow me to see where I was going.

Why, I wondered when I had finally achieved illumination, can't the Austrians put some proper lights in here?

Two long tunnels – called Gleinalm and Gratkorn, like a sinister firm of local solicitors – brought me to the unlovely outskirts of Graz, and no more than forty geographically chaotic minutes later I was parking in the sepulchral garage of the Hotel Daniel.

I don't know why this should be, but I always seem to have bad experiences in Austrian underground car parks. Maybe it's just that I drive more in Austria than I do elsewhere on my travels – it's the only way of getting to the A1-Ring – or perhaps there is a sadistic streak deep in the Austrian psyche, expressed by the tricks their architects get up to below the surface. Freud did most of his best work in Vienna.

Whatever the reason, my problems in Austrian garages usually follow a familiar script, regardless of whether I am at the Best Western in Salzburg, the Sheraton in Vienna or here at the Hotel Daniel in Graz. I drove up to the garage entrance, expecting the barrier to rise in front of me. Nothing happened. I turned off the engine and dashed to reception to explain my problem. Both receptionists were busy checking guests in or out. Another car had pulled up behind mine and was hooting.

Eventually – from the concierge – I secured the ticket needed to operate the barrier and descended via a series of hairpins into the depths. As I wiggled the little Mercedes into a slot on the lowest level, all the lights in the garage went out. I completed the manoeuvre with headlights on, but had to remove my bags in total darkness.

I found the wall – this took a bit of doing – and groped my way along it, barking my shins on bumpers. I finally found what I was looking for: a circular light switch on a timer circuit. I whacked it with my palm and raced, blinded now by the light, back to the car. I grabbed my bags and looked around. I saw an exit sign above a blue door fifty yards distant and lumbered towards it, five-day bag bumping slowly off my left leg, laptop whacking the side of my right knee. Halfway there, of course, the lights went out again but I carried on in what I was sure was the right direction until my nose met concrete.

I edged left, found the door handle and dragged my bags through into a pitch-black chamber. I groped three more doorhandles. What was this, *Tomb Raider*? The first two were locked, the third opened on to a long flight of stairs. I found another light switch. The stairs ascended towards a grey steel door – closed, and, I told myself on the lengthy, bag-bashing climb, almost certainly locked.

I was wrong. The door swung open and deposited me outside the main entrance of the hotel. It swung shut with a clang behind me, and I saw in red letters and several languages the words: 'Fire Exit. Emergency Use Only.'

A grinning bellboy came out for my bags. 'Why didn't you use zer lift?' he asked.

That night I was the sole diner in the Daniel's restaurant, a monument to the domestic architecture of the 1970s, done out in dark green paisley patterns on a pale green background. The cuisine followed the colour code: every item on the menu featured 'Spargel' in some form: asparagus.

Fortunately, I like asparagus, and I munched my way through a green terrine, followed by a log pile of thick white stems dressed with butter. I thought of the character in a short story by Ian McEwan who rhapsodises on the smell produced by asparagus when converted into urine. He concludes, as far as I could remember: 'It is a matter for the poets, and I challenge them to accept their responsibility.' That is the great thing about dining alone: you can follow any train of thought and not worry about being considered a pretentious pillock.

After dinner I went for a random walk. Usual objective, invoking the Way of Baker: stroll until well and truly lost, then find a bus, tram or taxi to return to the hotel. I left behind me the Europaplatz, the ghastly concrete square on which the Daniel stood, and walked down a long, wide, traffic-crammed street called Annenstrasse.

Quickly it became clear that with my unerring instinct for tat I had chosen to stay in quite the nastiest part of Graz. With every street that passed, the city became prettier and more civilised. Soon I reached a river: the Mur, whose winding course I had crossed several times on the autobahn. Across the river the vistas improved still further: a floodlit white clock tower poking out atop a thickly wooded hill, domed and pinnacled churches, gilded statues and elegant arcades. I had walked from Wolverhampton to Florence in twenty minutes.

I plunged further into the old town, which was surprisingly quiet for nine o'clock on a summer Friday night. Grazers (as the locals call themselves) were grazing in a polyglot array of little restaurants: pizza joints, kebab houses, grills offering the best of wurst. I dodged trams across the terminus at Jakominiplatz and turned down a side street.

I passed an internet café and a Thai restaurant and then saw a sign saying 'Irish pub'. I was in like Flynn, and negotiated through sign language with the determinedly Austrian bartender a large glass of bitter. Half a dozen Grazers were glugging wheat beer around a fruit machine. I took my bitter into the deserted Guinness Room.

This little panelled chamber turned out to be a shrine to Grazgo Rangers, a football club who have not, so far as I could recall, figured largely in the annals of European competition. Yet they had been successful: twenty-two trophies of varying heights and degrees of hideousness were displayed in the window, all but blocking the light from the street. There was a pair of ancient boots, gilded and mounted on a plinth inscribed '*Torschutzenkonig*', which I translated as something like goal-shooting king. But there was no clue as to who the king had been. A glass case held an old shirt in a frame, and a number of CDs: Grazgo Rangers Volumes 2, 3 and 4. On the cover of the latter the team had been photographed (from behind, mercifully) racing nude across the pitch in a large, floodlit but deserted stadium.

Armed with my second pint (or was it a litre? Or two?) I prowled around the Guinness Room examining in minute detail the artefacts of Grazgo Rangers. I felt like an anthropologist who had stumbled on a lost civilisation, which tells you something of the strength of the beer. It was fascinating stuff. What on earth was on the CDs? *Schottische Lieder*? What was the significance of the Christmas card signed by seventeen members of the ticket-office staff at Ibrox Park?

I pulled myself together. The locals were starting to stare, nudge each other and whisper. Time to head back to the Daniel.

I had failed to get lost, an infringement of the Way of Baker, but at least this made the return journey possible on foot. Soon, though, the beer worked its way to the end of the line and I realised I should have used the facilities in the Irish pub. It was late by now, and the taxis were all occupied. I dared not risk a tram in the wrong direction.

It is difficult to run with your legs crossed, but that is the manner in which I returned to the Hotel Daniel, high-speed hobbling down the corridor to my room before unleashing a torrent into the lavatory.

I inhaled deeply and reached for the wall-mounted phone. 'Reception?' I said. 'Would you be kind enough to send me up a poet?'

The next morning I woke early and breakfasted mightily and Germanically: wurst, ham, a mountain of cottage cheese. I was a man with a mission.

At the track the previous day one of the British F1 writers had mentioned that he had read something on the Internet about an Arnold Schwarzenegger Museum in Graz: an estab-lishment dedicated to the achievements of Styria's most famous son, Mr Universe, the Terminator and – some time in the future – the Governor of California. I was the only one among the group staying in Graz (the others had cunningly billetted themselves in B&Bs much closer to the track) so I had promised to check out the museum on their behalf.

I did not even have to ask for directions. Driving into Graz from the motorway the day before, I had passed the home of Sturm Graz, the top local football team, a handsome concrete edifice proudly named Arnold-Schwarzenegger Stadion Graz-Leibenau. A bit of a mouthful compared to Anfield or Highbury but home, surely, to my coveted museum.

I drove past the usual outer-city shabbiness, railway yards and peep shows, and the unusual, a supermarket dedicated to equestrian equipment. I parked on a dusty side street with the stadium in sight, and passed a pair of pistol-packing policemen on early lookout for fans attending the afternoon's match.

The ticket office was shut, as was the stadium's main entrance and the Café Wurm (yum, yum) next door. Not encouraging. I followed a walkway down one side of the stadium, past a long line of locked gates that led into the grandstands. Eventually, I found one that swung open to my touch.

The pitch was bare, but the stands were speckled with maintenance men, checking seats, distributing cushions in the VIP area, installing PA cables. I interrupted a chap who was setting up a stainless-steel bar table in the VIP concourse. He wore a T-shirt with the logo of Puntigamer beer, Sturm Graz's sponsor. It was, his chest declared: 'Das Bierege Bier': the beeriest beer? The most beersome of beers? A beer's beer? Beer, anyway.

'*Entschuldigung. Sprechen sie Englisch?*' My standard opening.

'*Nein.*' Rats. '*Ich suche Der –*' (*Das? Die?*) '– Arnold Schwarzenegger Museum.'

'*Ach, ja,*' he said. '*Kein problem.*'

That much I understood. But the directions he proceeded to give me were incomprehensible. It's not just that I don't speak German. It's that Austrians don't speak German either. Their dialect is so weird that tourists from Munich and Berlin stood around on the streets of Graz scratching their heads and consulting phrase books, as nonplussed as me.

The man's gestures had seemed to indicate that I needed to go underground in some way. Sure enough, back where the policemen were standing was the entrance to a subterranean car park, and a signpost to a gymnasium. Still no mention of a museum, but promising.

I walked down into the dark and deserted car park,

wondering what it was about Austria that compelled me to spend so much time under it, and wondering also how safe the subsurface areas of an Austrian football stadium might be. Another sign suggested I turn right for the gym – into a deserted and underlit parking area the length of the football pitch. 'I am a mole,' I sang to myself, 'and I live in a hole.'

I came to a door – locked, of course – and another gym sign, this one pointing up a curved tarmac ramp. This is how the gym gets its members fit, I mused, puffing upwards. They walk them three times around the stadium before they arrive.

I crossed yet another floor of the car park and emerged into daylight. To my right, an indoor mini soccer pitch. To my left, the creak of machinery and the unmistakable melodies of HitRadio Drei: the gymnasium.

Arnie was much in evidence. A placard at the entrance detailed his achievements in a manner that gave equal prominence to his Austrian regional muscleman titles and his Hollywood megahits. On the walls of the staircase that led down into a weightlifting hall there were photographs of Schwarzenegger visiting this very gym with his visibly pregnant, Kennedy-related wife. There was also a life-size and extremely unattractive pop-art portrait of the great man by someone called Hiro Yamagata, and a paean to the painter by his subject which led me to believe that Arnie's artistic sensibilities had not developed in line with his musculature.

More of a gallery than a museum, I thought, reaching the bottom of the stairs and attracting the glares of a trio of blimp-armed men in singlets. A young lady in a black suit hurried up to me, dragging a toddler behind her.

'Excuse me,' she said, diagnosing my nationality immediately. 'Zis area is for members only. You have come to look at zer museum, *ja*?'

'Yes,' I said. Did I really look like a tourist?

We turned around. The toddler – it was a boy, I think – followed us up the stairs, whacking the backs of my calves and shrieking '*Argh! Argh! Argh!*' Seen too many action movies, I suspected.

At the top of the stairs the lady turned left and made an elegant gesture, welcoming me to the Arnold Schwarzenegger Museum. It consisted of a dozen items of superannuated gymnasium equipment cordoned within a red rope ten feet square. On these cracked red leather benches, I assumed, and with these ancient iron dumbbells, was built the body on which Schwarzenegger built his career.

It was a less than magical moment. I think my guide must have sensed this, because she detached her son from my knee, which he had been trying to bite, and directed me to the photographs on the wall. 'Zese are very rare,' she said. 'People are coming from America to see zem.'

I could not vouch for their rarity, but they were certainly very funny. Here was pre-Hollywood Arnie, five years or more before his long-forgotten movie debut in *Hercules in New York* (1969). The young Schwarzenegger was preposterously overdeveloped, chest like an oil drum, arms like legs, lantern jaw, limbs scribbled with worryingly bulging veins.

In the best of the photographs, taken at the Mr Austria competition in Graz in 1964, Arnie, clad only in a minute pair of white bathing trunks, strikes a classic Charles Atlas pose on a wooden stage. Behind him stand a mop-topped, bow-tied beat combo, Austria's answer to The Beatles. They don't know where to look.

'Thank you very much,' I said to my guide. 'Do you get many visitors to the museum?'

'*Ja, ja,*' she said, walking me to the door and restraining her son from a parting nip at my ankles. 'We get some.'

93

I winked at her. 'I'll be back,' I growled.

She sighed. 'Zey all say zat.'

Back into the car, back on to the autobahn, back into the tunnels. In my best Boy Scout manner, I'd worked out a routine for them: change arranged for the toll booths, normal glasses on the passenger seat ready to be swapped with my shades at the tunnel entrance. I even knew where the headlight switch was.

The worst of the tunnels was the boredom, and the nagging notion that any involuntary twitch would precipitate a collision with a juggernaut at a closing speed of 80 mph. The Gratkorn tunnel is more than five miles long, and every half-mile or so there is a recess in the tunnel wall painted with a sign that tells you how far you have come and how far you have to go. In each recess there is a fire extinguisher and a mysterious doorway which presumably leads to some kind of service tunnel.

Two and a half miles into the Gratkorn tunnel, the central recess holds something else: a wall-mounted glass cabinet, lit by a dim fluorescent tube, containing a small white statuette of the Madonna about nine inches high. I had passed it the previous day and it had registered on my peripheral vision like a ghost. Had it really been there? This time I was ready to make sure, and pulled away from the traffic behind me in order to slow as I passed the shrine.

It was there: the glass of the cabinet encrusted with accumulated exhaust particulates, the illumination feeble, the isolation absolute. I thought of the thousands of religious statuettes leading happy lives in churches and devout homes, frequently dusted and prayed at, cherished and adored. And here was this forlorn little lady, entombed and traffic-tormented, the Madonna of carbon monoxide.

The blast of the horn made me gasp aloud. In my rumination I had slowed almost to a halt, and the driver of the gravel truck behind me was none too happy about it.

Attempting to frame apologetic gestures between gear changes, I accelerated away.

I arrived at the track in time for lunch, which I took in the same Benetton motorhome where I had interviewed Button the previous day. There is an element of cheek involved in scrounging food in the paddock: act as if you have a divine right to nourishment, and it may come. Or you might be thrown out. On this occasion I plonked myself down at a table with a bundle of timing sheets from that morning's free practice session, and appeared to absorb myself in the serious study of sector times and speed-trap readings. A kindly waitress recognised me from the previous afternoon, and produced a plate of delicious mushroom ravioli scattered with the finest parmesan, and a little glass of lovely red Italian wine.

In the far corner of the motorhome, Flavio Briatore, the team's caramel-tanned, chain-smoking boss, was deep in discussion with two suited and sunglassed executives from one of the team's sponsors. The lounge-lizard looks, trattoria accent and penchant for the company of supermodels might make Briatore a figure of fun among some in the paddock, but no one underestimates his Machiavellian skills or eye for talent.

This is the man who took Michael Schumacher from greenhorn to race winner to world champion, assembling around him the team of designers, technicians and strategists who would move with the German to Ferrari and provide five more titles there. Italy, not just Benetton, owed Flavio Briatore a debt of gratitude.

But, it seemed, he did not owe me lunch. As I shovelled away the pasta, the quizzical glances from Flav's table were growing more and more frequent. Now he was conferring with the waitress. I glugged back the last of the wine, swiped a napkin across my mouth and made for the sliding door, giving Briatore a full-beam grin. He shrugged and reached for another cigarette.

I wandered, burping, through the paddock, sidestepping gaggles of gawping corporate guests and trying not to bumble into television interviews. A faded-looking blonde in a sixties-style short suede dress was surrounded by autograph hunters and supplicants with microphones. I stared, but I couldn't place her.

'Who's that?' I asked an Austrian microphone-wielder.

'Big star,' he said. 'She tells the weather.'

You get this kind of cultural dislocation at every Grand Prix. Teams like to please their local sponsors, so they bring in local stars, and the poor drivers have to endure endless photocalls with chat-show hosts, politicians, footballers, actors and models, thinking 'Who are these people?'

I walked up to the far end of the paddock, past Bernie's bus, the unspectacular seat of power, and beep-beep-booped out of the gates. I was off-duty and I fancied a ramble.

A motor-racing track might seem like a peculiar place to commune with nature, but the A-1 Ring was built on acres of woodland and meadow, and despite the developers a little woodland and meadow had remained within the loops of tarmac and steel barriers. I walked past the two MedEvac helicopters, hoping that neither would be employed that weekend, and climbed the steep hill that rises behind the paddock. Within a minute the road had become a farm track, and the hubbub had given way to a chorus of crickets. To my right, wild grasses, poppies and buttercups waved in the wind. To my left was a dark, intriguing wood.

I was trying to locate one of the crickets among the long grass when I heard footsteps on the path and excited chatter. Over the crest of the hill came what looked like the entire female cast of *The Sound of Music*: a score of beautiful young Austrian women in brightly coloured traditional costumes – dirndl skirts, laced suede bodices, floaty white blouses and sensible shoes. The grid girls.

Before the start of every Grand Prix the cars line up on

96

the grid next to the pit lane. In order to aid the crowd in identifying their favourites, and to keep the glamour levels hovering close to overload, each car is accompanied by a pretty young lady holding a placard bearing the driver's name and the flag of his country. Each host nation has a different style of dress for their grid girls, but most can be summed up in one word: skimpy. In Melbourne, for instance, the girls wear hot-pants; at Silverstone, mini skirts. In Japan, where there are magazines and websites devoted solely to the grid-girl phenomenon, they wear one-piece swimsuits and shimmery tights.

But in wholesome Austria there was barely an ankle to be seen; attention was drawn instead to the girls' fresh, clear-complexioned features. As they tripped, chattering, down the hill, one or two of them shot quizzical glances in the direction of the sweaty, bearded little fellow up to his midriff in grass. I just smiled inanely back at them, hoping to be taken for no worse than a harmless loony.

I soon gave up on the cricket hunt (I suspect that they can throw their voices, or their legs, or whatever it is that they chirrup with) and walked further up the path to the crest of the hill. Next to a grassy bank stood a line of little white wooden boxes: five beehives, a little dilapidated but still evidently home to thriving swarms. One or two orange-bottomed sentinels buzzed out to have a look at me, so I scuttled off up a steep path into the wood. Funny place to make honey, I thought. Wonder if it tastes of exhaust fumes?

The wood was mostly conifer – the track is more than 1,000 feet above sea level – but the trees were close-packed and the canopy was dense. The air was sultry and dusty, the sense of isolation quite extraordinary. I found a narrow, mossy path of the sort that might be used by commuting badgers, and followed it up a steep hill with no clear idea of where it might emerge. I wondered – as I often do, when walking somewhere strange and unasphalted – how numerous and deadly the local snake population was, comforting myself with the probably erroneous notion that snakes like to bask in the sun, and that precious little sun penetrated to the floor of the wood. Nonetheless, I avoided any wiggly-looking sticks.

After crunching warily along for five minutes or so I came to a little sunny clearing, a space no more than five yards across where the sun cut through a gap in the trees and illuminated a circle of bright green bracken and a solitary tree stump, bleached white. I inspected it for vipers, and sat cautiously down.

Two bees swung by to investigate some strange blue flowers, and then – good grief – an orange wasp-like thing the size of a Chicken McNugget buzzed past my left ear. A hornet, I supposed, and I certainly didn't want another look. But it hadn't seemed interested in me, and nor were the bees, and it was a most beguiling location. I pulled my cap down lower and shut my eyes. I don't know how long I dozed – no more than two or three minutes, I suppose – but I will never forget the manner of my awakening.

A shattering scream burst upon me, and I shot up and off the log like a startled pheasant. I heard another scream approaching, and stuck an index finger in each ear. In this manner I pushed through the bracken to find myself behind a debris fence and a steel barrier, and about five feet from a Benetton-Renault travelling at 180 mph.

Hi, Jenson. No, no. Of course you didn't disturb me.

I walked back down the hill through the wood, which now echoed and re-echoed to the wails of Formula One cars in their final qualifying session. I realised why the wood was short of substantial fauna: anything with ears would have relocated for the weekend. Emerging on to the trail that led back to the paddock I nearly trod on what looked like a small, fresh, human turd. I bent down for a closer inspection. The turd was moving. It was a slug: a slug

coloured a rich, shiny, milk-chocolate brown. I knelt down
to watch the little creature make its slow and slimy way
across the track. It simply boggled my mind. No doubt
everybody knows that the slugs of Styria are brown; no
doubt there are brown slugs all over Europe. But where I
come from slugs are black, and always have been, and I
found this exception really rather exciting.

I was still marvelling away at the little blighter when I
heard closely approaching footsteps and looked up to see
a track marshal in fireproof safety gear glaring down at me
from behind an aggressive moustache.

'*Wie gehts?*' he said, or something like it.

I clambered to my feet, brushing dust from my trousers.

'*Kein problem, kein problem,*' I said, pointing at the little
invertebrate now nuzzling its way into the field. 'Brown slug.'

The moustachioed marshal said nothing, but looked at
me for a good half-minute, as if thinking: How am I going
to report this? Then he turned and walked away, and I
resumed my study, one curious little creature examining
another.

Later, I sat in the circuit car park and called home, where
it was teatime. Lucy's fourth birthday was coming up, and
she wanted to know if there were any good present shops
in Austria. I said that unfortunately there were not.

'Oh. Is there anything nice there at all?'

'Well, yes. Pretty mountains. And lots of cows.'

'Good. Will you bring me back a cow for my birthday?'

I said goodnight to the rustling static.

That evening I walked back to the Irish pub and had a
couple of powerful beers in the Grazgo Rangers shrine,
followed by a tramp's shoe disguised as a Wiener schnitzel
in the half-timbered, half-empty restaurant next door. Given
the consistency of the veal I wasn't surprised at the lack of
diners. But it wasn't just the restaurant I had chosen that
was nearly empty: all the cafés and bars on my walk back

to the hotel were sparsely populated, and several were closing. At a quarter to ten. On a Saturday night.

I'd hate to misjudge a place on the evidence of one weekend, and I was probably on the wrong side of town – I usually am – but even so, it was pretty clear to me that Grazers are not ravers. In the party stakes, I decided, Graz makes Leamington Spa look like Las Vegas. This theory was confirmed when I walked into the Hotel Daniel and found the bar, which occupied one third of the lobby, monopolised by a coachload of geriatric Germans, all drinking small glasses of beer and cackling.

I went straight to bed.

The incredible thing about the Austrian Grand Prix is not the setting, though the foothills of the Styrian Alps are jolly pretty, or the circuit, which is short and relatively unchallenging. The really amazing thing is that on the morning of the race you can just drive up, park your car, and walk in.

No traffic jams. If you drive to the British Grand Prix at Silverstone, you can reckon on sitting immobile in your car for at least three hours on the way. Most Grand Prix venues get snarled up, even in hyper-efficient Japan and laid-back Australia. But the Austrians have cracked it. You pootle off the dual carriageway, wave at a couple of policemen, are directed into a meadow and there you are, ten minutes' walk from the track. The only potential snag – and the one that got me that Sunday morning – is the cow pat adjacent to the driver's door.

Still smelling faintly of recycled grass, I assembled my equipment at desk 157 in the media centre. Laptop, mobile phone, notebook, timing sheets from practice and warm-up, nice fat paperback thriller . . .

I know, I know. There are sports fans who would give significant portions of their anatomy to be allowed into the paddock at a Grand Prix; who, once there, would be sure to hoover up every last molecule of atmosphere. They'd get driver autographs, have their photos taken with models and actors, gaze longingly at the racing cars, and phone all their friends to tell them where they were, what they were doing and how wonderful it all was.

Well, I'm sorry. There is a limit to the amount of purposeless wandering you can do in a paddock, and I had reached it on Friday afternoon. I didn't want any autographs, I didn't recognise any of the actors and if I had been photographed with a supermodel all that would have appeared in the shot was the crown of my head, at roughly the level of the smiling lady's elbow. I already knew what the cars look like, and my friends had long ago grown weary of my boastful phone calls.

So a paperback it was.

The thriller occupied me until the pit lane opened for the cars to make their way to the grid. I scoffed some black bread, smoked ham and cheese from the lovely buffet that the Austrians lay on for the press, then took my place at the windows running the length of the media centre, overlooking the pit lane and the starting grid.

This is a slightly uncool thing to do, implying perhaps that you are sufficiently inexperienced to find the start of a race still intriguing. But it *is* intriguing. It is also imperative to get to the window at least fifteen minutes before the start of the race, i.e. before the real novices work out that it is a good idea. You then have to defend your position with a fair bit of elbow work, paying particular attention to local photographers who may seek to use the top of your head as a resting spot for their telephoto lenses.

Rasping and screeching with impatiently suppressed power, the cars trickled on to the grid for the second and final time. Then the engines roared in chorus, and they were off – all except Mika Hakkinen, whose McLaren eventually chugged away behind the rest sounding very sorry for itself.

I strolled back to desk 157 and sat down to watch television.

There is a common misconception that sports writers watch motor racing from the track-side or the pit lane. Not true. They watch it on the telly, just like the millions back at home. The only difference is that the millions back at home are considerably better informed, with expert commentators and pundits to tell them what is going on, and reporters roaming the pit lane to sniff out stories and interview drivers. The sports writers have to work it all out for themselves, with the help of three large televisions: one showing the pictures that everyone at home will be seeing, one displaying the location and lap times of every car, and one devoted to official announcements from the race stewards and a graphic depicting things like humidity, track temperature and rainfall. The teams themselves get the same stuff; if you ever wonder what Jean Todt, the Ferrari sporting director, is frowning at on the pit wall, it will be one of those three screens.

There is a knack to employing all this information in an efficient manner as a race unfolds – a knack I don't have. For instance, I was peering at an announcement from the stewards that car so-and-so was under investigation ('prob jumped start', I noted) when there were whoops from all around me and I looked up at the TV satellite feed to see Michael Schumacher in the gravel trap at the second turn, spinning his wheels irascibly as half the field drove past him.

Thank heavens for instant replays. Schumi had been bumped off the track – not for the first or last time – by Williams' Colombian driver Juan-Pablo Montoya. The incident engendered an outbreak of cheering and ribaldry in the media centre, for while most neutral journalists are properly admiring of the elder Schumacher's driving skills, they find him personally unendearing. And he wins far too many races.

It didn't look like he was going to win this one. David Coulthard, the square-jawed Scot in the second McLaren, had taken the lead with the aid of a cunning pit-stop strategy. With just a handful of laps to go he was comfortably clear of Schumacher's team-mate, the smiley Brazilian Rubens Barrichello, and big Schumi himself, who, amazingly, had battled his way back through the field to lie third. I was beginning to wonder what on earth I was going to write about.

But what was this? Todt, on the Ferrari pit wall, could be seen muttering urgently into the microphone of his headset. Surely it was too early in the season for team orders? Murmurings of discontent spread around the media centre. The laps counted down, with Barrichello remaining stubbornly in second place. Coulthard crossed the line to take the chequered flag, and the two Ferraris turned in to the long, final right-hander with the Brazilian in front . . . and emerged with him behind.

The entire press room rose as one, booing, hissing or simply yelling abuse. The sense of outrage was almost palpable. In the grandstands on the far side of the pit straight, fans in Ferrari red had their thumbs down, and some were throwing away their banners in disgust. It was result-manipulation worthy of a North Korean election, and it outraged the fans and almost all of the writers. In the smoking section of the media centre, it was easy to identify the two or three people who thought that Ferrari had done the right thing: the Italian writers, now surrounded by furiously gesticulating Brazilians.

Before they could move on to fisticuffs, the drivers arrived for their press conference, to be greeted, for the first time in my experience, by loud and almost unanimous booing.

Schumacher reacted as he always does to hostility, by raising his formidable chin by five degrees, and setting his mouth in a thin line of defiance. Barrichello looked close to tears, Coulthard smugly amused.

The motor-racing writers tried their best to make Schumacher squirm, but he had obviously not been in the queue when God was handing out embarrassment. He stuck stubbornly to the line that he might need the extra points by the end of the season, which was mathematically feasible but still made him look ridiculous. You could have run the Flying Scotsman on the steam escaping from Barrichello's ears, but he controlled himself manfully and instead of punching his team-mate's lights out, muttered: 'I do not want to say anything about this. I need to clarify the situation with the team.' We got his message.

I felt I needed a soupçon more righteous indignation for my article, and I knew where to get it. The paddock was seething with people: mechanics stacking and packing race equipment, hangers-on waiting for autographs, hacks sharking for quotes. I dodged and excuse-me'd over to the Ferrari motorhome and joined a dozen or so journalists loitering outside.

I spotted our prey before anyone else did: Todt, the tactical genius, Schumacher's apologist-in-chief, heading for one of the motorhome's blue-tinted *Star Trek*-style sliding doors. I was standing at the foot of the steps as he walked down them, notebook and pen at the ready.

'Monsieur Todt, how can you *ooof* . . .'

Something hard and heavy landed on top of my head. A television camera, placed none too carefully by an Austrian cameraman who wished to use me as a human tripod. Print journalists elbowed in from either side of me, radio interviewers stuck their microphones in front of my nose. I couldn't believe this. I'd been there first . . .

Within moments I had been forced to crouch at Todt's

feet, my view of him almost completely obscured by portable broadcasting equipment. The diminutive Frenchman gave an eloquent defence of Ferrari's divine right to do whatever they wished whenever they wanted, of which I can remember very little.

But I do recall that the inside of Jean Todt's nostrils are, appropriately, Ferrari red.

Back at the Hotel Daniel, the lobby bar was almost deserted as I sat down with my paperback. The place was empty apart from a rumpled and melancholy-looking fellow in jeans and a West McLaren T-shirt, alternately pulling on a gigantic beer and a Marlboro Light.

The barman set a beer of more modest dimensions in front of me. 'He's a Finn,' he whispered, as if that explained everything.

'I *am* a Finn!' the McLaren man confirmed, quite loudly. 'I am a Finn,' he said, reflectively, and burped.

'Good for you,' I said, and picked up my book.

'You are not a Finn,' the McLaren man declared. 'So you will not understand.'

The intelligent response here would have been: 'No, you're right, I won't, so don't bother telling me, I'll just get on with my book.' But instead I put down my book and said, with a sigh: 'What won't I understand?'

The Finn's name was Keke. He pronounced it something like 'Kayo', but when he wrote it down for me on a napkin it was Keke: 'Just like Keke Rosberg, the great champion.' He looked to be in his early thirties, and had lank blond hair, a sunburnt complexion and three days' worth of stubble. After the race, Keke had gone to catch a boat – a ferry of some kind, as far as I could ascertain – but the crew had been unwilling to let him on board.

'They said I was too drunk,' he lamented.

'Really?' I said.

'I was a little bit drunk,' Keke admitted. 'The captain said, "No, no, you have been drinking, also smoking I think, and I do not take you in here." He took my friend, who was riding my motorbike, but not me. I was only drinking because of what happened to Mika. If the captain of the boat had been Finnish he would have understood.'

The real source of Keke's grief was not the missed ferry but what his wife would think if he did not get home when he was expected. He was going to call and tell her what had happened, he said, he just needed a couple of drinks beforehand to work up the courage. His mobile phone sat next to his glass in a pool of beer. Every now and then Keke would glance at it as if expecting it to explode.

I bought him another gargantuan beer and we talked about the race – I reminded him that the other Finnish driver, Kimi Raikkonen, had scored a couple of points, which cheered him up – but then his phone gave a shriek and I did the proper journalistic thing: I made my excuses and left.

The hotel restaurant was deserted, which suited me fine. I took a corner table overlooking the unlovely Europaplatz, and ordered asparagus in several permutations. Across the square, a large red-on-yellow sign above what seemed to be a hardware store advertised 'Kock Service'. Framed on the restaurant wall were signed souvenir photographs of the many stars who had chosen to stay in the Hotel Daniel over the years: rock legends of the calibre of Nazareth, Uriah Heep, Boney M and The Serendipity Singers, and a man whose career had not, perhaps, scaled those heights: Herman Duer, zither soloist. I hope they all liked asparagus.

I stopped by at the lobby bar for a nightcap, and was not remotely surprised to find Keke still present, although somewhat slumped. He was chirpy, though, by Finnish standards, so I asked if he had talked to his wife. 'Yes, yes,' he said. 'She is drinking schnapps at home. She is sad about Mika as well. So I have decided to have some schnapps myself. Will you join me?'

No way. I had a glass of Austrian Riesling, and listened to Keke babble about the incompetence of McLaren's technical staff and the villainy of Ferrari. As he rambled on, his head sank lower and lower until his forehead rested on the bar, and he was talking to the floor.

'I must go to bed,' I said. 'Early plane. Don't you have to go to work tomorrow?'

Keke giggled and burped, and looked up at me with one bleary blue eye. 'That's not a problem,' he said. 'I'm the boss.'

'Really?' I said. 'Good grief. What exactly do you do?'

He giggled again. 'I'm a bank manager,' he said, and passed out.

In 2003 I went back to Austria for what looked like being the final Grand Prix at the A1-Ring. The Formula One calendar had become crowded and the old place was going to have to make way for a more cigarette-friendly venue in the Far East.

Nothing much had changed. Ferrari had fixed the 2002 race as well, in an even more blatant manner than before, and this time the outrage was so extreme that Michael Schumacher – sort of – said sorry, and the FIA – sort of – changed the rules to prevent such fixes happening again.

I stayed in a lovely hotel in the pretty part of Graz, but still got stuck in the underground car park and had to be rescued by the receptionist.

The people of Styria were still inclined to wear leather-lapelled jackets and elect extreme right-wing politicians, but one extraordinary change had come over Graz: it had been selected as European City of Culture for 2003. The manifestations of this honour seemed to me unimaginative: an exhibition devoted to the art of car design, another exploring the appeal of erotic clothing. But there was one startling innovation. In a little square next to the Jakominiplatz there is gilded statue of the Virgin Mary atop a stone column. It is a modest monument – in columnar terms, no more than a half-Nelson – but the Grazers had decided to make it a feature of their cultural year. An artist, or architect, called Richard Kriesche, had designed a glass-walled lift to be built next to the column. For one euro, the lift transported the curious to the height of the Virgin and suspended them there for one minute before returning them gently to the ground.

According to Kriesche: 'This change of the accustomed perspective will allow people to actively experience social change, away from pyramid power structures towards an egalitarian democractic society.' According to me, that's cobblers, but the lift was irresistible. As I waited my turn, feeling self-consciously touristic, a very striking brunette in her late twenties walked up to me and asked in German if I had one euro. I held out my hand with the coin in it: she took it, and replaced it with a fifty-cent piece.

The Asian family who had ascended before us emerged, giggling. The young lady put our coin in the slot, and the doors slid shut. As we rose slowly above the square I asked her if she lived in Graz. She sighed.

'I used to,' she said. 'Now I live . . . somewhere else.'

'It is a beautiful city,' I said.

'Yes,' she sighed again. 'The best in the world. There are lakes close by where you can go at the weekend, and the people here are so friendly. But these days I am just visiting.'

We came to a halt. I looked across at the shining figure of the Madonna, who bore a striking resemblance to Queen Victoria.

'To the people in the street,' my companion suddenly said, 'there are now two statues.' She smiled. She had unusually dark blue eyes. 'The Virgin, and us.'

I was still trying to think of an appropriate response when the lift doors opened at street level and the young woman walked briskly away.

Conclusion: Austrian slugs are brown.

Chapter Five

Who Let You In?

Objectives: Attend the Laureus Awards ceremony in Monte Carlo. Mingle with the sporting aristocracy, shake hands with Monegasque royalty, interview a giant of sumo wrestling, and take a taxi around the Grand Prix track. Arrive on time for a synchronised swimming show, and try to avoid the Sports Editor. Time allocated: three days.

I was walking up the hill to Casino Square in Monte Carlo when I heard the voice coming the other way. Before I could make out individual words I could tell that the accent was more Midlands than Midi. There were visual clues, too: pink, furry limbs protruding from straining burgundy shorts, tented yellow polo shirt, puce face, mirror shades and baseball cap.

He might have looked like an outsider, but he was at home. He was chatting to a slimmer, clean-shaven version of himself: son, or nephew, or business acolyte. As they passed by me, the fat man was saying, in unreconstructed Brum: 'I'll tell you, if this place ever loses its independence, I'm stuck with a worthless, tiny apartment in a shithole.'

Such is the patriotism of the typical citizen of the principality of Monaco.

Monaco and Monte Carlo hold a place in the public imagination wildly out of proportion to their size and clout.

The tiny state is promoted as the global epicentre of glamour, the party HQ of the planet, home to the stars and their favourite bars. While I was there I heard the then President of the International Olympic Committee, Juan Antonio Samaranch, describe the place as 'the worldwide capital of sport'.

It is none of these things. The glamour (both human and mechanical) is expensively imported, the parties are flaky, the stars spend as little time there as possible and when you see the prices in the bars you can understand why. As for the 'capital of sport' bit: Monaco has a decent football team who play in front of tiny crowds. It has a rally which takes place almost in its entirety outside the principality on French roads. It has a middle-ranking tennis event and used to have a decent golf tournament, which lost its place on the tour because the weather (contrary to the brochures and popular belief) was too foul too often. Of course it has the Monaco Grand Prix, which is the world's loudest traffic jam, and the excuse for some of the most flagrant abuse of corporate funds the planet has seen. Do these factors combine to form a worthy sporting capital of the world? I think not.

Samaranch, like me, was in Monaco for the Laureus Awards, the *soi-disant* 'Oscars of Sport'. The ceremony and its attendant parties – largely bankrolled by Mercedes-Benz and Cartier – are carefully scheduled to attract stars who have just finished their promotional duties at the annual film festival in nearby Cannes, and high-rollers of all kinds assembling early for the following weekend's Monaco Grand Prix.

Such people need constant entertainment. As well as the awards ceremony, Laureus had laid on a cocktail reception, a golf tournament, a regatta on the harbour, an 'Evening of Sport and Film', and a farewell brunch. Guests of Laureus – indentified by dinky little enamel lapel badges – were ferried from swanky event to swanky event in a fleet of fifty Mercedes limousines, which had rear-seat vanity mirrors to allow last-minute adjustments to cosmetics and coiffure. They were pretty good for nose-picking, too: there's nothing worse than hopping out into a blaze of flashbulbs with a half-excavated bogey dangling from one nostril.

I was there, armed only with a threadbare tuxedo and a powerful sense of inadequacy: in the limos, at the parties, trying to keep my cheat's bow-tie straight and wondering if people could tell how much my shoes had really cost. The British hack pack, twenty-odd strong, had flown in together to Nice airport where we were to be met by the aforementioned limos. I affected great nonchalance strolling through the customs and passport formalities, exuding familiarity with the airport and its procedures and general South of France *savoir faire* for the benefit of my fellow journalists.

Forty minutes after landing, they had all disappeared, as had the pretty lady holding the Laureus sign, and I realised that I had been standing at the luggage carousel for the easyJet flight that had landed five minutes after ours. As nonchalantly as possible – as if I had been studying other people's luggage for deep purposes of my own and had reached satisfactory but inscrutable conclusions – I sauntered over to the British Midland carousel and retrieved my suitcase, which had been revolving in solitary splendour.

Outside in the concourse I located the only remaining Brits, Paul Trow from the Hayters agency, and Harry Pearson, an unfeasibly tall freelance who contributes regularly to the *Guardian* and has written the only interesting book ever published about Belgium.

'What happened to you?' asked Paul, a slightly shambolic and endearingly tactless figure. 'We saw you standing by the easyJet carousel.'

'Ah yes.' I smiled knowingly. 'I was just checking a few things. Now where's our limo?'

On cue, a large grey Mercedes glided up to the kerb. As we settled into the teak and leather interior, the driver asked if we wanted to go by the scenic route or the motorway. The motorway, we decided. Dammit, we're not tourists.

Half an hour later, as we completed our third serpentine tour of the suburbs of Nice, it became clear that the scenic route was the only route the driver knew. And it wasn't the route to Monaco.

'You're . . . not from these parts, I take it?' I said to him.

'No.' He gave a sheepish shrug.

'Where exactly are you from, in fact?'

'Belgium.'

This was bad news from a punctuality point of view, but good news for Harry, who misses no opportunity to add to his store of knowledge of all things Belgian.

Eventually, by a process of elimination, we found the autoroute through the mountains and, two petty tollbooths later (the French extracting final tributes from those heading into tax exile) drove past the modest road sign that announced our entry into the principality of Monaco.

'Are we on the Grand Prix track yet?' asked Paul.

'I don't know,' said the driver, pointedly. 'I don't come from here.'

'Look, there's the casino!' Paul exclaimed.

'That's a bank,' I said.

'That must be the Grimaldi Palace!' Paul cried.

'That's another bank,' I said. 'But now we are on the Grand Prix track.'

We went down the steep hill to the old Station Hairpin, at which celebrated curve our driver took a course which in a week's time would have caused extensive bodywork damage, but now led through a gap in the steel barriers and on to the forecourt of the Monte Carlo Grand Hotel. The Grand is built on the site of Monte Carlo's old railway station, and has the distinction not only of abutting several corners of the Grand Prix circuit, but also sitting smack on top of another chunk of the track. The tunnel, a long curve negotiated in near darkness by the drivers, takes them under twenty bedrooms and the Grand's Piano Bar.

The hotel is much too big to be pretty – there are 619 guest rooms – but the swimming pool on the roof is lovely, and I went and sat up there with my paperback and sipped beer and gazed at the panorama of the cruise-ship-crammed Mediterranean. Then my mobile phone rang, and I heard the Sports Editor's voice accompanied by a chorus of sea-gulls.

'What are you doing, Andrew?' he demanded.

'Just – um, just checking out one or two things,' I said. 'Where are you?'

'I'm on a yacht in the harbour,' the Sports Editor said. My God, probably looking at me through binoculars. I moved my beer behind a sandwich menu. 'There are a couple of press conferences you might be attending, aren't there?'

'Yup, sure,' I bluffed. I hadn't even looked at the schedule. 'I'll be down there in a couple of minutes. Don't worry. I'll get it all covered. *Bon voyage.*'

Damn.

As I scampered through the hotel foyer I almost bumped into a substantial figure in a lurid Hawaiian-print shirt. Dave.

'Where you off to, then?'

I told him.

'Nah, bollocks to that. Complete waste of time. I'm going up to the casino. Why don't you come with me?'

'Because I don't want to lose my job and all my money,' I said.

Dave laughed. 'Wimp.'

The press conferences, like the awards ceremony itself, were taking place in the Grimaldi Forum, a futuristic convention palace on the sea front not far from the hotel. Like most of the modern bits of Monaco, the Forum is built on land reclaimed from the sea. The Grimaldi family, who have ruled the principality for a little more than 700 years, have proved most inventive in extracting the maximum value from their limited patch of ancestral real estate. They build in three dimensions: apartment blocks go up; car parks, road tunnels and auditoriums go down; roads, football stadiums and marinas go out where the sea used to be.

The Grimaldi Forum went out to sea and down. When I stood on the stage of the auditorium for a moment that morning in a break from the awards-ceremony rehearsals, I was standing at a point which, five years previously, had been a hundred yards offshore and a hundred feet under the Mediterranean.

None of which had any relevance to what I was supposed to be doing. I was, as usual, lost, and had blundered backstage while trying to locate a press conference. Any press conference, in fact, since several were apparently scheduled and I wasn't fussy. But the Grimaldi Forum is a large and complex place, being further complicated by teams of carpenters erecting temporary partitions which would later protect the stars from the public and – particularly – the press.

Large South African security men patrolled the corridors, denying and granting access to different bits of it seemingly on a whim. I walked into a room full of photographers, and another occupied by off-duty limousine drivers, munching baguettes and watching football on a small television. Eventually I found something called the Auric Room – named, presumably, after Auric Goldfinger, eponymous Bond villain and Monaco-style multi-millionaire – which was occupied by a dozen or so journalists scattered around seating for a hundred.

A press conference. Good. Now, who was doing the

talking? A Laureus operative handed me a sheet of paper headed 'Media Alert'.

Hmm. A Slovenian who had skiied down Mount Everest. An American endurance mountain biker. Two Italian ice skaters. Jennifer Capriati, tennis queen . . . great! Except that a colleague had interviewed her last week. A French paraplegic swimmer. A Russian gymnast, and a Chinese one. Cathy Freeman, Australian athletics megastar . . . who had been interviewed by a colleague of mine yesterday afternoon. A South African who had circumnavigated the globe around the Equator. An American swimmer. A Chinese badminton player. An Australian paraplegic sailor. A sumo wrestler.

Hang on, though. Not just a sumo wrestler. *The* sumo wrestler. Konishiki. Six feet three and thirty-five stones of Hawaiian-Japanese blubber, he hauled himself on to the little stage at the far end of the Auric Room and took his place – took two places, to be accurate – among the other guests at the press-conference table.

Before the questioning could commence, though, we had a spiel from Edwin Moses, the legendary American 400-metre hurdler who is chairman of the Laureus World Sports Academy. Moses reminded us that the World Sports Awards were not just about glamour. They were also intended to showcase the work of the Sport For Good Foundation, the charitable side of Laureus, under whose auspices academy members – famous ex-stars, like Moses – travelled the world donating money to sports-related charities and inspiring young people to do good through sport.

I already knew about all of that since I had tagged along on several Sport For Good project visits, and interviewed some interesting people in even more interesting locations: Moses in downtown Richmond, Virginia; the Indian cricketer Kapil Dev on a housing estate in Berlin; the wheelchair athlete Tanni Grey-Thompson next to a lough in Northern

Ireland. But today I needed some juicy quotes from Konishiki, since nobody else present was likely to tickle my newspaper's fancy. What could I ask him?

'How many of your opponents have you actually eaten?'

'You recently got married. How is the wife bearing up?'

'When did you last see your penis?'

None of those would really do, I thought. I'm not very good at interviews, to be honest: much too self-conscious about the whole process. I care a great deal more than I should about not asking boring or obvious questions when the subjects, I am sure, don't really give a toss and are quite happy to trot out the boring or obvious answers. The thing to do is just to pitch in there, which as usual I let somebody else do for me.

'Here, Konishiki, how did you get so fat?'

It was Dave, evidently finished with his business in the casino.

For a moment Konishiki's formidable brow furrowed – it looked like a bum seen sideways – but then he smiled. 'It is much harder than you think,' he said, evidently holding Dave's portly form in poor regard. 'We have to eat a very great amount of healthy food and then sleep. A sumo sleeps for four hours after his lunch, just to put on weight.'

Dave looked interested. This was a career opportunity that had never previously occurred to him. 'Blimey,' he said. 'What's the money like, then?'

Konishiki shook his great head. 'There is no sponsorship in sumo,' he said. 'We dress in traditional costumes, and they cannot have sponsors' names on them. So all the wrestlers – there are nine hundred or so professionals – are paid a salary by the Japan Sumo Association. Perhaps only fifty of them are really paid a proper salary.'

Dave was downcast. I chipped in.

'Is it true that you have to book two seats when you are flying?' I asked.

'Sure,' Konishiki beamed. 'But it makes check-in faster. I get the aisle seat *and* the window seat.'

I scribbled all this down, and at the end of the press conference dutifully telephoned the sports desk. 'I can offer you a five-hundred-word piece on the celebrated sumo wrestler Konishiki,' I told the sports news editor.

'And I can offer you a two-word response,' the sports news editor replied.

I had been wasting my time at the press conference. But my boss, whom I was likely to encounter at that evening's reception, would rather I wasted my afternoon taking notes in the Grimaldi Forum than sitting by the hotel pool with a succession of beers. And while the Sports Editor was at large in the principality – very likely armed with a pair of binoculars – I was going to do what I was told.

Inspired by Konishiki, I decided to walk back to the hotel by way of the Japanese garden, an unlikely oasis of calm on the sea front that is one of the better things the Grimaldis have done for their principality. The thing I like about Japanese gardens – and this is particularly appropriate in Monte Carlo – is that there is no pretence of untamed nature. The garden is artificial, and the more blatantly so the better. The central feature of Monte Carlo's Japanese garden was a lake fed by a cascade and filled with giant, slow-moving koi carp. Little humpbacked wooden bridges connected miniature islands, while around the water's edge stood ornamental pavilions and placards explaining the meaning and symbolism of the various features in the land-scape.

The park was tiny, probably no more than an acre, but it was beautiful and near-deserted. I shared it with two young ladies of Scandinavian appearance, who might have been tennis professionals, or pop stars but were probably aspiring trophy wives, and a nonagenarian lady in white culottes and a white T-shirt, her arms wrinkled and brown like bark, face protected and almost completely hidden by a wide-brimmed straw hat and giant sunglasses. You see a lot of these crones tottering around the streets of Monte Carlo, usually taking a miniature dog to do *un dou-dou* on the pavement, which their owner will leave for someone else to tidy up. The pampered relics are barely living evidence of the longevity of the human female compared to the male, widows of the bankers, arms dealers and dodgy aristocrats who brought them here to escape taxation and left them here when they succumbed to life's other inevitable.

I had been staring at the old lady while wondering what her late husband had done to buy her jewellery, and I felt hostility radiating back from behind her sunglasses. Any minute now, I thought, she's going to call the police and have me arrested for being poor in a public area.

Back at the hotel I asked for a taxi, briefing the concierge on the route I wanted to take.

'But it will not be possible, monsieur,' he protested. 'The traffic, the roadworks . . .' he shrugged expressively.

I was firm. 'Just get me a taxi, and we'll see what the driver says.'

What the driver said, when I told him that I wished to be driven around the Monte Carlo Formula One track, was '*Merde.*'

I waved a fistful of francs at him, and his attitude modified subtly. '*Merde alors,*' he said, pulling out of the hotel forecourt and on to what is for ninety-eight per cent of the year an ordinary road, and for two per cent of the year the most famous racetrack in the world.

The hotel stands on the outside of what used to be known as the Station Hairpin, and from there the road/track runs downhill into the corner known as Portier. This ninety-degree right-hander is where Ayrton Senna once crashed

119

while leading the Grand Prix, and was so cross with himself that he climbed out of the car and walked straight to his nearby apartment to sulk.

My driver, who was called Didier, negotiated the corner with more aplomb than Senna and pointed his battered Mercedes saloon at the entrance to the tunnel. The long, blind, subterranean right-hand curve under the hotel is one of the fastest places on the course, with the cars topping 180 mph as they reappear into daylight. Didier proceeded at a more sedate 25 mph through the tunnel, which echoed to the sound of bolt-guns as workmen prepared the crash barriers for the race.

At the exit of the tunnel, where the Japanese driver Takuma Sato would, in a week's time, find himself on three wheels at full speed, the road runs quite steeply downhill, something you never appreciate from the television. That must make braking for the subsequent chicane all the more difficult, but we had no opportunity to test the theory. Where the track jinked left at the chicane, the racing line was occupied by parked cars, and Didier was obliged to drive straight on down the Avenue President John F. Kennedy. To our left, beyond the racetrack, bobbed the mega-yachts of billionaires. To our right the shop windows displayed models of the same vessels: these were the offices of the yacht charter companies, handily placed to keep an eye on their assets.

Didier quickly manoeuvred back on to the Grand Prix route – we'd missed about fifty yards – and we pootled along the harbourside between ribbons of newly installed steel barriers. Just past the swimming-pool chicane, we came to a halt at the rear of a sizeable traffic jam. '*Merde*,' muttered Didier, opening his window and lighting a cigarette.

It was a very Monégasque traffic jam: a low-speed auto-motive beauty contest. Immediately in front of our modest Mercedes were not one but two late-model Ferrari coupés, one scarlet, one metallic blue. Next up was a black Porsche 911, then a little Smart car, then a Bentley. Around the steel barrier at the next corner peeped the butch rear end of a Lamborghini Diablo.

Didier ran through an impressive catalogue of French profanities as we crawled towards the hairpin at La Rascasse, named after the fish restaurant that stood for years on the inside of the bend. We came to a halt again here as a middle-aged man in a dark blue BMW saloon made a hash of the entry to the underground car park next to the Formula One paddock. It was Jenson Button's dad, John, and he looked rather embarrassed as the massed supercars honked and hooted at him.

Released at last, Didier accelerated as we pulled on to the pit straight. We flashed past the winner's podium (surprisingly modest) at, oh, at least 20 mph, and I barely had time to notice the branch of Barclays Bank adjacent to the start/finish line. Handy for the winner to cash his cheque.

At Sainte Devote the Formula One cars go around the outside of a traffic island adorned with a statue of the race's first winner, a pseudonymous Englishman called Williams. This spot traditionally provides some of the liveliest photographic material in sport, as on the first lap the drivers often experiment – involuntarily – with aerial overtaking.

We nearly had some carnage of our own as we approached the traffic island. The driver of the scarlet Ferrari in front of us suddenly changed his mind about turning right and swung left instead, right across our bows. Didier stamped on his brakes and, as I unpeeled myself from the upholstery, treated the Ferrari man to a frank discourse on his ancestors and their carnal activities with members of the animal kingdom.

'*Merde*,' Didier concluded, and swung us right up the Avenue d'Ostende, the sinuous ribbon of uphill tarmac that leads to Casino Square. Here are branches of Europe's swankiest boutiques: Gucci, Lalique and Prada, where big winners can buy little somethings for their glamorous companions, and perhaps a guilt-gift to take home to the wife. The Monaco heart hospital is close by, its proximity to the gaming tables no doubt very good for business.

A gentle left-hand turn took us into the square itself. On one side, the Hotel de Paris, temporary abode of Laureus's grandest guests; on the other, the celebrated casino, a cathedral of kitsch that was currently being gawped at by a busload of Japanese tourists. We crested the little hump on the left-hand side of the road that so disconcerts the Formula One cars – barely discernible through Didier's saggy suspension – and trundled downhill past the Tip-Top and Tiffany's, ancient nightspots enlivened by rakish British drivers like Mike Hawthorn and Graham Hill in the days when hangovers were as common on the grid as helmets.

We were off the racing line for the only possible overtaking spot on the entire circuit, the right-hander at the foot of the casino gardens, but the Porsche behind us was unambitious and stayed dutifully behind as we ran down the hill towards the Grand Hotel. Here we were delayed one last time by a bus in the middle of the road – the hairpin is no better suited to public transport than it is to Formula One cars – before the taxi trundled to a halt in front of the hotel.

'Seventeen minutes and thirty-four seconds,' I announced. 'Not quite good enough for pole position, I think.'

'*Merde*,' said Didier.

Back in my room, I commenced preparations for the evening's cocktail party. The invitation stipulated black tie, so it was time to exhume my tuxedo from its polythene shroud, and tackle the tricky business of cuff-link insertion.

Most of the time I can wear whatever I want, so unless I'm up a mountain I'll generally wear a T-shirt and jeans and training shoes. Once a month, perhaps, for a lunch or an interview with a minister or a millionaire, I'll put on my suit (note the singular). Once in a blue moon I'll reach for the tux. So I'm not as comfortable as I might be with the practicalities of formal dressing. It normally takes me several goes, for instance, to produce a perfectly ordinary neck-tie knot. And cuff-links? I generally set aside half an hour.

First of all, I put the links – miniature Scrabble squares with my initials on, highly amusing – in with the shirt off, then found (as I had expected) that I couldn't get my hands through to the end of the sleeves. So I took the links out again, put the shirt back on, and started again. After ten minutes or so of fingernail-splitting, I succeeded in getting the left one in. But the right proved impossible, mainly because I am so right-handed that it is as much as my left can manage to pick up a fork.

Eventually I gave up, slung on the rest of my kit and walked down to reception with the undone cuff hanging out of the end of my sleeve. I might as well have been wearing a badge that said 'Social Outcast'. Surfing a wave of derision, I presented my sleeve and the recalcitrant link to the concierge, who performed the necessary service in moments.

I was much too embarrassed to hang around outside the hotel with all the other black-tied guests waiting for Laureus limos to ferry them to the party, and decided instead to walk. The party was at the Monte Carlo Beach Club, and since, to my certain knowledge, there is only one beach in Monte Carlo, the artificial one next to the Grimaldi Forum, I knew it wouldn't take me too long.

Sure enough, a quarter of an hour later I was standing on the promenade above the beach, coming to terms with the fact that there was no club adjacent to it, and therefore no party. Yards away, Laureus limos purred past me, heading out of town in the general direction of Italy.

The Monte Carlo Beach Club, I discovered, is approximately forty minutes' walk from the centre of Monte Carlo. Here are some other things I discovered: that my new black shoes caused blisters on my left heel and right little toe; that I had omitted to bring a handkerchief with which to wipe the sweat coursing from my brow; and that my left cuff-link – the one that I had put in without assistance – had come undone.

Perhaps I should have hitched a lift in one of the Laureus limos that swept past every couple of minutes, spattering dust and gravel at my ankles. But there is something about wearing a black tie and a dinner jacket that seems to rule out standing at the roadside with a cocked thumb. And if I were to be truly honest, I wasn't in too much of a rush to get to the party in any case.

Most people, I understand, would jump at an invitation to the Monte Carlo Beach Club; my instinctive response to the phrase 'champagne reception' is a shudder. Canapés give me indigestion, and I am positively allergic to speeches. I would rather have spent the evening reading my book in the hotel bar. Party Animal? No. Super Pooper.

But with the Sports Editor in town, shirking was unthinkable. He would be at the party, in a tuxedo that fitted, with a real bow-tie and cuff-links he had inserted without professional help. He would be doing his diplomatic thing, securing the newspaper a year's worth of celebrity columnists, while simultaneously scanning the gathering for signs of misbehaviour by his staff. Therefore I had to be at the party, though my role was unspecified. Don't fall into the swimming pool, don't cheek royalty, and don't throw up on anyone important, I supposed.

I waved my little Laureus tag at one of half a dozen South African goons at the gate, and sauntered nonchalantly into the grounds of the Beach Club, trying not to limp. I was immediately surrounded by beautiful people: tall, good-looking, suave and sophisticated. And they were just the waiters. My fellow guests were from a different planet: Planet Glamour, where all the beings wear permanent tans, where all the teeth are dazzlingly white and everybody's body is honed to perfection.

God knows who they all were. I recognised one or two global sporting megastars, but the idea of marching up and introducing myself to, say, Ronaldo, did not appeal, and in any case he and his ilk were hardly short of attention. I took a glass of champagne and walked on to a jetty which led away from the Beach Club out into the bay.

When I could walk no further, I turned and looked back at the party. Lanterns illuminated the gathering dusk, while waiters flitted from group to group like butterflies. I would happily have stayed on the jetty all evening, given the opportunity and frequent refills: a sort of Gatsby figure, only with less money, enigmatically alone on his dock.

That was the fantasy. In reality I was the first thing that most people saw when they arrived at the party, and rather too many of them were nudging each other and saying: 'Look, there's a scruffy little man with no friends. Do you think he's contemplating suicide?'

Time to mingle.

The throng was most concentrated around a vast outdoor swimming pool, the illuminated water of which glowed an iridescent blue. Long tables had been laid along one side, and these were groaning under the weight of an ambitious buffet. Out at sea, I imagined, were just one or two lucky lobsters looking around and wondering where the hell all their friends had got to.

The knack to concealing social isolation at a party is constant mobility. Don't look as if you are searching for your mates: look as if you have spotted them across the crowds and are making your way determinedly towards them. If the party is sufficiently large, no one will notice that you never actually meet anyone.

In this manner, nodding, waving and winking at non-existent acquaintances, I made two slow circumnavigations of the poolside, gathering bits of lobster and conversation as I squeezed politely between bronzed shoulders and satin lapels. Anyone witnessing my performance – the Sports Editor, perhaps – could surely only conclude that here was a man on good terms with half the population of Monaco. Or a man with some kind of obsessive compulsive disorder.

But the conversations were tasty.

'Did you bring the Bentley tonight?'

'No, the Ferrari.'

'Which one?'

'The blue one. The red needs a wash.'

And . . .

'I told him thirty million dollars, closed, finished.'

'You're a monster.'

'I'm a monster deal-maker.'

And . . .

'Have you seen his yacht?'

'Don't tell me . . .'

'Marble walls. So vulgar.'

Eventually I found myself in a corner next to the three diving boards, somewhat hemmed in by men in dinner jackets, a number of whom were mumbling with South African accents into little microphones on their lapels.

Suddenly, one of these gentlemen turned and started to shove me backwards. 'This area must be clear of everybody,' he declared. 'Now, right?'

Flipping heck, I thought, go easy. Can't a man mingle in peace?

'I'm sorry, sir,' the shover continued. 'This area is private.'

'Since when?' I asked.

'Get out of the way, please,' said Johannesburg Jimmy, with a final shove that forced me up on to a foot-high wall bordering a flower bed. 'The Prince is coming.'

Indeed, the Prince had come. His Serene Highness Prince Albert had materialised under my nose, and was shaking hands with a Laureus bigwig.

'Welcome,' the Laureus man said, and then laughed nervously. 'So sorry. How can I welcome you to your own country?'

'I'm very happy to be here anyway,' the Prince said. Then he glanced up at me, teetering on the wall above his head. 'What are you doing?' he asked. Then I watched his shining pate move on down the receiving line, and I recalled Prince Edward doing his meet'n'greet routine in Malaysia. What is it, I wondered, about minor royalty and hair loss?

'Who let you in here?' hissed the South African shover, as he moved away, covering Prince Albert's serene back.

Later on I found Harry, Dave and Paul, and we settled in a little pavilion some way from the main throng to engage in moderate champagne consumption and immoderate speculation about our fellow guests. Dave was of the opinion that most of the women present, 'at least eighty per cent, no less', were not the genuine spouses or partners of the men they were accompanying, but were being paid for their presence. Or, as Dave put it: 'This place is heaving with tarts.'

This was clearly nonsense, but we were still hard pressed to prevent Dave from testing his theory by walking up to the wife of the chief executive of an intercontinental luxury-goods brand and asking her how much for a quick one. Just as we were contemplating physical restraint, Dave was distracted by an extraordinary vision. So were we.

A slender teenage girl wearing a silver swimsuit and a lot of make-up walked elegantly past, followed by a similarly attired blonde and then ten more young ladies. As the last silver bottom swayed past us, Dave lurched to his feet and started to follow the line of taut posteriors through the crowd, an ugly duck to the flight of beautiful swans. 'I'm not fucking missing this,' he muttered.

The girls and their shambling stalker walked all the way around the pool to the diving boards. Four of them climbed on to each board, and we could see the South African security men restraining a bulky figure who seemed to wish to join them. In quick and elegant succession, the girls dived into the floodlit water.

'Of course,' I groaned to Harry, 'there would have to be synchronised swimmers.'

The party organisers had selected their team with care: they were well matched in physique, strength and aquatic ability. When required, hands, elbows, arms and feet broke the surface quite simultaneously. But the organisers had failed to take into account a fundamental aspect of synchronised swimming (on which, since Malaysia, I considered myself something of an expert): if you aren't sitting in a pretty high grandstand, or watching a television picture shot from above, you don't have the first idea of what is going on. Since the Monte Carlo Beach Club was equipped with neither grandstands nor television screens, most of the display was lost on the audience, who quickly returned to their chatter of convertible bonds and convertible coupés.

The girls finished their routine with a long line of scissoring legs, leapt like silver seals out of the water and processed, at a trot, back around the pool, with their biggest fan doing his best to keep up.

Dave was quite out of breath by the time he returned to us. 'Wonderful sport, synchronised swimming, isn't it?' he gasped. He looked wistfully at the gate through which the swimmers had disappeared. 'I wonder if I shouldn't go and ask them a few questions. About technique and such . . .'.

We thought that the security personnel might not go for this idea, and instead I fetched us all some more champagne.

The thing about having your glass refilled, unbidden, with good bubbly every fifteen minutes is that very soon you are starting a lot of sentences with 'The thing about . . .' but not getting the chance to finish them, because your friends are all saying 'The thing about . . .' about whatever the thing is, at about the same time.

The other thing about production-line champagne-drinking is that the finished article is frankly but unwittingly pissed.

So when I finally lost track of whatever is was that I had been talking about and decided to make my way back to the hotel, my progress through the throng was pretty erratic. It is nice, at a party, to bump into a lot of people whom you know. But I was bumping into a lot of people I didn't know, and bumping into them pretty hard. Like a tuxedoed pinball, I ricocheted my way through the crowd to the entrance, where I burped in a friendly manner at a patient Laureus representative, who summoned a Mercedes and ushered me aboard.

But then they had to blow it all by letting Dave and Paul aboard as well.

'Right,' said Dave to the driver. 'The casino, mate, and quick about it.'

This was not at all my plan. I was just sufficiently sober to realise that I wasn't sober at all, and just sufficiently sensible to remember that I have never, ever, walked out of a casino with more money than I had when I walked in. I explained all of this to Dave, who dismissed my objections as those of an amateur and an intimate portion of the female anatomy.

'The thing about Monte Carlo,' Dave declared, 'is the casino. So we are going to go to the casino, we are going to win a lot of money and then,' he licked his leering lips, 'we're going to make some friends.'

I could tell you a tremendous story here about how, against my better judgement, I was frogmarched into the casino and up to the roulette table where, using a combination of my daughters' birth dates, I garnered a mountain of chips at the first spin of the wheel. About how, when converted, the mountain provided enough cash to sponsor a crate of champagne at Jimmy's, the most expensive nightclub in the world, where we met . . .

What really happened is that when the limo pulled up in front of the casino, and an elaborately liveried flunky opened the door, I wriggled out of Dave's grasp and ran away across Casino Square, pursued by a volley of insults but, thankfully, nothing more corporal. Slowing to a walk, I stumbled past the Tip-Top, where the ghosts of Hawthorn and Hill were chatting raffishly over cocktails, and, gathering momentum once more, trundled down the steep hill to the hotel. I went through the lobby at a full clip, bounced off a jewellery boutique, and felt safe only once the lift doors had closed behind me.

I looked at myself in the mirrored walls as the lift climbed. Bow-tie askew, collar stained, flecks of ash and canapé on my lapels. Not sober, not smart, but solvent.

'Wimp,' I said.

The next morning I woke very early, for some reason, and being unable to get back to sleep (something to do with the municipal workers erecting crash barriers ten yards from my window), breakfasted heartily on Nurofen and mineral water and decided to go out for a walk.

Coming out of the hotel I met Dave, who was sitting on the rockery, cradling a glass of what seemed to be flat champagne. He was wearing a Monte Carlo Grand Hotel nightshirt, tucked into the trousers of his formal suit.

'What happened at the casino?' I asked.

'I lost my shirt,' he replied.

*   *   *

I wanted to revisit Fontvielle, a recently developed marina at the northernmost extreme of the principality that had been the scene of an embarrassing interview a couple of years earlier. It was about a mile and a half, as the crow flies, from the hotel, but crows don't accept passengers, and the other transport options in Monaco are all fraught with difficulties.

I could have taken a taxi, but as I had found the previous day in company with Didier, taxis (like Ferraris and Bentleys) get stuck in jams. The same applies to the local buses, which exist largely to ferry non-residents to and from a day's skivvying: if you want to know the difference between those who work in Monaco and those who live there, keep your eyes on the roadside. The workers are the ones queuing at the bus stops.

I could, theoretically, have travelled by boat or helicopter, but either would have made for budgetary problems. So I decided to walk, though even this would be in no sense straightforward. Monaco is crammed on to a narrow and precipitous strip of land between the Alpes-Maritimes and the sea. The roads are necessarily convoluted and often subterranean. In some cases the fastest way to travel between two adjacent streets is by public elevator.

A three-dimensional model of my morning stroll would resemble the DNA sequence of someone with severe genetic abnormalities. I went up, left, up again, left again, down, left, down again, left, right, up, left, up, right, up, left, through a tunnel and finally, with relief and on my second large bottle of Evian, straight on into Fontvielle.

This area is the most dramatic example yet seen of the Grimaldi family's expansionist tendencies. The ruling family survived in relative penury for generations largely because their rocky little kingdom was too small to attract the attention of the acquisitive local grandees. But modern-day Monaco, with its ever-increasing population of tax exiles and high-spending tourists, is becoming short of space in which to accommodate them all.

The apartment blocks have got higher and higher, but as each new edifice obstructs the sea views of its prede-cessors, so the acrimony of existing residents has risen with each new erection. The Grimaldis have tried building under the sea, as at the Grimaldi Forum, but when a squillionaire shows up here looking for an apartment with a Mediterranean view he is not usually expecting to gaze up at the yachts from beneath. They have tried demol-ishing public utilities: my hotel was built on the site of the former station, subsequently moved inland. That replacement station has itself now been demolished, and station number three has been built not so much inland as under land, into a colossal man-made cavern under the mountains at the rear of the principality. Station number two is being replaced by – *naturellement* – more apartments. But faced with a simultaneous shortage of car parking and yacht moorings, and a high-achieving but modestly housed football team, the local planners went for the big one: they shoved half a mountainside into the sea and built a new port, a stack of new apartments and a multi-storey garage with – nifty touch, this – a football stadium on the roof.

For all of which spectacular achievement, I thought, wandering around the nondescript new streets, the place still looked like an unusually sunny sector of central Reading.

Two years earlier, I had been dispatched at an hour's notice to interview the distinguished Australian motorbike racer Mick Doohan, who was languishing in his Fontvielle apart-ment while recuperating from a smashed leg, and suffi-ciently bored to accede to requests from his various sponsors to talk to the press. I ran out of the house clutching my passport and a notebook, expressed myself to Heathrow, caught – just – my British Airways flight and then a bus to the heliport at Nice airport.

My ticket for Heli-Air Monaco looked like a regular airline ticket, with a flight number, and specified departure and arrival times. My journey was scheduled to take six minutes, which presumably ruled out drinks from the trolley and an in-flight movie.

I was waiting dutifully in the little departure lounge when a Heli-Air official dashed in from the apron outside and demanded to know if there were any passengers present. I raised a hand sheepishly and explained in halting French that my flight was not due to leave for twenty minutes – but by then he had tagged my bags, torn my ticket and was hustling me across the tarmac to a whirring chopper that had seen better days.

The good thing was that there was no time to be worried. As I, the sole passenger, sat fiddling with my lap strap and wondered how secure the doors were, the pilot lifted off from the southern end of Nice airport and banked steeply out over the sea. We flew low over the waves, low enough to discern the nipples on the yacht-bound sunbathers sailing below us, an observation that entertained me more thoroughly than any in-flight movie might have done until we touched down on Monaco soil or, more precisely, Monaco landfill.

After all that frantic travel I was nearly an hour and half early for the interview. I checked into my hotel, a swanky edifice that apparently formed one end of the football stadium, and wandered off with my notebook to find Doohan's apartment.

It was not all that difficult. He lived in a block not far from the heliport which would not have looked out of place in a reinvigorated British slum: Gorbals-sur-Mer, if you like. I selected, by trial and error, the correct entrance, and was just about to press the buzzer marked 'Doohan' when I noticed some of the other surnames on the buzzer panel. Surely he's a former Formula One driver, I thought. And he's a middle-ranking tennis player, she's an athlete and he drives rally cars for a living . . . good grief. Of course, none of them would be at home – Doohan was there only because he had a broken leg – but on paper the apartment block could put out one hell of a pub-quiz team.

I wondered, riding up in the lift, what kind of palace of opulence I was about to enter: ultra-modern, all blinding light and sharp angles? Heavily swagged rococo, illuminated by antique candelabra? Or suburban Gothic, hand-tooled leather with oaken trophy cases?

A PR flunky opened the door, and led me into a building site.

To my left, where once there had been a wall, was a sheet of clear polythene, taped to the floor and ceiling. The noise was deafening. Either someone was doing some serious renovation work, or I had walked in on a bring-a-pneumatic-drill party.

Doohan was sitting in a battered modern armchair, with one leg propped up on a stool in front of him. Slim steel bars projected at right angles through strategic rips in the left leg of his jeans, and joined another steel bar that ran most of the leg's length.

'You'll forgive me if I don't get up,' he said, as I leaned over to shake hands. 'Can't you complain to the neighbours about that?' I asked.

'I am the neighbours,' Doohan replied. 'I bought the apartment next door, and I'm having it knocked into mine.'

The seigneur of the site was surrounded by the PR and three foreign journalists: a German, a Scandinavian of some kind, and a Japanese fellow. We all perched around his slight figure, and took turns to ask not terribly probing questions about the thrills of speed, his chief rivals on the track, and what it feels like to smash your leg into tiny little pieces. His answers were barely audible above the workmen's clattering.

In the brief pauses between outbreaks of drilling, choppers clattered into the heliport across the road. I suppose I should have been sticking to bike-racing, but I was appalled by the lifestyle that millions bought in Monte Carlo.

'Don't you ever get fed up with the helicopters?' I asked.

'Nah, mate,' Doohan replied. 'It's just like living next to a bus stop.'

The conversation trailed to a desultory close. The Japanese journalist had not asked a single question, and it struck me that in all likelihood he spoke no English, and would simply present his tape recording to a translator when he got home.

We said polite goodbyes, and as I headed for the door I heard Doohan saying to his PR: 'Is that it for the day?'

'Nearly,' said the PR. 'There's still some bloke called Baker. Should have been here by now.'

Bloody cheek, I thought, and left them to wait for me.

I wondered, as I stood in front of the same building two years later, if Doohan had by now knocked the entire block into one noisy, nondescript mansion. He had certainly never achieved the comeback that he assured us so confidently he would, and perhaps an ex-bike racer with time and money on his hands would turn to property development to pass the time – at least while he waited for 'some bloke called Baker' to show up.

I became aware that the gallons of Evian I had knocked back that morning had finally started to filter through the dehydrated assault course of my internal organs, and that pretty soon I would need a piss. I flirted momentarily with the idea of knocking up Doohan ('Hi, mate, sorry I'm late, mind if I use the facilities?') but decided instead to walk for a little: there had to be a loo nearby.

Sure enough, there was, a public convenience nestled conveniently into the shadow of the car park/football stadium. The only snag was that I had spent the last of my change on mineral water, and there was a basket sitting on a little table inside the door for customers' contributions.

Never mind, I thought, there's no one around. I sauntered in and was reaching for my zip when from one of the gentlemen's cubicles emerged a miniature crone in a sort of maid's uniform, with sharp dark eyes and an improbably raven hairdo.

'*Bonjour, monsieur,*' she trilled, taking up her place at the desk. '*On doit payer ici.*'

'*Vraiment?*' I went on to express, in schoolboy French, my astonishment at this turn of affairs, my temporary lack of funds and my determination to return with same as soon as I had, er, what was the verb . . .

'*Monsieur,*' the crone pronounced, '*on doit payer maintenant.*'

Now? Goodness me, what a pity. My felicitations, madame, and I shall take my custom elsewhere.

I should have taken my custom, of course, straight back to the hotel, but that switchback route seemed an awfully long way to take a rapidly filling bladder. I figured that if I headed back towards the centre of town I was sure to find a free, or at least unattended, public facility.

No such luck. I plodded up past the building site at the old station, through the modern shopping centre behind the casino, down the dowdy street which accommodates the principality's unglamorous boutiques: dry cleaners, pharmacies, tobacconists. I passed countless tall apartment buildings, all distinguished by common clues to their layout: on the seaward front there were balconies with pretty awnings and umbrella-protected tables for *monsieur* and *madame*; on the road-facing rear the balconies were smaller and sported clothes-lines bearing cheap, bright, damp outfits: the servants' quarters.

I took the public elevator from the shabby avenue down to a smarter boulevard, in the hope that the subterranean tunnels to and from the lift would boast public conveniences. They didn't, notwithstanding the aromatic evidence that the tunnels themselves had frequently been used as conveniences.

My bladder now felt like a molten cannonball, but I refused to succumb to the temptation to have a quick whizz in a corner next to the lift. There were bound to be security cameras about, and the penalty for indecent exposure in Monaco would be severe: confiscation of credit cards, at least.

I emerged on to the boulevard, turned left and headed for the beach, contemplating, as a last resort, shedding most of my clothes and diving in to pollute the local ecosystem. Not necessary. Next to the beach – entirely artificial, packed with families and, unusually for Monaco, full of low-key charm – was a public changing room with equally public and equally free urinals.

Shortly thereafter, weak-kneed with relief, I leaned for a moment against a café wall and watched the children scampering around the beach-side playground. A hundred yards to my left was the principality's eastern border. Fontvielle, where I had started out, was the nation's westernmost point. Not bad, I thought. I've walked from one side of a country to the other while looking for a loo. A new personal best.

I had to spend a little while in the afternoon renovating my formal suit for the awards ceremony that evening. I raided the bathroom for Q-Tips and cotton wool, and swabbed away the worst remnants of canapé and ash. I was hanging everything up to dry when my mobile went.

'Daddy?'

'Yes, Lucy.'

'Daddy?'

'Yes, Lucy?'

'Daddy, um, Mummy says you're at the seaside.'

'That's right.'

'Are there seagirls?'

'Seagulls, Lucy.'

'That's right. Are there seagirls?'

I looked out of the window. All I could see was cars and apartment blocks.

'Yes, Lucy, lots of seagirls.'

'Good. What are you doing now?'

'Getting ready for an awards ceremony.'

'What's a wards ceremony?'

'It's a kind of party where people get prizes for being good.'

'Oh. Will you bring me home a prize?'

'Of course I will. Can I say hello to Emily?'

'Yes. Wait a minute.'

There was a long pause, distant dialogue.

'Um, Daddy?'

'Yes?'

'It's Lucy again.'

'Yes, Lucy?'

'Emily isn't old enough to talk yet.'

'Fair enough.'

'But she wants a prize as well.'

Tuxedoed up again, stains mostly concealed, cuff-links self-inserted in just twenty-seven minutes, I stood among a throng of sharp-elbowed paparazzi in a pen – that's what it was called, a 'media pen' – watching the rich and famous arrive. I felt like mooing.

Limo after limo swept up, and the paparazzi dutifully fired

off a cannonade of flashbulbs at each one, regardless of whether it contained an Olympic gold medallist, a Hollywood starlet, or the senior vice-president of promotional affairs at a Swiss bank.

Mysteriously, though, when I brandished my invitation and made my own way up the red carpet, the only things flashing were the eyes of the security guards. They couldn't touch me. Whether through generosity or administrative error, I had actually been invited to the cocktail party that preceded the awards ceremony, and to the ceremony itself. Imagine! I accepted a glass of champagne from a hovering waiter.

The Sports Editor loomed instantly in front of me.

'Ah, Andrew. Nice to see you.' His shirt-front gleamed; his bow-tie was effortlessly symmetrical; his powerful teeth demolished a canapé. 'I've been thinking about your role this evening.'

'Stay out of the way and don't throw up on anyone important?' I suggested.

'A little more specific than that,' said the Sports Editor. 'We'll need a news piece for the final edition rounding up all the winners, with one or two quotes. Do you think you could put that together for me? Of course, you won't be able to go into the ceremony itself – they're not letting anybody out again once it's started – but you can watch it on the monitors in the press room. OK? See you later.'

Mission accomplished, he moved smoothly off into the party, like James Bond's slightly more substantial brother.

The ceremony was awful, but all I needed to do was tap out the names of the winners on my laptop. In the press room, there was no obligation to applaud or laugh at unfunny jokes. I filed my little piece, rebutted some of the more robust allegations of freeloading from the night sports editor and, with my denials still echoing, went in search of more canapés and champagne.

Upstairs, the post-awards bash was gathering steam. Black ties had been loosened, sarongs had strategically slipped. Carefully crafted fitness regimes were crumbling in the face of aggressive hospitality. I saw . . . actually, I saw a number of well-known people who retain very expensive lawyers doing things that the lawyers will expensively claim they never, ever did.

The next morning, our little band of hacks were decanted from our limousines at Nice airport, and settled down to some desultory shopping and hangover-assuagement. I bought some chocolate 'prizes' for the girls, a T-shirt for Ingrid, and treated myself to a potent mixture of Resolve, vitamin C tablets and lemonade.

I had operated among the movers and shakers and felt shaken, if not moved. Dave, too, had been deeply affected by his experiences in Monte Carlo. He sat in the airport bar with a rip in the neck of his hotel T-shirt, wearing dark glasses, a day's stubble and a smug grin. In front of him on the little table stood a brimming litre of lager and a small mountain of receipts.

'The expenses on this one are going to be monstrous,' he mused, arranging the crumpled papers into piles.

'But Dave,' I said, 'everything was free.'

The dark glasses swung my way. 'Amateur,' Dave said.

Conclusion: Didn't throw up over anyone important.

Chapter Six

Wavy Necking

Objectives: Attend the University Games in Beijing, meet Chinese journalists and envisage the Beijing Olympics of 2008. Take a walk through the Forbidden City, and try not to eat any insects. Time allocated: Three days.

I've lost plenty of tennis matches, but this was the first time I had failed to find one. At Wimbledon, when assigned a contest to cover, it is the work of a moment to look up which court it is on, and the work of a few aggressive minutes to reach said court. But in Beijing? Not so straightforward.

The match I was looking for was the semi-final of the girls' singles at the World University Games, which were being held in the Chinese capital by way of a long-range rehearsal for the Olympics of 2008. I wanted to get an idea of what a Chinese Olympics might be like. Instead, I got lost.

Sometimes I get lost for fun, but this time I got lost by accident, despite being equipped with a map and a taxi. The taxi driver's name, according to his licence, was Hang, and for a short while after we left the hotel, I amused myself by calling out 'Hang, a left' or 'Hang, a right' every time we approached a junction. Hang, like all the other taxi drivers I had met in Beijing, spoke not a syllable of English (why should he?) and responded to these instructions with game grins.

I'd shown him the map, which purported to display all the event sites for the University Games, and pointed at the venue marked 'tennis'. Hang had nodded, which had seemed to me to indicate that he knew where I needed to go.

That was an hour ago, and it had long become clear that we were going round in circles: that bowling alley, for instance, I had seen twenty minutes ago; the pink gates of some kind of amusement park had just made their third appearance. Such an aimless tour would have been pleasant enough if I had had time to kill, but I had a particular tennis match to see, and a particular player to interview, and by my watch the players should just about be knocking up.

I did some knocking myself, on the Plexiglas screen between myself and Hang. He looked around, and I mimed: 'If you don't find this place soon I'm going to tear your head off.' He nodded, shrugged. And a few moments later, gave a cry of triumph. On the other side of the road – or, to be more accurate, the other side of the dual carriageway – was the Beijing International Tennis Centre.

Hang found a gap in the central reservation and aimed his taxi through it. There was an instant chorus of hoots and threats from his fellow road users, but Hang ignored it and shot across a line of traffic to deposit me at the Tennis Centre gates. I pressed a wad of yuan into his hand, and cut short his pantomime of relief and apology. As Hang's little Chinese-built Citroën put-putted away, I was trying the first of a series of comprehensively locked doors.

Everything looked right. The place was festooned with University Games banners, and I could see the floodlights of some kind of show court; but where was the thwack of racket on ball, where the roar of spectator approval?

They were somewhere else. Perhaps the unsmiling soldier who was bearing down on me would know where. I stopped kicking the Tennis Centre door and flashed him my accreditation pass. He blanked me.

I lobbed an imaginary ball on to my imaginary racket and swept it into the far corner of an imaginary court. No response. I looked at the balls in my hand, chucked one contemptuously, Sampras-style, back to the ball boy, bounced the remaining one a couple of times on the ground, tossed it up and whacked an ace down the middle. Nothing.

Some kind of female receptionist in a khaki twin-set appeared from inside the building, but instead of helping out just stood next to the dim private, giggling behind her hand while I added a backhand and a chopped volley to my display. By now I wasn't expecting directions so much as a round of applause.

Instead of clapping, the soldier wandered off and re-appeared with a smiling sergeant. I performed a terrific fore-hand smash. 'Tennis?' I said.

'No,' said the sergeant.

'Well, what do you think it is?' I asked. 'Paperhanging? Origami?'

But he was pointing at the buildings behind me. 'Not today,' he said.

OK. This was something. Not good news, but progress of a sort. I pulled from my bag the map of Beijing on which were superimposed the thirty-odd venues, mostly gymnasiums, being used for the University Games. The sergeant ummed and ahhed for a minute before poking a dirty finger at a spot seemingly around the corner, the Beijing Muxiyuan Tennis Gym. Oh, I see. *That* Tennis Centre.

Fortuitously, a taxi was waiting at the gate. Less fortuitously, it was the one I had vacated five minutes earlier. Hang turned around to me and spoke a couple of sentences in welcome. I spoke as much Chinese as he did English, but his meaning was clear: 'Who's the idiot now, then?'

He was still chuckling as he took me first to a volleyball centre, then to a hockey match, and finally to the Muxiyuan Tennis Gym. As he drove off clutching another fistful of yuan, I sprinted into the venue to discover that, one hour and forty minutes after the scheduled start time, the match was barely underway.

The British player I had come to watch lost her match, and I never did use any of the quotes from the interview. But on the other hand I did manage to hitch a lift back to the games headquarters on the team's bus. For Hang, it was over.

'Chinese are enthusiastic for sport, yes?' said a young man named Wang Luhui. He had walked up to me as I watched the athletics competition at the National Olympic Sports Centre, which despite its grandiose title was a collection of crumbling facilities built in crummy, Communist concrete for the Asian Games of 1990.

After surrendering my cigarette lighter to the inevitable security check (thus ensuring that I could neither incinerate any athletes, nor sniff myself senseless), I had wandered into a section of grandstand inhabited by young Chinese people wearing yellow T-shirts and waving giant red banners.

Many of them stared at me in a way that would have been the prelude to a fight at, say, Millwall's New Den, but which here was the prelude to a shy giggle. After a few minutes, during which a female Chinese competitor the size of a tractor let go of her projectile too soon and demolished the hammer-throw cage, Wang voted himself fans' spokesman and came up to shake my hand.

He was slim and slight, with untidy, spiky hair and an embryonic moustache. He wore a yellow T-shirt with scarlet characters on the chest: Beijing United University Sports, he explained. 'Where do you come from?' he asked.

'UK,' I said. No reaction. 'GB. England? London?'

He smiled at last. 'London,' he said, nodding emphatically. 'Near Switzerland.'

'Well, yes,' I said. 'Nearish.'

'Manchester United,' Wang declared.

'Not so far off,' I said.

'They are favourite football team in China,' Wang said. 'Wavy necking.'

I thought for a moment. 'David Beckham?' Enthusiastic nods, thumbs-up from some of Wang's friends, who had clustered around to listen in. 'Oh, yes,' I said. 'He's very good. Silly hairstyles, but useful at a set-piece. So which is the best football team in China?'

Wang conferred with his chums. 'Dailin. Very strong. Like Manchester United.'

'And what about the Beijing teams?' I asked. 'Any good?'

No conference was necessary. Everybody shook their heads.

'Best team is called Beijing Guo An,' Wang said. 'They play at Workers' Stadium. Once they were good, but they are not good any more.'

'I understand,' I said. 'Like Manchester City.'

Even so, I wanted to see Beijing Guo An's home, and as it happened the British Universities' side were playing there that evening, against Japan.

I arrived at dusk, and the Universiade flame high above the stadium roof flared dramatically against a dark blue sky, a symbol of Olympic ambition that would be visible for miles around. A monumental statue in the classic Communist-heroic style stood outside the main entrance, depicting a muscular man and woman in football kit striving nobly for a better future, or perhaps going up to contest a high ball. The stadium was vast but simple in design, an elegant oval within the exterior walls of which were housed a luxury hotel, a smart restaurant, a barber's shop and the Beijing Guo An fan shop, which was open but empty. Some of the residents from the adjacent tower blocks were strolling around outside the stadium in the warm evening air, stopping every now and then to exchange gossip and cigarettes with their neighbours. One or two people were roller-skating, and one young couple played netless badminton between a pair of parked buses.

It was all very tranquil, and hardly prepared me for the atmosphere inside the stadium. Imagine a similar fixture – say, a student match between Malaysia and Germany – being staged at a stadium in central London. How many people would show up? One hundred? Two hundred?

There were, at a very conservative estimate, 10,000 people inside Workers' Stadium for a fixture between two teams with only one thing in common: both were former enemies of the Chinese people. Maybe that's it, I thought: all these people have come not to watch football but to jeer at their past oppressors. I was half right. As the teams were introduced over the public-address system, each British player was cheered as if he were wrapped in the Chinese flag, while the names of the Japanese side were completely inaudible beneath a blanket of booing and howled imprecations.

It was a pretty appalling football match. The British – wouldn't you know – lost on penalties, but by then I had become more interested in the spectators than the game. Most were in their late teens or early twenties, and they had clearly seen a lot of European football, for their behaviour was modelled on European crowds. They could do the slow hand-clap and the synchronised chant, had a couple of stabs at a Mexican Wave and sang 'Olé, olé olé olé, olé, olé', although they had trouble with the central consonant.

But there was a self-consciousness about it all, a sense of parody.

So, too, with the abuse of the Japanese. It was sincere: the atrocities of the war between the two countries in the 1930s have never been forgiven, and the Chinese media makes sure they are never forgotten. But every chorus of boos was followed by an outbreak of giggling: the crowd were being naughty, and they knew it.

Such mass self-expression would have been unthinkable even a decade ago, and the young people of Beijing still felt uneasy with their limited freedom and unsure what to do with it. Just before half-time I felt a hand grip my elbow.

'Excuse me, please,' said a thin young man with a poor complexion. 'You are British, I think? Please may I ask you some questions?'

Henry, as he introduced himself, sat down next to me. He was from the Xinhua News Agency – an enormous and powerful organisation – and he was very worried about his fellow citizens. 'Please tell me what you think about this . . . this behaviour towards the Japanese team,' he said. 'Do you not think it is shameful?'

I mumbled reassurance: youthful high spirits, heard worse at Crewe on a wet Wednesday night, that sort of thing. But Henry was unconvinced.

'It is not right,' he declared, with painful earnestness, putting his hand rather disconcertingly on my knee. 'Sport and politics are not the same. We must behave well to the guests in our country. You are journalist, yes? Do not write bad things about this. This is not that way that sport is in China.'

'Oh, don't worry,' I lied heartily. 'I'm only going to write good things.'

In his relief, Henry bound himself to me like an Elastoplast, chatting away while the footballers flailed up and down the pitch towards the inevitable shoot-out, and afterwards insisting on accompanying me on the shuttle bus back to the Press Centre.

We were the only passengers, and Henry leant very close as he pressed me for greater detail on the transfer system in European football, the sponsorship budget of Manchester United, David Beckham's hairstyle and my salary.

'You make a lot of money in your job,' he pronounced, putting his hand on my knee again. 'How old do you think I am? Look, and tell me.'

I stared, in the orange motorway light, and I didn't have a clue. Seventeen? Thirty-eight? What did he want me to say? And how could I get his hand off me?

'Twenty-eight?' I guessed, uncrossing my legs and placing my notebook across my knees.

'Twenty-three,' Henry announced, with an unmistakable note of triumph. 'Very young, yes? You are old, I think . . .'

And so we rumbled on around Beijing's equivalent of the M25, while Henry discoursed haltingly on the excellence of sport as a builder of bridges between nations, on the fineness of the British university system (which he wished to experience at first hand) and on the many cultural differences between our countries. I tried to keep my end of the conversation up, while wondering what to do if he tried to snog me.

As we drew up outside the Press Centre, Henry started asking for a detailed itinerary of the rest of my stay, clearly determined to spend as much time in my company as possible. I blustered and prevaricated, cited deadlines, meetings and the unpredictability of the British delegation, but he was most insistent on a further chat. 'There are so many questions that I still need to ask you,' he said.

Eventually, I agreed to meet him at nine the next morning in the Press Centre, where at least there would be witnesses.

I think I may have been very unfair to Henry, for his motives seem to have been neither perverted nor political. We met, as arranged, the next morning, and he had brought along a colleague, Gerry, a smiley, chubby, mop-topped young man who covered German football for the Xinhua agency.

We talked for an hour or more, about Chinese youth sport programmes (regimented, tough, successful, according to Henry), the role of the military in Chinese sport (widespread and, to Henry's mind, largely beneficial) and why the Chinese prefer ping-pong to basketball (they are not – at present, said Henry – very tall. But sports scientists are working on this). Gerry's contribution was limited. 'Rudi Voller?' he would say every now and then. 'Carsten Jancker? Good, yes?'

Eventually I said I had to be getting along, but Henry insisted that I must have more questions for them. OK then. Taking a deep breath, I asked: 'Do you wonder why people did not want the Olympic Games to come to China? Do you know why people worry about the Olympics in China?'

Henry nodded sagely. 'This is human rights, isn't it?' he said. 'You know, this I think is a big cultural problem between our countries. What we think of as human rights and what you think of as human rights are quite different things.'

I had heard this line before. It was one often used by the Chinese leader, Jiang Zemin, and it continued: 'Human rights for us are about the right to food and clean water; only when these are freely available to all will we be able to address other concerns.'

It was a pointless conversation, really, but I tried one more tack. 'Tell me about religion,' I said. 'Tell me about Chinese attitudes to religion.'

'I know what you think,' Henry said. 'You think that we are hard on religion. But that is not true. We respect people who follow a true religion: there are cathedrals in Beijing where people may go without interference. The religions that you worry about are not true religions at all, but – what is the word? – cults. Cults which are harmful to people.'

I was smiling by now, and to his credit Henry grinned too. 'I know,' he said. 'It is no use. Whatever I say to you, you will believe that the security services have told me to say it.'

'Yes,' I said. 'You're absolutely right.'

'Oliver Bierhoff?' said Gerry. 'Fantastic.'

I had escaped from Henry and Gerry claiming that I had an urgent appointment at a table-tennis fixture but, in fact, my plan was much more sinister: I wanted to go for a walk. I nipped back to my room in the Continental Grand Hotel next to the Press Centre.

As an honoured guest of the Universiade I had been al-located a room on the top floor: the thirteenth floor, as it happened, indicating that the number holds no fears for Chinese numerologists. The Continental Grand bills itself as one of Beijing's swankier hotels, and awards itself four stars. The accolade might have been more credible had not fully half of the hotel been shut down and stripped bare, presumably for renovation.

The remaining restaurants and public rooms were smart enough, and populated by endless flunkies and security guards. The guest rooms, however, matched those of an ordinary British motorway motel, only with rather harder mattresses and a lot of interfering notes from the manage-ment.

'Not free water!' declared a card collar on the neck of the bottle of Evian on the desk. 'Turn off lights, heating or air, TV and radio,' said another notice, despite the fact that all these switched off automatically when the key card was removed from its socket next to the door. 'Please don't waste water,' read a sign in the bathroom. That was super-fluous: the bath boasted a maximum depth of four inches, and took approximately twenty minutes to fill. 'Using my linens twice is just as nice,' said a card placed next to the bed. 'Please leave this card on your pillow,' the notice continued, 'and your sheets will not be changed that day.'

Supervision reverted to human form as soon as I left the room. At the end of the corridor, a junior hotel operative stood all day and night behind a desk decorated with a Universiade poster. Whenever I left my room, they would spring into action and summon a lift for me. And whenever I returned, they would be there to welcome me back.

Once – only once – I emerged from the lift to find the desk deserted. Curious, I looked to see what it was that kept the youngsters so busy, and found a book containing the arrival and departure times of all the residents of the thirteenth floor. The trainee returned as I was leafing through the pages, and indicated by way of polite mime that it was none of my business.

The same trainee was there as I set out for my walk. 'I'm going for an innocent stroll,' I said to his uncomprehending smile. 'No need to alert the military.'

'You wreck room,' he said in return, which I think meant that I was welcome.

'Thank you,' I said, sniggering in breach of the vow I had made in Malaysia concerning funny pronunciations.

'Itma pressure,' said the notekeeper.

I had four hours before I was due at a press conference for Jacques Rogge, the president of the International Olympic Committee. I planned to walk for three and a half of them, then take a taxi back to the Press Centre. Beijing was too big, too flat and too featureless for the mapless Way of Baker, and since this looked like being my only chance for a substantial walk on the trip, I needed an objective. I chose the Forbidden City.

The hotel was in the north of the city, next to the outermost of Beijing's three peripheral ring roads, a six-lane highway with a further lane on each side dedicated to bicycles and rickshaws. I crossed at one of the many underpasses, noting the public-protection officer, a sort of auxiliary policeman, fast asleep on his little stool at the foot of the stairs, and soon worked my way round to Anding Lu, a wide avenue that ran south towards the centre of the city. This was to be my main route.

One major difficulty for the Beijing pedestrian immediately became apparent: breathing. The haze that wobbled the sides of buildings half a mile away had not seemed too problematic while travelling in a bus or a taxi, but a brisk walking pace soon had the back of my throat coated with what felt like iron filings which no amount of coughing would dislodge.

I bought a bottle of mineral water from a roadside kiosk and plodded on, pausing at the imposing entrance to the National Olympic Sports Centre. Just now, the entrance was about all that existed of the NOSC, but a giant poster showed an artist's impression of how the surroundings would look by 2008. There would be elegant towers reflected in an ornamental lake, and splendid stadiums amid sculpted parkland. I stared at the poster for five minutes, wondering how many acres of residential neighbourhoods would need to be bulldozed. It was captioned: 'Build New Beijing! Hold Great Olympics!' but none of the locals hurrying past gave it a second glance. Never mind: they had seven years to become enthusiastic.

A hundred yards down the road from this prospect of sporting glories to come was a ghost of sporting glories past. It was another triumphal gateway, and on it rusting scarlet letters a foot high announced: 'Beijing Asian Games Village Automobile Exchange.' Beyond, sullen rows of rusting Suzukis awaited optimistic new owners.

Next up was a bicycle showroom, then a row of rather careworn restaurants, advertised to passing trade by battered

red paper lanterns hanging from their eaves. All were empty – it was mid-morning – but in one, the Hong Kong Nice Food Restaurant, scarlet-clad girls stood to attention in rows behind the empty tables, a terracotta army of waitresses waiting for the opportunity to serve.

A complex, curving pedestrian bridge – fitted, for some unfathomable reason, with a brown carpet – led to an area where Anding Lu was flanked by residential tower blocks. Here the pavements became more crowded, and the going more hazardous, as exponents of the great Chinese hobby of public spitting crowded the way, dredging up ever more loathsome gunk from their bronchial tracts before letting fly around my feet.*

I crossed a large and terrifying junction – where cars, bicycles and rickshaws dodged each other in a ceaseless lethal dance – by sticking closer to Chinese pedestrians than their own shadows. On the other side, the character of the avenue changed once more. Now it was lined with ancient, low-built workshops, interspersed with gateways that led into intriguing alleyways, dark even in the bright sunshine.

These alleys were *hutong*, ancient lanes not dissimilar to those found in the old City of London, where among a jumble of outhouses tradesmen both worked and sold their goods. Here was a hut crammed with seventies-style telephones; there one with the carcasses of bicycles. Beyond a tray of glistening baked pigs' trotters stood a row of caged birds: some kind of pigeon, I thought, doing their best to look on the bright side.

An entire block of *hutong* had recently been demolished, as many more would be, to make way for the Olympic works. A woman of indeterminate age, hunched and determined, was scrambling among the debris to retrieve splintered

* This was before SARS had mutated out of the Chinese backwoods, by the way. Otherwise I'd have remained in my hotel room throughout my stay, wrapped in clingfilm.

planks of wood, which she then stacked onto a precariously overloaded trishaw, for use perhaps as fuel, or even shelter.

The road narrowed as the buildings became older and more ramshackle. Tall trees with dappled bark – some kind of birch, I reckoned – now provided constant shade from the sun, and shadow in which customers of little front-room cafés could sit at pavement tables sipping green tea. I was getting closer to the Forbidden City, the old heart of Beijing, but there was no hint of tourist-friendly, cosmetic civic tidying.

Quite the opposite. A soldier barred my way at what I had taken to be the entrance to a park. Go away, he gestured. Go a long way away. It was a barracks.

Across the road, a woman who must have been in her seventies was putting the men to shame, working out at a kind of street gym, a playground for adults that is common in Chinese parks but less so on street corners. I grinned at her: she grimaced and spat.

Moments later, the canopy of trees gave way to bright sunshine and I found myself facing the blank walls and rank moat of the Forbidden City.

Decision time. Due to an elementary miscalculation of map scale, my walk had so far taken up almost three of the three and a half hours I had. Should I therefore wander around aimlessly for half an hour or so, or race through one of the largest and most complex ancient palaces on the globe in thirty minutes?

I opted for the scamper through Chinese history.

So, from one side of the Forbidden City to the other in half an hour. A nifty rock garden, on which 'Climbing Is Forbidden'. Perhaps that is how the city got its name. Refreshment shops and camera-film emporiums. An old-style Party poster: 'Value the cultural heritage of our ancestors. Shoulder the historic mission of conserving their relics.' Hundreds of Chinese visitors milling around, shouldering their historic mission to drink Coke and take pictures of each other making funny faces at ceremonial bronze lions. I hurried on.

Then palaces: individual buildings the size of tennis courts, the exteriors lavish with carved animals, the best of bestiaries. They had grand and poetic names: the Earthly Tranquillity Palace and the Eternal Spring Palace. In a large square next to the Palace of Preserving Harmony, a detachment of troops drilled, preserving harmony in the modern Chinese manner. The neck of my T-shirt was wet with sweat.

After the palaces, the servants' quarters, now housing exhibitions and ancillary services: there was a Hall of Ceramics, a Hall of Bronzes, a Hall of Paintings, a Hall of Tacky Souvenirs, and a Hall of Slightly Dodgy-Looking Fast Food. I was running out of breath.

Outside the Hall of Preserving Harmony there reclined a 250-ton block of marble ebulliently carved with lotus blossoms, clouds, waves and dragons. 'This fine stonework,' a nearby sign read, 'was carved during the Ming, and has great artistic value. Funded by American Express.'

I staggered out of the final, colossal gate of the Forbidden City, out of China past and into China present: Tiananmen Square. Soldiers stood to attention scanning the vast open space for the slightest hint of dissent while above them, on the wall of the old palace, a gigantic portrait of Chairman Mao looked down on his people. I sat down on the pavement for a rest, and tried to think suitably sombre thoughts about democracy and so on. But I was too knackered, so I waved down a taxi instead.

By a stroke of luck I had found a taxi driver with a sense of direction and morality, and was delivered back to the Press Centre in time for President Rogge's address, which was a model of charm and diplomacy and therefore about as interesting as his tie, which was brown. Sixteen Chinese film crews focused on Monsieur Rogge's every syllable, and when the time came for questions, Chinese journalists struggled to wrest the microphone from each other.

The Chinese moderator of the conference yapped at them to try to keep order, and helpfully provided a translation of his commands: 'You must obey my rules!' he yelled. But the questions themselves were curiously anodyne: What did President Rogge think of Beijing? Would the Chinese host a good Olympics? How was the weather? Was he enjoying himself? They put me in mind of a puppy who had brought its master a slipper, and was waiting to see if it would get stroked or kicked. Rogge stroked.

The moderator asked for questions from the Western press, and a bloke from Reuters made the obvious enquiry about human rights. So did the chap from the Press Association, and the lady from Agence France Press. The mayor of Beijing, next to Monsieur Rogge on the platform, worked on his smile.

Rogge insisted, as he always has and always will, that the Olympics were nothing to do with politics. This is bollocks, as he undoubtedly knows, but it makes his life easier at press conferences. His disingenuous message was that human rights had nothing to do with the IOC, but that, incidentally, the Olympics would help to make human rights better in China. Having made everyone happy, he toddled off to be lunched and shake more hands. I felt rather sorry for him.

I went to watch some table tennis, which in atheist Chinese society has acquired something of the status of a religion. A very loud, happy-clappy sort of religion, if the crowd in the Beijing Haidian Gym were anything to go by. I watched Wang Liqin, who according to *China Daily* is the world's best player, team up with Tie Yanan to take the mixed-doubles title from a South Korean pair called Park and Ryu. Actually, 'take' is little too genteel: this was a smash and grab, a mugging with little padded bats. Wang was indeed wonderfully gifted, and Tie displayed great dexterity and skill in her efforts to get out of his way.

The crowd, of course, went crazy, waving their crimson flags and chanting incomprehensible slogans every time the Chinese won a point. During play, they were silent, glued to the progress of the tiny ball, but the average ping-pong rally lasts approximately four and a half seconds so the intervals between outbursts were distressingly short. It was like listening to a malfunctioning CD at maximum volume. I couldn't share the euphoria. I don't harbour a visceral dislike of Koreans, for one thing, and for another, table tennis fails to move me. There is such a comical disparity between effort and effect, so that even the mightiest smash still produces no more than a tap when the ball hits the table.

From ping-pong to Yingdong.

The National Olympic Sports Centre's Yingdong Natatorium might have been named by Spike Milligan. The building was not as splendid as its name: the exterior walls were showing the strain of repelling a decade of humidity and pollution, and the interior was plain to the point of austerity.

At the main entrance a sign read: 'Dangerous articles like weapon ammunition controlled knives flammable and explosible stuff are forbidden.' The security guards X-rayed my mobile phone, frisked my wallet and, once again, confiscated my cigarette lighter, so that I could not torch the pool. But I perked up a bit when I got into the arena, because the atmosphere was as warm as the wet air.

Swimming is right up there with table tennis and spitting in the pantheon of favourite Chinese pastimes, and several thousand local people had crammed into the Natatorium's grandstands. As usual, there was a suggestion of the state's guiding hand in their yellow T-shirts and vast crimson flags; but equally typical was the fervour of their cheering whenever a Chinese student ploughed a winning furrow through the water.

The Chinese had recently won many, many international medals at both swimming and diving, and in several instances the winning athletes were not found guilty of using banned substances. Why had the state made such an obvious effort to excel in the pool?

There are some prosaic reasons: more kids swim than (for instance) hurdle, so there is plenty of potential talent to cherry-pick. Swimming is low-tech and fairly easy to coach at junior level, and being largely a matter of strength rather than skill there is a good risk/reward ratio for those who seek greater performance through ingesting turtle blood and/or steroids, two substances that had proved popular among Chinese athletes.

There are also cultural and even political reasons. Although the great majority of her billion citizens will never see the sea, China is a land of great rivers: the Red River, the Yellow River, the Mekong, the mighty Yangtze. Along the banks of these waterways swimming is a necessity, and those who practise it are not only learning to safeguard their own lives, but imitating the example of China's greatest leader. For Chairman Mao, swimming was much more than a hobby. It was a demonstration of his vitality, athleticism and fearlessness, and since he embodied the qualities of the nation, of China's too. Nor did he restrict himself to a few laps of the pool in his official residence: on 16 July 1966, at the age of seventy-three, Mao swam ten miles down the Yangtze River in just over one hour. Newspapers and television stations all over the world carried photographs of the old man's beaming features as he bobbed up and down amid the driftwood and turds, and even the staunchest enemies of Chinese Communism were forced to concede that Mao was a truly remarkable individual.

The Great Helmsman needed no boat, and that is why the Chinese love swimming.

I left the pool at quarter past ten, with the Universiade

anthem and Chinese cheers ringing in my ears, and realised that I was ravenous. Hunger at a vaguely appropriate time was a sign that I was becoming fully accustomed to the Beijing clock – just in time to fly home the next day. Anyway, I was spoiled for choice. Chinese food is globally famed, but the sheer variety of the cuisine can barely be appreciated in the export versions.

Never mind sweet-and-sour chicken. Within a mile of my hotel I could find – and I'm not kidding about any of this – donkey dumplings, deep-fried scorpion, caterpillar kebabs and several kinds of casseroled dog (or several kinds of dog, casseroled). I could go for a Mongolian hotpot, which you cook yourself, like a fondue; or Hunan fish-head stew with a side order of ant soup (Beijing is the only city in the world where you complain if there *isn't* a fly in your soup). I could sample Imperial-style sea cucumber with deer tendon, or camel paw with shallots, or simply settle for a homely bowl of cat's-ear noodles.

You know what? I went to McDonald's.

Dereliction of duty, I know, and gross cultural impertinence. But I was very, very hungry, and I needed something I knew. Also, I had nine hours on an aeroplane the next day, and I didn't want to spend them with a paper bag clamped to my mouth.

The next time I'm in China, I promised myself as I chomped deliriously on a quarter-pounder with cheese, I'll hit the local cuisine hard. Maybe I'll come back for the Olympics in 2008, and then, my goodness, animal, vegetable, insect, household pet or beast of burden, fried, boiled, puréed, I'll try the lot. But first – straight away, in fact – I needed another cheeseburger.

Conclusion: Ate too many cheeseburgers and not nearly enough insects.

Chapter Seven

A Bullet Train to the Funfair

Objectives: locate and describe the World Cup training base of the England football team in Japan. Watch a J-League football match. Have a word with Mika Hakkinen. Report on the Japanese Grand Prix. Time allocated: five days.

The Japan Airlines Boeing 747-400 was equipped with a forward-facing video camera connected to a large screen in the main cabin, so that all the passengers could share the excitement of final approach and landing. That, I imagine, was the theory. In fact what we all shared was profound anxiety as the giant plane bucked and creaked through driving rain and dense cloud.

Only seconds before touchdown did the lights of Narita Airport become visible, and the pilot must have been so delighted to see them that he almost forgot how to land. We hit the runway with a spine-compressing bump, bounced, then slid sideways for a hundred yards or so through blinding spray before the brakes were applied, a sensible heading was restored, and 414 people exhaled.

We had landed in mid-afternoon, and I scampered off the aeroplane keen to embark on the 500 miles that separated me from my bed for the night. But my dash from the jumbo had brought me only to the end of a glum line of non-Japanese people snaking through six concertinaed, taped-off passageways to a trio of immigration officials. While the massed Europeans and Americans shuffled grumpily forwards, a sprinkling of returning Japanese nationals sauntered up to any of the half-dozen desks devoted to them.

There were lessons here. Whatever the jolly airport signs might claim, we were not entirely welcome to Japan. Furthermore, a long queue for a simple task represents core Japanese values, such as obedience to authority and submission to bureaucracy.

Forty minutes later I emerged with my passport stamped, changed some travellers' cheques (two offices, two officials, three forms) and joined another queue at the information desk. My first target was Awaji Island, destined to be the hideaway for England's footballers during the forthcoming World Cup. No British reporter had visited this obscure location, and I was supposed to be the first to describe the facilities and amenities that Beckham and Co. would enjoy.

At this stage, six weeks before the draw for the World Cup was made, no one could be certain that England would be playing in Japan – they might just as well have been selected to play their games in South Korea, the country co-hosting the tournament. But the Sports Editor has connections, and he had become convinced that England were going to Awaji.

So, therefore, was I. But how?

'First of all,' the lady at the information desk explained, 'you must go on the Narita Express to Tokyo station. Then you must take a Shinkansen train to Shin-Kobe, where you will find a boat that will take you to Awaji Island. You will enjoy the whirlpools very much.'

Whirlpools? She pointed at a brochure on the desk. 'Whirlpools,' she said. 'Very famous. Everyone goes to Awaji to see whirlpools. And earthquake park.' She prodded at another spot on the map.

I explained that I was more interested in football than

life-threatening natural phenomena. Could one get to Awaji Island without encountering whirlpools and earthquakes? The lady disappeared behind the desk again, and emerged with an old timetable. 'Bus,' she said. 'Safer than boat.'

The first part of the journey was straightforward. The Narita Express takes exactly an hour to get from the airport to the centre of the capital, and there is an electronic route map on the end wall of each carriage on which illuminated blobs track the train's progress. But all that this does is to lull the traveller into a false sense of security, because there is nothing comforting, predictable or informative about Tokyo station, the most intimidating transport interchange on the planet.

Sensible cities, like London or Paris, have a number of large railway stations distributed around the compass points, each serving a different range of destinations. All are of a manageable size and offer no great challenge to the sensible traveller, whether native or foreign.

Tokyo, though, has one central mainline station, and it is a nightmare.

Tokyo station has forty-eight platforms, distributed over six different levels. Eight different types of train run though it on fourteen different lines, each type of train and specific line requiring a particular kind of ticket. A ticket that is valid only for a particular seat in a particular carriage of a particular train leaving at a particular time. Difficult enough. But all the signs are in Japanese, and few of the staff speak even rudimentary English.

This was my third visit to Japan, and the fifth time that I had attempted to change trains at Tokyo station. Familiarity, they say, breeds contempt. I was still waiting for familiarity to breed familiarity. Japan Railways may claim that the primary function of the place is to unite passengers with trains, but its secondary purpose is to reduce foreign visitors to the status of rats in a maze.

I got off the Narita Express and looked up and down the bright, neon-lit platform for clues. It was crowded with scurrying office workers, known in Japan as 'salarymen'. There were signs everywhere, signs of every colour and size, subtle signs and emphatic signs, all of them in Japanese. I saw an escalator, and headed up.

I had done some research while on the Narita Express, and thought I should be looking for the Sanyo Shinkansen, one of Japan's mightiest bullet trains, to whisk me south towards Kobe and Awaji Island. But where . . . ? I walked down long, wide, white-tiled corridors. Lugging my suitcase and laptop, I felt like a supertanker in a sea lane full of speedboats: every time I tried to change direction I would capsize a salaryman or hole a secretary beneath the hemline.

I stood on another upward escalator while junior executives swarmed past, hurdling my bags and cursing under their breath. It slowly began to dawn on me that I was tackling this vast monument to confusion at rush hour. At the top of the escalator I turned right, winging a schoolgirl, and headed for what looked like an atrium or some kind of central meeting point. An information centre? No, a shopping centre. My feet were hurting now, and my arms were stretching; the air was warm, air-conditioned, fuggy. Sweat stung my eyes.

At the bottom of the next escalator I turned left, went through a group of junior executives like a bowling ball through pins, then made a right into . . . another shopping arcade. Sticky buns, pastel-coloured rice confections, dinky wooden boxes of sushi and marzipan engines in abundance. But real trains? No.

I sat down on my suitcase in a corner next to a news stand crammed with garish magazines. Manga cartoon heroines with big puppy eyes, beachball bosoms and wasp waists, gazed down at the moping Englishman without sympathy. Perhaps this was as far as I was destined to get in the search for the England camp. Perhaps I would spend the rest of my life here, cadging change and subsisting on coffee and rice cakes from the vending machines while my beard grew long and straggly and I forgot my name and where I had come from . . .

Something wet dripped off my nose on to my knee, and I wondered if I had started to cry. But it was just sweat, and it ended the bout of morbid introspection. Helplessness breeds desperation, and desperation masters embarrassment. I began buttonholing passers-by with an urgent request.

'Shinkansen?'

'Shinkansen?'

'Shinkansen?'

The first three people veered away, as if from a madman. But then an old man with white, bushy eyebrows and thick, black-framed glasses took pity on me. He took my arm and pointed back the way I had come. 'Shinkansen', he said.

I repeated my enquiry every few yards. Back down the escalator, past a row of bars and doughnut stalls – God, I was hungry, but there was no time – up another escalator and into a great underground hallway, where one sign said 'Shinkansen tracks' and another said 'Shinkansen tickets'. Saved.

Almost. I queued for ten minutes, but the clerk wouldn't sell me a ticket for the Sanyo Shinkansen. He pointed, unnecessarily crossly, at another queue across the hall. Another queue, another clerk. Yes, I could buy a ticket for the Sanyo Shinkansen here. But not with a credit card, no. That would be one further queue, over there. Stay polite, I told myself. Tearing the head off a booking clerk and drop-kicking it across a crowded concourse is not how the British behave abroad. The High Commissioner would not approve.

The queue for credit-card purchases was longer than the

others had been. This was because it was in a sort of travel agency, clearly a cut above the ordinary ticket offices: an immaculate spider plant sat on each desk, and the staff all wore red bow-ties. Here Tokyo's suburban citizens were arranging not only their rail tickets home, but their weekend activities. The clerks juggled timetables, hotel brochures, maps and guidebooks. Each transaction seemed to take about a week.

At last I reached the front of the queue, and told the snaggle-toothed female clerk: 'Sanyo Shinkansen – Kobe.' She said 'Hai!', which I was confident meant Yes, and started flailing away at her computers, keying in numbers on a touch screen, reading little print-outs, glancing up at the clock. She asked me 'Shin-Kobe?' and I said 'Hai!' because it sounded sort of right and I was almost past caring. She asked me three more questions, and I replied 'Hai!' to each of them, hoping that she wasn't asking if I was happy to swab the buffet between stations, feed the driver raw fish, or complete my journey on the roof rack.

Eventually she handed me a ticket almost entirely covered in Japanese script, with just four numbers in Roman numerals.

'Thank you,' I said. 'Where do I go now? What platform?' A blank smile. 'Track?'

'Track fourteen,' she said in English, then pointed urgently at the clock. 'Seven minutes.'

Oh my God. I burst out of the travel agency like a finalist in the Olympic 100 metres for people with bags, and waved my ticket at the first official I could find, having first removed it from my mouth. He frowned at the toothmarks, then gestured vaguely in the direction from which I had just come.

More running, more collisions, more officials. Up some stairs – where had the escalators gone now that I needed them? – and up to a ticket barrier of the snapping-jaw variety, which tried to eat my laptop as I struggled through. More stairs, and on to Platform 14, where the ground suddenly started to shake beneath my feet.

An earthquake? No, my train. The Shinkansen, the fastest train on earth, had a long, sharp, visored nose that tapered seamlessly back into its body, so that it looked like a 1,000-ton earthworm in sunglasses.

I was too worried about missing the train to concern myself with looking for the right carriage. I bundled myself and my luggage aboard and waited for the other passengers to settle before approaching a conductor with my ticket. He indicated the Roman numerals on my ticket – IX – and pointed towards the rear of the train.

Car number nine was like the interior of a wide-bodied executive jet. On either side of a generous aisle ran a single row of large circular armchairs of the kind favoured by cat-stroking Bond villains. As I settled into mine I found that it not only tilted but swivelled, so that I could look at the night-time neon of downtown Tokyo as the train gathered speed.

While I arranged my belongings, the doors at the end of the carriage slid apart and an attractive, high-heeled hostess appeared. She gave a deep bow, then passed among the new passengers distributing hot towels.

The Tannoy went 'bing bong' and a calm female voice said in subtly accented English: 'Welcome aboard the Shinkansen. This is the Hikari Super Express bound for Okayama . . .' I gripped the sides of my seat, preparing to spring up and – what? Jump through the window? 'We will be calling at Shin-Yokohama, Odawara, Nagoya, Maibara, Kyoto, Shin-Osaka, Shin Kobe . . .' Ahhhhh.

From that moment on I was in train-travel heaven. Mobile telephones were banned. The ticket inspector bowed and smiled. A trolley girl sold me cold beer and a packet of 'Western-style' sandwiches, with recognisable fillings: ham, egg, lettuce. An alien landscape whistled past my window at 200 mph: floodlit golf-driving ranges, shopping plazas blazing with orange light, and vast industrial complexes belching flame and smoke into the dark and rain.

It was eight o'clock at night, five hours since the 747 had landed. This was the first time that I had felt comfortable since leaving London. I didn't want to fall asleep, because I had a horrific premonition of missing my stop, and I had no notion of how long the trip from Tokyo to Kobe would take. But the combination of fatigue and the gentle rocking motion of the Shinkansen defeated me.

Some two and a half hours later I felt an insistent nudging at my left shoulder, and blinked blearily at the hostess. 'Shin-Kobe,' she said, with a bow and a smile. What service.

It took me ten minutes to find a member of staff at Shin-Kobe station and a further thirty seconds to establish that it was too late to catch a bus to Awaji Island. My first object-ive, to locate England's training base, would have to wait for the morning.

I found a high-rise hotel close to the station. My room was on the seventeenth floor, with a view of distant road-works. All I can remember of the place is the English trans-lation of the 'What to do in an earthquake' leaflet I found on the bedroom table. It said: 'Do not stand by the window. Do not stand under the table. Do not stand in the cupboard. Do not use the lift.' Doesn't say anything about staying in bed, I thought, as I fell asleep once more.

I woke to find the hotel intact, and was soon at the station looking for the bus to Awaji Island. I won't dwell on the manoeuvres required to buy a ticket and find the right vehicle – they had a lot in common with the Tokyo-station pantomime – but within an hour I was on a smart, modern bus on a motorway out of Kobe, and one of the destinations on the video screen next to the driver was 'Tsuna – Awaji Island'.

I had found a leaflet that described the route in English,

so I knew that we were heading first for the Akashi Kaikyo Ohashi, and I even knew what that meant. It is a bridge. The longest suspension bridge in the world, the leaflet claimed, though it seems to me that there are more pretenders to this title than there are to that of world heavyweight boxing champion. The bridge was, when originally constructed, 3.91 km long. It became a metre longer in the Great Hanshin Earthquake of 1995 that had flattened most of Kobe and presented Awaji, the epicentre, with some new tourist attractions in the shape of some previously non-existent gorges and cliffs. As we crossed the Inland Sea, high above oil tankers, ferries and motor yachts, I wondered how a bridge constructed of concrete and steel could stretch by more than three feet without collapsing, and then tried hard to think of something else. That water looked an awfully long way down.

Safely landed on Awaji, we trundled through gentle hills terraced with paddy fields, and along a coastal road beside shellfish beds roped off in the shallows of the sea, with fishermen in wooden rowing boats harvesting from them. They wore baseball caps, which cost them points for picturesqueness.

Soon we came to Tsuna, the main town on the island, which in May 2002 would become England's training base. As the bus drove away, I looked around, hoping for something obvious like a football pitch or a banner strung across the street saying 'Welcome, Sven-Goran Eriksson's Brave Boys'. All I could see was an empty ferry terminal.

I walked into town. Next to the ferry terminal was a little fishing port in which half a dozen rusty trawlers rode lazily at anchor. A line of upended trestles and a powerful smell of deceased marine life indicated the site of the fish market, but today was not market day in Tsuna. Today was not anything day in Tsuna.

Main Street was mainly shut. Was it lunchtime, or early-closing Wednesday, or mass bankruptcy? I walked inland, down a street of low-rise buildings of whitewashed breeze-block. I counted four florists' and three monumental masons, their yards crammed with regiments of tubby Buddhas and prides of ornamental lions. The few people I passed on the street were elderly, walking along bent over bicycles that seemed more support than transport. I imagined they had not ridden their machines for years, but couldn't bear to let them go. No wonder the funeral business was booming.

I could see little of the infrastructure to support a squad of lusty footballers. There was one promising bar, called Come Come Cat, but it had clearly been shut for at least a year. The hairdressers', Airy Hearts, might expect great custom from England's players, but the staff seemed better suited to pampering Japanese matrons than shaving a millimetre off Rio Ferdinand's cranial crop or grooming David Seaman's ponytail.

Where was the five-star international leisure resort with attendant training facilities? There was a four-storey hotel on the outskirts of town, surrounded by paddy fields that came right up to the windows. I walked into the deserted reception area, and spent five minutes clearing my throat, whistling and tapping on the counter before a bespectacled teenage boy in a scarlet waistcoat and wonky scarlet bow-tie appeared.

'England football team?' I enquired. 'Coming here?' He grinned, looked around helplessly in the hope that some senior member of staff would arrive to rescue him, grinned some more. 'David Beckham? Michael Owen? Here?' The boy started giggling, shaking his head, then nodding. Sources in Tsuna would neither confirm nor deny, I thought, heading for the door.

There was nothing else to see, no one else to talk to. I felt frustrated and confused, and I had had my fill of Tsuna. I walked back to the ferry terminal, where at a snack stall I bought the only item on display that I could understand, a packet of Spicy Soy Pringles, which I munched while waiting for the Kobe bus. I wondered how the multi-millionaires of the Premiership would enjoy their stay in Tsuna. Was this a masterstroke of cunning from England's wily manager, to secrete his players far from the probing lenses of the media and the temptations of big-city night-clubs? Did the luxury resort really exist outside the imagination of the English Football Association?*

What this sad place would need, I thought, if it were to feature in the World Cup headlines, would be a marketing ploy, a catchline, something to bring the tourists flocking. 'Tsuna – it's a great place to die!' I said aloud, to the surprise of the girl behind the snack counter. I looked at her shrink-wrapped sushi meals. 'Tsuna,' I announced, 'the town that put the "s" in Tuna!'

Just then, much to the relief of the snack-counter girl, the bus drew in and I walked out.

I collected my bags from the left-luggage office at Shin-Kobe and caught a Shinkansen – the Hikari Super Express once more – to Nagoya, where I found a room in a high-rise city-centre hotel. It was nothing special, but it had a sepulchral cocktail bar that served little sausages on sticks and potato wedges. I had three plates of each, and two Asahi Super Dry beers, which were in fact wet.

Friday morning was bright and warm. I caught a local train from Nagoya to Shiroko, the nearest town to the Suzuka motor racing circuit. This was no Shinkansen Express, but an ancient slam-door local service, with dark green velvet-covered banquettes flanking a wide central standing area to accommodate the morning rush-hour crowds.

* Sven-Goran Eriksson's cunning was undone by a fluky Brazilian and a pensionable goalkeeper. But the resort, as the world's television viewers now know, was there all along, on the outskirts of Tsuna. I should have turned left at the second monumental mason.

The train was only moderately full, but still a dozen people hung from straps as we swayed from station to station. One stood out, like a splendid doll in a toy-shop window: a geisha. I could not help staring. It was too improbably appropriate, like a Japanese tourist encountering a Beefeater on the Bakerloo line.

The geisha wore a pale pink kimono intricately embroidered with flowers, a white belt and a kind of stiff tablecloth folded like a backpack between her shoulder blades. Her hair was drawn up into a tight bun and covered with a net spangled with gold stars. On her feet were strange, wedge-heeled shoes, part-clog, part-sandal, but much too short for her feet, so that her heels overshot the rear edge and her balance, swaying beneath the strap, was most precarious.

At the next halt I realised how rude I had been to stare, and offered her my seat. We mimed a diplomatic exchange: 'I insist', 'No, *I* insist', before she accepted with a series of deep bows, which I, of course, returned. For the rest of my journey she beamed at me, middle-aged features almost indistinguishable beneath a slick of cosmetics, a Patricia Routledge of the tea ceremony.

At Shiroko Station, a line of shiny black Nissan Cedrics waited to take racegoers to the circuit. All Japanese taxis and their drivers are well turned out, but these were worthy of a showroom. The boxy bodywork shone, while inside crisp white cotton covers shielded the seats from sweaty customers, and the driver flicked his column-mounted gearstick with a white-gloved hand.

I climbed out at the main entrance to the strangest racetrack in the world.

Suzuka was built by the Honda car company in the early 1960s. The track itself is a convoluted figure of eight, fast, challenging and dangerous, and the drivers love it. But it is the surroundings that make Suzuka so remarkable. The course has spawned a theme park, Suzuka Circuitland, that draws Japanese in their thousands even when there is no racing scheduled, and which provides an extraordinary backdrop to the final race of the Formula One season, the Japanese Grand Prix.

Two giant rollercoasters twist around the approaches to the grandstands, and a Ferris wheel that has become the circuit's trademark overlooks the main straight and the paddock. There is an aerial motorbike ride, and a replica of the Suzuka circuit for hefty go-karts. I longed to try them all, but I had to find Mika Hakkinen instead.

At most racetracks the entrance to the inner sanctum is discreetly hidden, but here a bevy of security staff checked my talismanic paddock pass, then waved me through to a railed-off stairway down the middle of the crowded grandstand. Hundreds of Japanese fans stared as I walked down, and I fondly imagined that they were mistaking me for an unusually tubby racing driver.

A tunnel under the main straight of the track led to the turnstiles at the paddock entrance. I headed for the McLaren-Mercedes office, next to Ferrari at the bottom end of the paddock. Assorted silver-shirted staff stood around outside the office door, consulting clipboards and whispering urgently into walkie-talkies and tiny mobile telephones. I was looking for Wolfgang Schattling, head of corporate communications for Mercedes, a nice German who might be able to procure a few minutes of Hakkinen's time for me.

But it was a long shot. Hakkinen is a monosyllabic Finn who hates giving interviews. What is more, this was to be his last race before a year's sabbatical that most close observers of the sport reckoned would turn into permanent retirement. Polite approaches had been made on my behalf while I was in transit, and they'd been equally politely rebuffed. Mika was not doing any one-on-one interviews this weekend.

'Mika is not doing any one-on-one interviews this weekend,' Wolfgang reiterated, when I finally tracked him down at the back of the team's pit.

'Not five minutes?' I asked. 'Not one?'

'Not one.' Wolfgang shook his head with a rueful smile.

I turned dejectedly and started to walk off.

'Of course,' Wolfgang called after me, 'He is appearing at the official press conference.'

'Oh, really?' I said. That would be a lot better than nothing. 'When?'

'Oh,' Wolfgang looked at his watch with a sly grin, 'about now.'

Why do I always end up running?

Formula One press conferences are not spontaneous affairs. A handful of drivers and team officials are rounded up, plonked behind microphones and politely grilled by the sport's master of ceremonies, a charming Englishman of Greek extraction called Bob Constanduros, who speaks five languages fluently but is incapable of asking a spiteful question in any of them.

That Friday in Japan, Hakkinen shared a cramped annex to the Suzuka press room with the young Malaysian driver Alex Yoong and three team principals: Craig Pollock of British American Racing, Eddie Jordan of the eponymous Silverstone-based squad, and Hakkinen's boss, Ron Dennis of McLaren.

As everyone was settling down, Jordan threw a cup of water over the shirt of Dennis, a man whose racing philosophy is built on the immaculate appearance of his cars, his drivers and himself. While Dennis sat with a face of stone, an outraged McLaren flunky disappeared in search of a cloth and Jordan smirked. It occurred to me that F1 resembles a travelling boarding school, and that we had just witnessed the equivalent of a staff-room prank.

In the front row of the class, Hakkinen the senior prefect

and Yoong the new bug dutifully ignored their masters' misbehaviour and waited for the first question. Constanduros asked Hakkinen about his impending break from the sport, and received a polite but non-committal reply, which is the most he or anyone else has ever been able to elicit from this particular source. Hakkinen is often referred to as the Ice Man of Formula One, but that suggests a chill in the personality that is not present at all. The tag is apposite because he has blond hair, blue eyes and comes from a cold country, but it makes him sound altogether too unfriendly. Granted, conversation with Hakkinen is as free-flowing as a glacier, but there is humour behind the taciturnity.

Constanduros, who knows this routine very well, pretended to probe a little deeper. Was Hakkinen's motivation gone? Had he lost his competitive edge? Had recent fatherhood hampered his ability to express himself in the car? Hakkinen placed a finger either side of his nose, as if in deep thought. His orange-shaded sunglasses blanked fifty journalistic stares. Five seconds passed. Five more.

'No', Hakkinen said. I had come to Suzuka for a word with Mika Hakkinen. Now I had it. As a corner of the Finn's mouth quivered, almost smiling, the regular Formula One hack pack cheered. They may never have got much in the way of quotes out of Hakkinen, but they would miss him.

Ron Dennis was more forthcoming on the topic of Mika than Mika himself had been. Dennis uses a language that is thought to be related to English and is known among the Grand Prix fraternity as Ronspeak, an amalgam of American management jargon, technological terms and public-relations euphemisms. A major crash might be 'an unscheduled vehicular impact', a screaming row 'a vigorous discussion'.

Tom Clarkson of *F1 Racing* magazine helped me to translate Dennis's thoughts on Hakkinen, which amounted to the fact that he was a good bloke and would be sorely missed, although whether or not he would be giving up for good was anybody's guess.

Not much on which to base a major feature, but it would have to do. Fuelled by soy-flavoured Pringles and mineral water, I put together 900 Hakkinen-related words and, after a brief but intense struggle with what in Ronspeak is known as the telephonic interface of my laptop, emailed the piece back to London.

The sun had set, and the big wheel behind the grandstand on the other side of the main straight was illuminated by yellow floodlights. Every once in a while there would be a flash from high on its circumference as another fan recorded the romantic image of Suzuka by night, or (more likely) their companion's grin. I wanted to go on the big wheel, too. I consoled myself with a telephone call home, where it was breakfast time. I prodded sixteen times at my phone, and Lucy, (aged four and a quarter) answered.

'Daddy?'

'Yes, Lucy?'

'Daddy?'

'Yes, Lucy?'

'Daddy. Um. Where are you?'

'I'm in Japan.'

'Why?'

'To find a hotel where some famous footballers might stay, and to watch some people race cars round and round in circles.'

'Yes, Daddy. But why?'

'To make money so that I can buy you toys.'

'Oh. Daddy?'

'Yes, Lucy?'

'Do they have nice toys in Japan?'

'Yes, Lucy.'

'Good. Would you like to say good morning to Emily?'

'Yes, please, Lucy.'

'Emily, do you want to say good morning to Daddy?'

Emily (two and seven-eighths): 'Noooooh!'

I wanted to be at home. I wanted to rest. I packed up my kit and started the long schlep back to Nagoya.

Bus, train, taxi, hotel. Vain attempt to find English-language television channel. Sleep.

The next morning – Saturday – I asked the receptionist to write down for me, in Japanese characters, the name of the football stadium in Osaka – Nagai – and also a short message: 'I am an English journalist. I have come to watch the match.' Then I headed once more for Nagoya station. I had plenty of time, for once, because the match between Cerezo Osaka and Gamba Osaka did not kick off until four o'clock. So, for once, the journey was smooth and uncomplicated. I waved my piece of paper at the ticket collector at Osaka station, who directed me to the Midosuji subway line, which took me to Nagai.

There was a group of schoolboys in my subway car, eleven or twelve years old, spots on their faces, braces on their teeth. They spent the journey giggling at me. 'Ingrish!' they whispered. 'Hey, Ingrish!' They thought I was giggling back at them, but I was mean-spiritedly laughing at the motto embroidered, in English, on their jackets. It said: 'I have fulfilled my ideal of physical perfection.'

I did not have to worry about asking directions to the stadium: no one could miss such a vast, sculptural, concrete bowl. There was a bonsai market in the surrounding park, where fans in pink Cerezo Osaka shirts were stooping to admire the delicate little trees. It wouldn't happen at Old Trafford.

A fountain danced outside the VIP entrance, which was guarded by a large, round young man who might have

been a trainee sumo wrestler. I showed him the receptionist's message and one of my business cards, but he
remained impassive and in my way. I tried another entrance,
where a friendlier goon pointed to a lobby next to the VIP
door.

Here three young ladies in smart cappuccino-coloured
suits were distributing press badges. I gave one of them my
piece of paper, by now rather crumpled, and she smiled
and said: 'No need. I speak English.' As if this were not
good news enough, Aya Otani (as her name badge declared)
also produced a form with my name and newspaper already
inserted at the top. I was expected.

Once I had completed the form to her satisfaction, Aya
– who was pretty despite severe silver-rimmed spectacles –
gave me a pass to wear around my neck, a programme and,
I was amazed to see, a team-sheet in English. 'I translated
it for you,' she said.

Glowing with gratitude, I went for a walk around the
stadium. Fans of Cerezo ('It's the Spanish for cherry, cherry-
blossom,' Aya had told me, as if that explained anything)
and Gamba mingled happily at soft-drink stands. Most were
young – the average age about twenty-five – and there were
almost as many women as men.

Boys skateboarded in the car parks, while touts in shabby
suits waved discreet bundles of tickets. There were no takers.
A group of teenaged girls stood in a circle, singing a song
in unison. As I approached they stopped, and one called
out 'Hello!' 'Hello!' I said, and they giggled like synchronised dollies. 'Goodbye!' the girl said, and I replied
'Goodbye!' which she and her friends found funnier still.

On the quiet side of the stadium, away from the bonsai
stalls and fast-food stands, I came upon the strangest thing:
a tiny cemetery on a triangular plot no more than five yards
from the stadium wall, so close that it seemed to be part of
the complex. Two ladies, one old and bent, the other,

perhaps her daughter, middle-aged and stout, were tidying the narrow paths between the gravestones with wooden rakes. Each nodded solemnly at me as I squeezed past them. The monuments were stepped, like primitive pyramids, and although I could not make out any dates it was clear that most of them long predated the football ground.

On every gravestone stood a vase of flowers, most of them fresh, and I saw the old lady take a watering can and start to top up the vessels. Next to each vase stood a glass, or ceramic cup, or bottle, or can. They were offerings, or tributes to the deceased, containing, or so one bottle announced, *sake*.

I left the ladies to their tidying and the dead to their drinks and walked back to the press entrance. After one or two false turns – one of them into the royal box – I took my seat.

Almost immediately, a hostess in a Cerezo pink suit appeared with a pretty wooden box containing equally pretty morsels of raw fish and rice, and a bottle of clear liquid labelled 'Pocari Sweat'. I have never met a Pocari, and know nothing of their standards of personal hygiene. But their perspiration tastes like sweet lemonade.

The Nagai Stadium seats 40,000 people, but only 15,441 – according to the scoreboard – had turned up to watch what I imagined would be a match of keen local rivalries. The sparse attendance suggested that the J-League was hardly surfing a great wave of popularity, but those fans who had come along had certainly done their homework on football-crowd etiquette. Those at the Gamba end of the ground greeted their team with a blizzard of paper fragments, a South American gesture which prompted a Japanese response: nineteen ground-staff spent the entire first half on their hands and knees picking up the tiny pieces of litter. Cerezo's supporters were keen singers. They had a club anthem, the words of which appeared on a giant

178

scoreboard to encourage participation. 'Cerezo, Cerezo, we love you, Cerezo . . .' When they were done with this, they took up the theme from *The Great Escape*, the favourite tune of England fans, albeit with Japanese lyrics.

Beer sellers climbed up and down the grandstand stairs, hawking the local lager in plastic cups, while pink-suited Cerezo girls scurried back and forth among the VIP boxes with supplementary portions of sushi and Pocari Sweat.

Out on the pitch, things were not so busy. I tried to note the respective sides' tactical formations, but either I had got no better at this since the World Cup, or there weren't any. The two foreign players on each team stood out from their Japanese colleagues by virtue of their complexions rather than their abilities, while the home-grown performers charged up and down the pitch with more energy than invention.

At half-time it was nil-nil, and the action on the pitch livened up when the full-grown players were replaced by a Cerezo junior team, who did some ball tricks and then lined up to be presented with medals by a female pop singer and the club's mascot, some sort of steroid-bloated squirrel dressed, like the bimbo, in football kit. The man in the squirrel suit was obviously suffering impaired vision, because he kept stumbling into the footballers; he stuck his nose right into one little player's eye. Meanwhile, the pop singer kept a straight face until she reached the end of the line, where the two smallest players stood. As she presented a four-year-old with his memento, the three-year-old next to him swiftly yanked down his team-mate's shorts. Gazza would have been proud.

Unfortunately it was then time for the big players to come back, and they did not seem to have picked up any tactical tips in the interval. My attention kept wandering from the pitch to the crowd, so that when Gamba scored – it was a fluke – I almost missed it. Their fans let fly with another snowstorm of litter, and the ground staff, who had only just finished picking up the first lot, morosely returned to their task. Cerezo's manager – Brazilian, like two of his players – started to prowl the touchline, shadowed by his Japanese interpreter.

These two had quite a routine going. The Brazilian would wave his arms at one of his Japanese players, yell some instructions and gesture some directions. Moments later, the interpreter would repeat the process, translating the instructions and copying the gestures identically. This meant that anything more complex than 'Mark your man' took some time to get across.

But it seemed to work, for out of the morass of mediocrity Cerezo plucked a rather lovely equaliser, Yamashita and the South Korean Dong exchanging three headers before the latter nodded the ball into Gamba's net. The squirrel and the pop star did a little dance of joy.

It was still one-all when the referee blew the final whistle, and I was halfway down the stairs to the exit when I realised that the players had not left the field, but were gathered in twin circular huddles either side of the halfway line. I had forgotten that in the J-League there is no such thing as a draw. Extra time is played, during which any goal is golden and settles the contest. If the sides are still deadlocked the tie is decided on penalties.

I returned to my seat and signalled for another Pocari Sweat. But no sooner had I put it to my lips than the match was over. Cerezo's Okasaki tumbled for what seemed to me to be an extremely dubious penalty, and the same player converted it. Celebrations and lamentations over, each team then ran to the end of the stadium occupied by their fans, lined up and bowed deeply. The fans, en masse, bowed back. As the rest of the players trooped off the field, the pop star interviewed Cerezo's penalty hero while the squirrel tickled him with his tail. Any self-respecting Premiership player would have punched the rodent's lights out.

Meanwhile, I subsequently discovered, Gamba's Japanese manager was tearfully resigning his position, overcome with the shame of defeat by his club's local rivals. 'It happens quite often,' Aya told me as I thanked her for her help. 'He will soon have another job.'

I was dozing on the Shinkansen back to Nagoya when my expensively hired mobile telephone rang, for the only time on the entire trip. I hurried, under fire from disapproving eyes, to the end of the carriage reserved for such conversations.

'You are Baker of British newspaper?' enquired a male voice, none too politely.

'Yes, I am,' I said.

'I am press officer of Cerezo Osaka,' said the man, without mentioning his name.

'How nice of you to call,' I said. 'I am sorry I didn't see you at the match. I enjoyed myself very much.'

'Yes, yes,' he said. 'But you have taken away your press pass.'

I glanced down to see to see the crumpled square of card in its clear plastic sleeve hanging from a string around my neck. It had not occurred to me that such a flimsy credential would need to be returned.

'So I have,' I said. 'I'm very sorry.'

'You must bring it back to the stadium now,' the Cerezo man said.

I couldn't believe my ears. 'I am afraid I can't do that,' I said. 'I am on a train. I will send it to you, all right?'

'You are a very bad man,' my accuser said, and cut the line.

I still have the pass.

That evening, on television in my hotel room, I watched a chef dressed only in his underpants slicing a giant white radish while riding a bicycle. Sleep did not come easily.

*   *   *

181

I had a complicated itinerary for my last full day in Japan. Nagoya–Shiroko–Suzuka. Watch Grand Prix. Suzuka–Shiroko–Nagoya. Nagoya–Tokyo–Narita, and a night in an airport hotel.

First of all, I had to get rid of my suitcase, since I could hardly lug it around Suzuka and I did not wish to delay my evening transit by having to return to the hotel. I had spotted a left-luggage set-up at Nagoya station, and I headed straight there on Sunday morning. The transaction was suspiciously easy, so straightforward in fact that I wondered if I had not mistaken the purpose of the office altogether. Had I unwittingly pawned my suitcase and its contents? I would find out before 9.30 that evening, which was when the place shut. That deadline gave the entire day a sense of purpose, for the idea of a night in Nagoya without my suitcase followed by a horrifically early dash to Narita was too ghastly to contemplate. Come what may, I must be back at the station by 9.30 p.m.

The train out to the track was crowded with Japanese motor-racing fans, most of them draped in the colours of Ferrari. More climbed on at every station, so that by the time we drew in to Shiroko it was impossible to move without getting a mouthful of Michael Schumacher T-shirt or a poke in the eye from a scarlet flag-stick.

I shared a taxi to the circuit with a Singapore-based Australian investment adviser and a middle-aged Japanese lady who wore a hat on which perched a toy Ferrari. Neither had been to a race before, but the lady had memorised all of the elder Schumacher's previous Grand Prix victories, and kindly recited them to us throughout our journey. It was a relief to reach the circuit gate.

I deposited my laptop in the press room, where Tom Clarkson was already hard at work. 'You missed a great party last night,' he said. 'Honda hired the entire funfair. Every ride was free, there was masses of beer and quite a few of the drivers were there. We couldn't get Juan-Pablo Montoya off the roller-coaster.'

This was bad news. Not only might I have had a good time, I might also have gathered enough material for a splendid story which I could have finished before the race had even begun.

'I had a prior engagement,' I explained to Clarkson, 'with a short-sighted footballing squirrel in Osaka.'

But he had got me thinking: there was time to squeeze in a couple of rides before the serious business. I made for the big wheel.

A long queue snaked up to the entrance, so I looked for a mid-morning snack to munch while I waited. Suzuka is entirely bereft of Western-style food, so unless you can wangle a meal in one of the pit garages you have to take your chances among the stalls selling local specialities. Like many Japanese restaurants, the stalls display plastic models of their signature dishes in glass display cases on their counters. These were utterly unappetising, chipped and scuffed, playthings from a giant's doll's house.

I passed on noodles and mushroom omelettes (too messy) and rejected bean-curd fritters (ditto). I'd had my fill of sushi in Osaka, and pastel-coloured sticky buns held no appeal. Then I saw a stand advertising 'American Dogs' and a hot dog sounded just fine. I was handed a pair of deep-fried juggler's clubs on sticks, great blobs of batter which, when I cautiously bit into one, revealed sickly sweet processed pink sausage meat. There was no way that I was taking another bite out of these, but no way either that I was going to lose my place in the queue in order to throw them away. The big wheel was surrounded by couples taking little naps on the grass. One pair had chosen to lie down right next to the queue, and I laid my dogs, like an offering, at their feet.

At the front of the queue a skinny young lady in a Suzuka

Circuitland T-shirt beckoned me forward, took my 500 yen, and opened the rickety gate of one of the wheel's little capsules. Suzuka's big wheel is not like the London Eye. There is nothing modern or high-tech about it, but that is part of the charm. The capsules would seat four cosily, but I had one to myself, so I could swap seats from side to side and pretend that I had company.

As I rose gently into the sky I saw at first only the backs of the grandstands and the roofs of the refreshment stalls. But then I was above the buildings, and the sun-baked circuit stretched away into the distance like a Scalextric set. A saloon-car race was taking place, and as the noise of the engines and the size of the cars diminished, the contest started to look trivial and silly, no more than a child's game.

I swapped to the other seat – making the capsule wobble alarmingly on its axis – and looked away from the circuit. There was the rest of the funfair far below, and beyond it woods, and in the distance Shiroko. The air was clear and the sky was blue, and I felt that I ought to be able to look across the flat landscape as far as distant Mount Fuji and Tokyo, but the horizon was just an indigo shimmering line. Suddenly my car was at the apogee of the wheel's turn, and seemed to stop for a moment – an illusion, since I had simply been deprived of the relative motion of the other capsules. But an enjoyable illusion, all the same. There could be worse places from which to watch the race.

As my capsule gently descended on the other side of the wheel, I peered anxiously down at the sleeping race fans. The pair to whom I had donated my dogs were still snoozing obliviously, and no one was pointing up at the foreign litterer. I was tempted to stay aboard for another orbit, but I had one more mission to complete in the funfair. I had noticed from high above that the queues for the Formula Grand Prix go-kart track were relatively short, so that was my next destination.

Most of those competing were Japanese children, and I considered for a moment the embarrassment potential of the exercise. I reasoned that it was worth the risk. If I was too old, the attendant would tell me so. And if the unthinkable happened and I should be beaten on the track by a Japanese infant – well, who was to know?

At the front of the line a steward in a chequered-flag baseball cap fired a series of questions at me in Japanese. Was I aware that there was a weight limit for these karts? And an age limit? And was I the man who had left two partially devoured American Dogs next to a sleeping couple at the big wheel?

Actually, he had been giving me a safety briefing, as I discovered when he handed me a dog-eared printed card with instructions in English. It was all common-sense stuff – Rule number 1 was 'Do not crash into the other cars' – although elements of the translation could have been improved. Rule number 4 stated: 'Do not leave your can on the track even if it is broked.' I would try to bear that in mind.

The karts were parodies of Formula One cars with wide tyres, air scoops and wings that would have negligible aerodynamic effect at 20 mph (oh, all right then: 5 mph). There were to be five other competitors in my race, all Japanese: four children, the youngest aged about six, and a man in his early twenties who wore mirror sunglasses and a leather jacket and obviously fancied himself as something of a hot-shot.

We started in line in the narrow pit lane. The six-year-old boy was the only kart ahead of me, while behind lurked the leather-jacketed man and three girls. One by one the gantry lights blinked out, and as the last disappeared I flattened my right foot on the accelerator pedal. The engine roared like a mighty lawnmower sighting a lush meadow, and I shot off in pursuit of the six-year-old at the pace of a brisk walk down the high street.

No matter. Performance is relative, and none of the other vehicles was moving significantly faster than mine. The track climbed around a long left-hander and I weaved ponderously behind the young leader, seeking to intimidate him into an error. Hah! As we approached a right-handed hairpin he left a gap between his kart and the barrier, and I steered into it.

We rounded the corner with our fenders rubbing, much in the manner of Coulthard and Schumacher at Magny Cours, and as we pulled out of the turn and started on a gently sinuous downhill run, I was ahead. The spectators, had there been any, would surely have been on their feet.

I was too busy basking in the adulation of the imagined hordes to notice the little blighter edging alongside me once more. Before I could block him he was back in front. Worse, in my attempts to keep him behind I had lost crucial momentum, and now Leather Jacket was lining up a pass on my inside.

I held him off until the main straight, when he calmly motored past. Then a schoolgirl in a sailor-suit uniform chugged up behind me as we headed up to the hairpin for the second and final time. No way are you going to put a sucker move on me here, darling, I thought, moving over with a veteran's wisdom to hog the inside line.

So she puttered past me on the outside and – what was worse – waved and giggled as she drew away. Doddering back into the pit lane I saw a trio of European faces grinning at me. 'What happened out there?' one of them said, with a Lancashire accent. 'Couldn't you keep the little lass behind you?'

'Engine trouble,' I said, peering at the back of my machine. 'Must have dropped a cylinder. Gearbox problems. Couldn't get any heat into the tyres. And I think I might be getting a cold . . .'

To soothe wounded pride, I poured myself into my work.

The newspaper's motor-racing correspondent would do a straight race report, so I needed an angle for the accompanying piece. I decided to concentrate on the fortunes of Jean Alesi, a hugely likeable French-Sicilian driver who was to retire from the sport after this, his 201st Grand Prix.

A good choice, as it turned out. On the fifth lap of the race Alesi was following Kimi Raikkonen through the fast left-hand bend behind the paddock when the leading car suddenly spun around and Alesi could not avoid a collision. As his Jordan hit the rear of Raikkonen's Sauber the young Finn's car spun violently around and the nose slashed across Alesi's cockpit. Both vehicles came to rest in a storm of flying debris. There was a great gasp in the press room, and then a terrible silence as we watched for signs of movement in the wrecked cars.

At last it came, and both drivers climbed gingerly from what was left of their vehicles and vaulted the barriers to safety. Alesi walked back to the pits, waving at the fans, and I ran downstairs to see him wander, surrounded by a gaggle of well-wishers, into the back of the Jordan garage, where he watched the rest of the race with his mechanics.

It was a great story, and one that I was able to finish while, in the next-door room, Michael Schumacher was conducting his final victory press conference of the season.

'What is the quickest way to get to Shiroko station now?' I asked the multilingual attaché at the press help desk. 'Bus? Taxi?'

'Frankly,' he said, 'the quickest way right now is to walk. The traffic will be terrible. But it shouldn't take you more than an hour or so.' It was now five o'clock, and my suitcase became inaccessible in four and a half hours. No problem. . .

There is something quite satisfying about walking past traffic-jammed cars, but the satisfaction lasts only as long as the traffic jam. Once the cars start moving faster than you are, their occupants start to wear the same smug grin with which you strolled past them ten minutes ago.

The road became progressively narrower, from dual carriageway to two-lane highway, to single track with occasional bulges to allow two cars to pass each other. This is quite hair-raising for motorists, and doubly so for pedestrians, since there is no pavement, only a dusty margin between road and ditch. But there was safety in numbers. Hundreds of race fans had decided to walk to Shiroko, and I ensured that there was always a comfortable human cushion between myself and the oncoming traffic. Even so, there were a couple of occasions when passing cars – taxis, in fact – flicked at the trailing edge of my coat, and I was forced to reflect on what a second-rate death this would be: knocked into a paddy field by a Nissan Cedric.

It was quite dark by now, but that was no great loss in terms of sightseeing. Small fields of infant rice stretched away from the road on both sides, interspersed with simple modern houses. Dozens of tiny bats looped and swooped in the half-light. Every few hundred yards there would be a short stretch of sad roadside commerce: a garage, an off-licence, a dealer in military surplus clothing, a dusty slot-machine arcade. Nothing tempting.

Shiroko announced itself with the reintroduction of pavements and a marginal increase in street lighting. The little town square was packed with partying racegoers, slurping noodles and draining giant silver cans of beer. But the platforms of the station were not impossibly crowded, and I managed to climb aboard a local service to Nagoya.

Half past six. Not bad. On a British train, of course, my problems would only just have been beginning. But unpunctuality is unheard of on the Japan Railways system. Not only had all the trains that I caught on my visit departed on time, they had also arrived on time, and for good measure I had read in the *Daily Yomuiri* of the sad case of a JR driver who had hung himself for failing to adhere to the timetable.

So I was able to retrieve my suitcase intact at a little after eight o'clock. Things were going well – too well to last.

The difficulty arose when I attempted to buy a ticket for the next Shinkansen to Tokyo. The clerk in the ticket office scowled and frowned at his computer. 'Half past ten,' he said, gloomily. 'No seats until half past ten.' I was aghast. That would almost certainly be too late to connect with the Narita Express.

'What can I do?' I asked.

'Unreserved seat,' he said with a shrug, and his tone revealed the depth of my plight. Unreserved seat almost certainly meant no seat at all.

Sure enough, when the Shinkansen – my old friend the Hikari Super Express – trundled into the station, passengers were practically hanging from the baggage racks, and that was before the Nagoya contingent had boarded.

The waiting customers had formed formal queues next to where the doors would open, and I had obediently taken my place in the line, knowing that I was sacrificing any hope of a seat. The celebrated Formula One photographer who showed up just as the train was arriving was not so . . . I was going to say genteel, but I think the word is probably 'spineless'. The snapper took one look at the queue and barged straight to the front of it, earning himself a volley of 'Tsk, tsks' from the Japanese, and a nice comfy seat all the way to Tokyo. I stood in the aisle for the two-hour journey, barged aside every ten minutes by refreshment trolleys. Manners maketh man weary.

But at least I was on the last lap, and this time Tokyo station held no fears for me. I found the platform for the Narita Express, where a train was waiting. 'Narita airport?' I asked a Scandinavian youth standing in the carriage. 'Yes,' he said. Fantastic. It was half past ten, and there was a chance that I would be in bed by midnight.

It was not the Narita Express, but a rattly old local train that stopped at every suburban station on the way out of Tokyo. Still, there was no reason to suppose that it would not terminate at the airport. The Scandinavian had said so. But the Scandinavian was no longer on the train as it sat in Chiba Station, about halfway to Narita.

Indeed, no one else was still on the train, I realised, as the doors shut and we started moving – backwards. Towards Tokyo.

I got out at the next, deserted station and hunted down a blue-jacketed JR official. 'Narita airport?' I asked.

He shook his head. 'No more trains,' he said. He looked at his watch, then took a dog-eared timetable from his breast pocket and thumbed through it. 'Here,' he said, pointing down at the platform. 'Ten minutes. Narita. Then taxi.'

And that it is the way it happened. But before I got into the taxi I had to have a row with the inspector at Narita station, who felt there was a discrepancy between my pristine Narita Express ticket and the rickety rattlebucket on which I had arrived at his station. I agreed. In fact I felt I deserved a substantial refund. But that is not the JR way, and I ended up handing over 1,400 yen just to be released from the station.

I arrived at the hotel at half past one in the morning, requested an alarm call for six, and passed out. It had been a very long bit of Japan.

I am happy to report that take-off in the Japan Airlines Boeing 747 was smoother and more enjoyable than my landing in the same aircraft had been five days earlier. But no long-distance economy class flight is without drawbacks, in this case personified by the frail but single-minded elderly Japanese man who sat in the seat next to me and ate pickled fish all the way to Heathrow. So that even when I had put away my passport, slept off the jet lag and completed the last of my Japanese articles, an essence of the country still lingered in my senses, like an insistent ghostly herring.

Conclusion: I am a very bad man.

Chapter Eight

The Zoo in Room 605

Objectives: Travel to the port of Salvador on the north-eastern coast of Brazil and wait for Ellen MacArthur to arrive on her trimaran at the end of the Transat Jacques Vabre race. Try not to get mugged. Try not to get food poisoning. Try not to reinforce negative stereotypes of Brazilian society and cuisine. Time allocated: as long as it takes Ellen to get there.

I stopped for a moment at the top of a steep hill above the port of Salvador da Bahia. A ruined church stood just across the road, its stark profile straggled with jungly creepers. In the shell of the nave, market stalls were piled with green coconuts and giant watermelons. The jagged ramparts were silhouetted against a stormy gun-metal sky, where an ancient domestic jet lumbered towards the airport, spindly under-carriage extended. It was a spectacular tableau, but stopping to stare at it was a mistake: it made it apparent that I did not belong.

It was 11.30 in the morning of my first full day in Brazil. I was making for the port and the finish line of the Jacques Vabre transatlantic race. I needed to find some officials and discover what time Ellen MacArthur and Alain Gautier, the race leaders, were due to arrive. But I didn't get to the port that day.

Two men in their early twenties stood in the gateway of

a car park opposite the ruined church. They had watched me taking in the view, and as I set off again, down the hill, I registered a glance between them, felt their attention locking on to me like radar. I knew that they would follow, knew what would happen when they caught me.

I was not unprepared. I carried only about fifteen pounds' worth of *réis*; all the rest of my money, my credit card and passport were in the room safe in my hotel, the key to which lay between the sole of my left foot and its sock. I looked around for help: there were people walking on the wide street above outside the church, but the road downhill was free of pedestrians. The men had fallen into step close behind me. I needed to be back among the crowds.

I stepped into the road, intending to cross and jog back up the hill, but my pursuers ran forward, one murmuring 'No, no, no,' in an admonishing manner, and grabbed me in the middle of the carriageway. Taking an arm each, they frogmarched me backwards and shoved me against a parked car, a Fiat Panda, I remember noticing.

They worked silently and quickly. One shoved a penknife between my wrist and the band of my watch, popping off the strap; the other rifled the pockets of my shorts, then tore the plastic carrier bag from my arm. Within ten seconds, they were sauntering away down the hill. They threw behind them my paperback thriller and my company identity card.

I retrieved the former – much more important to me than a little Brazilian money – and was about to collect my card when a bus appeared around the corner, missing me but making a mess of my plastic image. Suddenly, rather too late, I felt vulnerable.

And cross. With myself, for wearing a watch, staring at a church, walking through a strange town in a strange land. With the young men who had mugged me, for so quickly confirming my worst preconceptions about their country. With the Sports Editor. And with Ellen MacArthur. Bloody woman, thinks it's clever to sail across the Atlantic. She should try walking across Salvador.

I'd been conned into this assignment, in the nicest possible way. 'Why don't you go and interview Ellen MacArthur?' the Sports Editor suggested one day, in his habitual tone of avuncular menace. 'She's in Le Havre, fitting out for a trans-atlantic race.' Interesting. I'd written about MacArthur's return to France in a heroic second place in the Vendee Globe round-the-world race the previous year, making copious use of her emotional emails back to base, but I had never met her.

Two minor blots on the plan: a public-relations person from MacArthur's sponsors would be attached to me throughout; and getting to Le Havre would involve an overnight ferry trip. Then I discovered a flight from London City, and bullied the PR into booking it.

Actually, it differed only in duration from the ferry crossing. We flew at wave-kissing height across the Channel, barely having to descend before touching down at Le Havre airport, which was the size of the average filling station. The PR (who I think was called Justin) and I were the only passengers to disembark from the plane, which was contin-uing to some other obscure destination. We woke the driver of the airport's only taxi. Over a cardboard pizza in a restaur-ant across the road from the hotel, Justin explained that he had not planned a career in PR, but 'just sort of fell into it, actually'. I wondered how long it would take me to bring about a similar manoeuvre at the harbour the next morning.

Justin stayed on the quayside pretending to make a series of important telephone calls while I leapt carefully on board MacArthur's trimaran *Foncia* (or, as Justin kept referring to it, with deference to the sponsor, '*Kingfisher-Foncia*'). The boat was huge – the size of a tennis court – and beautiful in a strictly functional way. MacArthur was tiny, and strictly functional. Slight, wiry, tomboyish; close-cropped hair, blue jeans and battered boat shoes, strong hands with nails worn to the quick, pink cheeks, eyes the colour of a stormy North Sea, no time for tossers.

We sat on the roof of the central cabin capsule while she batted back the questions she'd heard a million times before, intermittently firing volleys of French at the sun-tanned bloke adjusting the rigging. She paid a little more attention to questions specific to this race – how would she get on with Gautier, her senior both in years and experience ('should be fine – he chose me'), how much sleep would she get ('maybe four hours in four days') – and then took me bouncing across the trampoline-like netting between the hulls and down into the cabin.

This was spartan and claustrophobic, a fibreglass egg with a couple of shelves for sitting on, a wall of instruments and a lap-top computer for navigation.

'Where's the lav?' I asked.

She snorted with contempt. 'Over the back,' she said.

We went back up top, and MacArthur pointed out on the other side of the harbour the original *Kingfisher*, the boat in which she had finished second in the single-handed Vendee Globe circumnavigation race. 'I miss her,' MacArthur said. 'There will never be another boat for me like her.'

A crowd of French ocean-racing fans were queuing up on the side of the dock for MacArthur's autograph – on the Atlantic coast of France she is more famous than David Beckham – and I thought it was time to go.

'Will you have a chance to get to the finish?' she asked.

'I've no idea,' I said.

'Go on,' MacArthur said. 'Race you there.'

I left her to get on with fettling her cross-beams, or whatever it is that people on trimarans do to pass the time, and went off to extract a nice fish lunch from Justin's expense account. By way of retribution, he told me a lot of slightly fatuous stories about poltergeists at his public school.

The next day I was in the writers' room in the sports department, scrolling through the news wires and listening to one of the football reporters telling an extremely long and violently obscene joke when the Sports Editor loomed into view.

'Ah, Andrew,' he said, ominously. 'Would you pop into my office for a moment?'

It seemed that regaling me with his boyhood experiences of the supernatural had not satisfied Justin that his public-relations duty had been done. He now insisted on flying me across the Atlantic to Salvador to await MacArthur's arrival, and he would put me up at a sea-front hotel, all at Kingfisher's expense. Since this proposition allowed the Sports Editor to kill two birds with one stone, employment for one of his feckless writers, and a good story that wouldn't have to come out of his budget, he was politely insistent that I should go.

So I went. And this time, Justin didn't come with me.

One of the things that I like about Varig, Brazil's national airline, is that it is the only major carrier that I know of that persists in employing the McDonnell-Douglas MD-11 trijet on passenger flights. Since the company that made it long ago went out of business and the large and graceless aircraft is these days used almost exclusively as a cargo freighter, this seems to me a welcome variation on the ubiquitous jumbo.

Come to think of it, though, it is the only thing that I like about Varig.

The night flight out of Heathrow was uncomfortably full, and most of the passengers returning to Brazil were bringing with them the kind of hand baggage – hi-fi-systems, television sets, microwave ovens – that delights customs officers but represents something of a hazard to the loo-bound journalist in pitch darkness at 35,000 feet.

We landed in Rio de Janeiro ahead of schedule at nine o'clock in the morning, leaving me about an hour and a half to make my connecting flight – also with Varig – to Salvador. But as we taxied up to the terminal building, the MD-11 swayed to a halt. Ever so sorry, the pilot explained, but there's a bit of a traffic jam here: we'll have to wait for a couple of planes ahead of us to load up and clear their stands. So by the time that I sprinted down the ramp into a wall of humidity, I had just three-quarters of an hour to find my bags – not, as might have been expected, checked through to my destination – clear customs, check in for my Salvador flight and get on it.

This is where the good and bad sides of what one might very loosely call Brazilian organisation became clear. The transfer hall had its own baggage carousel, the idea being that passengers retrieve their own bags and then check them in themselves for their onward journey. An additional benefit was that passengers could monitor the length of the check-in queue while they waited with increasing frustration for their luggage to show up.

'Queue' is something of a misnomer. While the carousel remained immobile and the minutes until my Salvador flight ticked away, I wandered over to the check-in area and found a kind of auction by outcry taking place. It was pandemonium. The way to check in for an internal flight in Brazil, apparently, is to battle your way as close as possible to the scrum in front of the desk and then bellow your special circumstances at the clerk.

'I have a small child with me!'

'I have my disabled mother with me!'

'My wife is pregnant!'

'My bag is heavy!'

'I'm going to miss my fucking plane!'

The latter, rather unimaginative contribution was mine. The carousel had eventually spat out my bag, four minutes by my soon-to-be-filched watch before my flight to Salvador was due to take off. Naturally, I assumed that I had missed it and that was that.

But this was Brazil, where time flexes and twists like a party-entertainer's balloon. Having elbowed my way to the check-in desk, trampling grannies and infants in my desperation to get on the plane, I gasped my destination to the unruffled blonde behind the counter.

'Salvador?' she said. 'No problem. Gate seventeen.'

'But the plane has gone, hasn't it?'

'No, no, they are waiting. You have a few minutes.'

I sprinted to Gate 17, where another unruffled official tore my ticket and directed me to a half-empty bus. The bus continued to wait while a further score of passengers, mostly Brazilian and clearly more used to the timetable, ambled aboard. Eventually the bus coughed into life and the driver took us on a tour of the outer fringes of Rio de Janeiro's Galeão airport.

When, I wondered, had the war started?

There were shattered aeroplanes, and bits of shattered aeroplanes, lying around all over the place. The airport management could not have concocted a poorer advertisement for the locally prevailing safety standards had they erected a giant net at the end of the runway. A couple of wheels propped up against a fence; an engine rusting on a flat-bed truck; an entire marooned tailplane: had these bounced to their resting places after a spectacularly botched landing, or fallen off during the taxi to take-off?

The bus pulled up next to two derelict Boeing 727s, one windowless and wheel-less, the other with splayed cowlings on the port side displaying an empty engine-bay. Jesus Christ, I thought, which one is mine? The bus door opened on the far side from the two wrecks, revealing a practically pristine Boeing 737 with, as far as I could ascertain, its full complement of wheels and engines.

Pedro sat next to me on the two-hour flight to Salvador. His complexion was the colour of copper, his hair was like a Brillo pad and his eyes were bright blue. He wore jeans and a dusty blue sweatshirt that said 'USA'. He was going home to his family in Salvador with money he had saved working in some kind of food factory – an abattoir or curing-house, I couldn't work out which – in São Paulo.

He tucked in to the soggy cheese-and-ham roll as if ravenous, licking lumps off the stubble around his lips, scooping up stray fragments with his fingertips. He expressed approval in Portuguese, then when I smiled blankly tried again in English.

'Good, unh? And no money!'

He waved down the aisle for the stewardess to bring him another.

Pedro soon discovered where I was from, where I was going, what I was doing, or as much of that information as I could remember.

'I have been in England,' Pedro said. 'I was in . . . Guild Ford. Nice. Rich houses. My cousin was there. He find me work. I do . . .' Pedro's brow furrowed, his eyebrows meeting like two caterpillars disputing a twig. 'I do . . .' He started to mime some kind of vigorous construction activity, hammering away in thin air and spilling quite a lot of his coffee on to his second cheese-and-ham roll. He broke off from building a sort of oblong on the back of the seat in front of him and looked at me encouragingly.

'Bricklaying?' I suggested.

No, no. He started hammering again, then delicately sketched in the corners of his project.

'Picture-framing?'

No again. Seized with a sudden inspiration, Pedro leant across me – spilling what remained of his coffee – and pointed at the aircraft window.

'Window frames?'

He beamed, displaying a left incisor entirely of gold.

'You were installing window frames?'

He nodded happily.

'In Guildford?'

He nodded again, not so happily.

'They would not pay me. For two months I work hard, and then they will not pay me. My cousin has gone to London, I do not know where. These people in Guild Ford will not pay me. They say I am illegal.'

'And were you . . . illegal?'

'Yes,' Pedro said. 'But still I should be paid, I think. I do not like Guild Ford.'

'Never mind,' I said. 'Now you are at home.'

'Yes,' said Pedro, sucking the coffee from his roll as if it were a fruit. 'I am at home. And *you* are illegal.' Then he laughed very loud, showing his sharp gold tooth once more.

At Salvador airport I changed a hundred pounds into *réis*, fended off two stubbly middle-aged men who insisted that they knew how best I should spend them, and dived into a taxi. The driver was also middle-aged and stubbly – this month's look at Salvador airport – but gave a warm if patchy grin when I showed him the address of the hotel. 'Is far,' he said, with evident satisfaction.

We passed a battered Gloster Meteor jet fighter marooned forlornly on a pole at the airport gate and immediately entered a great tree tunnel, which the afternoon's bright sunlight pierced in dappled patches. On either side of the car bamboo trunks the thickness of Maradona's thighs arched upwards, a suburban trellis on steroids.

The jungle interlude was brief – it was probably soon to be light industrial units – and the freeway was long. Shiny skyscrapers appeared on the horizon, marched close by, receded. 'Salvador – downtown,' the driver said. Mmm-hmm, I thought. And where exactly are we going?

Off the freeway, it turned out, and along the edge of a beautiful park in which flamingos picked their way delicately through rock gardens on the banks of an undulating ornamental lake. All around were office blocks, flyovers, underpasses, the clutter of high-speed urban growth.

'*Futebol*,' the driver shouted, as we passed through the shadow of a craggy cliff of grandstand, sprouting rusting iron bars like weeds. 'You like?'

'*Futebol*? Yes, I like, I like.' This was Brazil. Why take chances?

There was another strange oasis, some kind of water park tucked among the roadways, with twisting chutes and slides curled against the sky like mutant spaghetti. It was called 'Wet 'n' Wild'. But it was dry and shut. Outside the padlocked gates two adolescent boys dressed in nothing but scarlet shorts were improvising, jumping in and out of a giant green-rimmed puddle.

The taxi meter was whirring as if supercharged, and I was trying to work out whether or not we were going round and round in circles. Soon I gave up. When you don't know where you are to start with, and you don't know where you're going, it is hard to protest about the route.

The ocean twinkled at the foot of a long, steep hill, and the driver pulled into a shadowy forecourt. 'Hotel Figeurel,' he announced, and shamed me for my suspicions by producing an official booklet detailing the official fares to and from certain city locations. He pointed at the airport figure with a defiant leer, and I guiltily over-tipped him.

The bellboy, a lean, silent, grinning character in a baggy grey uniform and bright white Nikes, showed me to Room 301, which had been the site of a recent orgy. Bedclothes, tissues and beer cans littered the floor, and a beige bra hung on the television aerial. The bellboy swivelled soundlessly and ushered me away.

Room 403 could not be unlocked.

Room 507 was sadly deficient in lightbulbs.

Room 605, though, was fine, or so the bellboy seemed to think. 'Television,' he announced, indicating the item of that name, which was without an aerial (or a bra). 'Cupboard,' he declared incontrovertibly, though he did not point out that the door was secured with some kind of heavy-duty sticking plaster. 'Window,' he finished with a flourish, and so it was, with two of the six panes cracked and a view of a shabby apartment block on the other side of the street.

I tipped him stingily and sat down on one of the narrow twin beds. The mattress was the thickness of a small-town telephone directory, and just as compressible. I fiddled with the television's Sellotape-bound remote control, and summoned six channels of static, one of soundless football and one – just about audible and visible – of some kind of historical soap opera.

I decided against unpacking, reckoning that even after a transatlantic journey in a Varig hold, my bag was probably a better home for my underwear than the Figeurel's drawers. I telephoned home, established that the family were well and happy, and reassured my wife that I was not here to sunbathe or otherwise enjoy myself. As I put down the receiver I realised that the highlight of my day had passed. Three-thirty in the afternoon. What now?

I looked longingly at my paperback, but I had barely 300 pages to get me through – what? Three days and nights? Four? Severe rationing would be necessary, unless Ellen got a move on or I could find another English book in Salvador.

Salvador. I would have to go out.

First, though, I secured my passport, credit cards and

dollars in the room safe, a rusty device somewhat like a wall-mounted waffle iron, and stuck the key down my left sock. It's a brave bandito indeed who takes on my whiffy footwear. I checked my apparel – T-shirt, shorts, sneakers, nothing too obviously plutocratic – and stuck on a pair of sunglasses and a baseball cap, for further invisibility.

You know what happened next. Clearly I had been insufficiently invisible.

As the muggers trotted away, eagerly examining their acquisitions, my heartbeat slowed to normal and I totted up the damage. I had a small graze where the blunt side of the knife had scraped the inside of my wrist, and what felt like a bruise on one hip caused by the door handle of the Fiat. I had lost a nice steel watch, but since it had been given to me for free at the world go-karting championships, I was hardly grief-stricken. I had lost a small amount of money, but no more than might have come in useful to buy a paperback and take a taxi back to the hotel.

The taxi, I now realised, I really, really wanted. I did not want to have to walk back through the same streets I had just traversed at the risk of being ambushed again. Why didn't muggers issue receipts, I wondered, or stickers: 'Already robbed', 'Freshly skint'? Why didn't the Government save everyone a lot of trouble by establishing official mugging squads at the airport, so that the arriving traveller would pass through baggage reclaim, immigration and customs and then get mugged, emerging to search for a taxi wearing a badge stating: 'Official muggee. Do not attack'?

Thinking about taxis again, dammit.

Abandoning my squashed ID card in the road (the newspaper's jobsworth-in-chief would subsequently demand ten pounds for a replacement), I started to walk back up the hill. One of the dozen or so people who had assembled to watch the assault – without offering any assistance – now sprang into life and started jabbering animatedly and gesturing at my card in the road. I replied with a pantomime gesture which I hope conveyed my contempt for muggers, Bahians and Brazil in general, and walked on.

I tried to re-adopt the I Am Local attitude that had slipped so disastrously opposite the church. Mentally, I ransacked the Way of Baker for the 'Safe Urban Walking' checklist. When walking through even the most remotely dodgy of foreign cities do not:

Carry a map, or consult one provided for public consumption;

Ask for directions;

Gawp at people, buildings or indeed anything;

Wander, amble or appear otherwise aimless, or (if in Brazil) wear a watch.

And if you get lost, get a taxi.

Bollocks. Thinking about taxis again.

I was sure I could remember the route back to the hotel. The street I was now on was lined with buildings of two halves: from the waist up, attractive, colonial-era townhouses, painted many years ago in pale pink or dusty yellow; below the belt, garish retail outlets. Most were clothes shops: loud T-shirts and shorts piled high in bins on the pavement, selling at around fifty pence per garment. Knots of people stood by each bin, rifling through the contents and adding further layers of grime to the already sullied fabric.

Further obstruction on the pavement was caused by fruit stalls and fast-food stands. I stood for a while beside one of these and watched the chef at work. She was a vastly overweight pale brown lady in late middle age, and her stall comprised a battered steel bowl of boiling oil set precariously over an open gas flame, and another bowl of what looked like sticky yellow porridge. At the approach of a customer, the lady would grunt, dip a large spoon into the porridge and dump a dollop into the oil, which would spit and sizzle mightily. The resulting browny-gold item – a doughnut, for the want of a more accurate term – was then consumed while held in a square of kitchen paper.

She asked in gummy Portuguese if I would like one.

'Under ordinary circumstances,' I said, 'I'd love to take you up on that. But unfortunately two of your young compatriots have made off with all my lolly.'

She shrugged, and mumbled something else, which might have been 'Oh, well, that's Salvador for you', or 'Sod off then, you tight-fisted gringo bastard', and I walked on.

I came across a bookshop, and dived inside, thinking: I'll find a paperback or two, put them aside, come back in a taxi (aaargh, yes, a taxi) and buy them. But the bookshop was exclusively Catholic, stacked with Jesus calendars and Holy Mother tea towels, cheaply bound gospels and paperbacks with titles I could not translate entirely but which were clearly religious self-help manuals: *God Is the Answer*; *Jesus Is My Workmate*; *Housekeeping the Holy Way*; *A Mugger's Guide to the Gospels*; that sort of stuff.

At the top of the street was a leafy square, with on one corner an enormous news stand: twenty yards of toothy, bosomy, shouting magazines arrayed under clear plastic tarpaulins, presumably to repel rain and thieves. There was a row of insistent pornography, three more of women's titles, another devoted to cars and guns, an entire section for football. I needed something to tag-team with my paperback and preserve my sanity over the next few days. The *Economist*? *Time*? *Newsweek*? Not here. *Country Life*? *Good Housekeeping*? The *Beano*? Nothing doing.

Beyond the news stand was a broad avenue overarched by gigantic, thick-leaved trees of a kind I could not identify. The trunks and branches were convoluted and mottled brown and had been trained, decades before, to create a wide path beneath for the sporadic traffic. The leaves were plain and broader than a big man's hand. So large, in fact, that when it suddenly started to rain I could hear the drops drumming on the canopy above, but none hit the road.

The avenue was lined with substantial buildings, modern villas in widely varying styles which shared one thing in common: each entrance-way boasted a purposeful gate abutting a sturdy gatehouse, and in each gatehouse a security guard sat with his eyes glued to a soap opera.

I walked through a square of the sort you used to see in the East End of London: a straggly central space surrounded by beaten-up houses and gaps where houses had once stood. On one corner stood a petrol station; on another (I noted, for future use) a McDonald's. I was close to the hotel now. The road ran downhill once more, past a police station. I toyed with the idea of reporting the mugging, but decided that my losses were not worth the hours of linguistic hassle and likely derision. ('Hey, José, you're not going to believe this: guy here went out wearing a watch!') I passed two empty hair salons and some kind of lingerie emporium, and there was the reassuring bulk of the Figeurel: nasty hotel, safe haven.

Back in Room 605 I locked the flimsy door and decided that I needed a treat. It was late afternoon: close enough to sunset, and in any case I had had an unpleasant experience. I opened the half bottle of Absolut Citron I had bought at the Heathrow duty-free shop, and broached the pair of free shot-glasses that came with it.

I had a drink.

In fact, I had a number of drinks, and then I lay down on my telephone-directory bed for a little nap until suppertime, and when I regained consciousness it was half past three in the morning and I couldn't think where I was or why, and when I remembered I didn't feel a whole lot better.

*　　*　　*

Breakfast at the Figeurel provided a surprise: the hotel had other guests. This was a real mystery. I had to be here, but these people were staying of their own free will, unless the Brazilian penal service had made a block booking for a rehabilitation weekend. There were a dozen people in the breakfast room. Two families of four (one lot fat, the other thin), two elderly couples. All, as far as I could tell, Brazilian, and none of them rhapsodising about the food. The place was silent apart from the occasional clank of cutlery and the massed mastication of the Fat Family. Reasoning that bread was probably the safest thing on offer, I swiped two slices of industrial white from the sideboard and manufactured a margarine sandwich, which I took from the sepulchral breakfast room to consume next to the pool.

It was a beautiful morning, the sun already high and bright in a cloudless sky, the cloying heat yet to build. I had nothing to do: Ellen, that slowcoach, was still a couple of hundred miles away from Salvador, though in her defence she was leading a fleet of the world's most eminent ocean racers.

Under normal circumstances (that is, almost anywhere in the world except Salvador) I'd have gone for a walk. But here, the prospect did not appeal. I went back up to my room, tried and failed to raise anything on the television except static and *Dallas* reruns overdubbed in Portugese, and gazed out of my window for a while, willing the occupants of the apartments opposite to do something violent or sexual, preferably on their balconies.

But no one did. It was Saturday, and on a sunny Saturday in Salvador people do what they do in every seaside town in the world: they hit the beach.

So I hit the beach as well. I put on a T-shirt and swimming trunks, locked all my worldly goods into the waffle-iron safe, and left my key at reception on the firm understanding that if my room was ransacked in my absence I would know jolly well who had done it, OK, pal?

You can tell how relaxed I was. But as I crossed the road to the beach-front promenade I started to mellow. After all, I reasoned, unless someone wants to steal my swimming trunks or murder me just for the hell of it, I really shouldn't be in a great deal of danger.

It was getting on for ten in the morning, and the beach was packed. The sand lay in a little bay between two rocky promontories, one of which boasted a sinister-looking old fort. Pre-teen boys were tumbling and somersaulting off the ramparts into the sea, which was surprisingly placid for an ocean, more Mediterranean than Atlantic.

There was a wonderful range of beautiful bodies on display, and it struck me what a fantastically diverse nation this was. There was every shade of brown here from deepest mahogany to my own off-white, the latter being by some way the least attractive. And everyone was so fit: the boys and young men playing volleyball and keepy-uppy were slab-chested and taut-tummied. The women were uniformly gorgeous, and wore bikinis so minimal that you would struggle to construct a teabag out of their constituent parts.

Not that I was looking, of course: eyeing up someone's girlfriend around here struck me as a sure-fire way of getting re-mugged. Eye contact in general was something I was keen to avoid, but there is only so much gazing at the horizon a man can do. I needed a focus.

I needed a sandcastle.

I lacked the correct implements, having thoughtlessly omitted my bucket and spade when packing to follow Ellen, but I had hands and I could improvise. I selected a spot as secluded as possible, close to the rocks on the right-hand side of the bay and as distant as could be from flying fris-bees and footballs. I decided on the classic approach and sketched out a circle two feet in diameter with an index finger, then set to with both hands to scoop out a moat and build up the centre.

The sand was a perfect consistency, not too dry and not too coarse, and before long I was quite preoccupied with volume and shape, circularity and moat depth. Every now and then I would remember with a twinge the last castle I had built, on holiday with my daughters, but I told myself off. Pull yourself together, man: there's a job to do.

It was a magnificent sandcastle. The central mound was smooth and steep, topped with an ornamental shell; the moat was deep, and the gatehouse was a nice touch. I doubt that Salvador beach had seen a finer example of the castle-builder's art, because to judge from the stares and sniggers I was getting from the locals, sand architecture was not a common hobby hereabouts. But I felt I had made my mark, and walked up the beach with a colonial swagger. One or two of the local boys smirked, and I heard a burst of laughter from behind me. I turned, in time to see a large black dog of indeterminate breed standing with one paw through the gatehouse, weeing on my keep.

By way of consolation, I decided on a McDonald's lunch. This was not going to win me any prizes for adventurous dining, but having seen the standards of hygiene prevalent among the roadside doughnut-makers I wasn't ready to sample the local specialities just yet. I nipped back into the hotel, changed out of my beach gear and grabbed a few *réis*, then walked the short way up the hill to the burger joint.

I wondered whether there might be some local variations on offer, since in Scandinavian branches you can get a Big Laks, which is a salmon burger, in Japan you can get teriaki burgers, in Athens you can snack on a Greek Mac (two burgers in a pitta) and in Australia – you have been warned – your McOz Burger will be garnished with beetroot unless you specify otherwise. Now don't tell me I'm not an expert on international cuisine.

The Salvador branch of McDonald's, however, stuck to the core menu, and I snaffled up a quarter-pounder at a window seat in the otherwise empty restaurant. The tray-mat, or underlay, or at any rate the piece of paper that prevents the staff from having to do much in the way of wiping, was most compelling. It depicted the national hats of some forty-eight countries: Mexico's sombrero, Russia's fur, America's Stetson and so on. Britain was represented by a bowler, which made me wonder whether or not the designer had ever set foot in my home country.

I stared at the hats for forty minutes or so, doing little gherkin burps, before reluctantly conceding that I wasn't going to eat any more and I really should get back out on to the streets. I was very taken with the idea of going back to my room at the Figeurel and reading my book, but if I finished my book I wouldn't have anything else to read and would shortly thereafter go insane.

I put the change from my burger into the charity pot on the counter – there was quite a lot of it, but I would rather give it than have it taken – and walked out under the incredulous and mildly aggrieved stares of the staff. I took a different route from the previous day, heading inland away from the port down a broad avenue lined with smart homes and what appeared to be exclusive clubs. But soon the swankiness wore off and the street narrowed, approaching a shabby square. I passed a young man carrying a vast translucent green bag crammed with empty drinks cans. He wore a little haversack, from which projected the head of a sleeping puppy. At least, I hoped it was asleep.

I found another bustling shopping street. Here the speciality of the vendors were little fish cakes, briskly fried in boiling oil: they smelled delicious, and for a moment I regretted my McDonald's. Then I saw the flies flocking around the raw materials kept in buckets under the stall, and felt good about my burger again. Call me picky, but I find that limiting the local gastronomy limits the risk of gastroenteritis.

Another innovative street stall consisted of an old-fashioned Bakelite dial telephone, a stool, and a large fan. I watched as a young mother came up with her toddler, perched on the stool with the child on her lap, and picked up the telephone. The proprietor, a middle-aged man wearing a pinstripe suit over a string vest, started a stop-watch and switched on the fan. The child giggled as the breeze ruffled her hair. At the end of the call, the man switched off the fan and showed the mother the stopwatch. She gave him some coins, and off they went. I liked that scene: it doesn't take much to start up in business in Salvador.

There was a bridge over a brown river flowing sluggishly to the ocean, and here I stumbled into a pop video. A handsome, bearded singer in long white robes was crooning along to the vaguely reggae-ish sounds emanating from a ghetto-blaster on the pavement. Around him jived four pretty women in black robes, while a colleague crouched in the road in front of the ensemble with a small video camera.

A policeman had approached, apparently with the idea of moving everyone on, but had changed his mind and decided to play a cameo role instead: he swayed behind the girls, waving his fearsome nightstick in a suggestive manner. Just for a moment I thought: I love this place. I don't get it, but I love it.

I walked on for a little while, then remembered that I didn't have any money for a taxi and thought I had better retrace my steps back to the hotel. When I got back to the bridge the singers were gone but the policeman was still there, differently engaged. He was holding a shirtless man face down on the parapet of the bridge, with his nightstick braced across the bare shoulders, shouting orders. Three other police-men stood by, one pointing a pump-action shotgun at the prisoner's torso.

Whatever the miscreant had done had been bad, and recent: spectators were starting to gather and exchange shocked gossip. I would like to have discovered the nature of the crime, but I didn't like the look of that shotgun, and I didn't like the thought that the barebacked baddie might have some chums in the neighbourhood. I put my head down, and got into Don't Bug Me, I Live Here mode.

I wondered, as I hurried along, am I being unfair to this place? There must be citizens of Salvador who lead blameless, crime-free lives. There must be things to see here that don't resemble out-takes from a Vinnie Jones movie. I had stepped out from the hotel three times so far, and had been robbed, witnessed an arrest, and had my sandcastle desecrated by a dog. Had I just been unlucky?

Quite the opposite, I decided, reaching the relative safety of the lobby of the Figeurel. I'd been especially fortunate to participate in the social life of Salvador in such an intimate way. After all, if you go out looking for experience, you can't complain when you get it.

There was a bar beside the hotel swimming pool. More accurately, there was a cupboard beside the swimming pool, with a little man sitting in it who would make you a drink called a *caipirinha*. This was clear, potent cane spirit with a chunk of lime in it, and it tasted quite nice. But the cheeseburgers being consumed percussively at the next-door table looked lethal to me, and I decided I would eat out.

I'd picked up a flyer in reception promoting a 'typical' local restaurant, so I hopped in a taxi outside the hotel and waved the leaflet at the driver. 'Is not far,' he observed gloomily.

'In a warm and featured place,' the blurb ran, 'you will find comfort, safety, air-conditioned and a finest full-service bar.' There's something funny about that, I thought, and it's not just the syntax. How many restaurant leaflets have you seen that go out of their way to advertise their safety?

The only security feature I noticed at the restaurant was the front door, which opened only from the inside, so that the staff could have a good look at each potential diner before they let them in. I apparently looked safe, or at least solvent, and was shown to a table in a corner of the cosy room, which was cluttered with artefacts – saddles, whips, prods – associated either with cattle-ranching or kinky sex. The place was crowded with early diners, so I guessed that either the food was good or the locals weren't fussy.

Unbidden, a waiter plonked a *caipirinha* in front of me, indicating that this was on the house. I studied the menu, which was written in Portuguese and a kind of English. The main dishes included 'roated goat', 'fresh water-grilled fish', 'lamp chop' and 'the most savoury roasted beff'. Accompaniments were limited to 'mush made with manioc flour and milk' and 'mixture of manioc flour with beans and green beans'. I went with the latter, to accompany my 'typical salted meat on barbecue'.

Nothing much happened for a while, so I sipped my drink and eavesdropped ineffectually on my fellow diners, concluding that Brazilian Portuguese sounded like Spanish without dentures. Then the waiter reappeared and placed in front of me a large white plate half covered with green-flecked goo: I might have been looking at the handkerchief of a man with a terminal cold. I must have seemed horri-fied, because the waiter put a comforting hand on my shoulder and said: '*Feijão verde.*'

'Bless you,' I said, and then a man dressed in white hurried towards me carrying a shining knife, three feet long and viciously serrated.

Oh, great, I thought. What a perfect way to end the day: I have been served a plate of snot and now I'm going to have my head cut off.

But the smiling executioner was only coming to serve my main course. In his other hand he held a hefty skewer, on to which a gigantic sirloin steak had been concertinaed. With his mighty blade, the chef cut strips of the meat which fell next to, but thankfully not into, my snot.

The beef was very good, but lip-puckeringly salty. Emboldened by my *caipirinha*, I even tried some of the snot, which tasted like a sort of savoury semolina and necessitated another shot of liquor to cleanse the palate.

The knifeman came back, this time with an entire peeled pineapple on his skewer. This had clearly been barbecued alongside my meat, and he sliced it on to my plate. Then he was off again to fetch me more beef. He kept coming backwards and forwards from the kitchen, alternating fruit and steak, until I felt that I had eaten half a cow. It doesn't do to disappoint a man with a scimitar, so I munched gamely on until the skewer was bare, and congratulated the chef on his work.

The bill was surprisingly large, but so was my stomach. I really needed a healthy walk to aid the digestion process, but since night had fallen and I couldn't swear that I knew the way back to the hotel, a stroll would have been asking for trouble. With a megaphone.

I called a cab instead and was shortly back by the pool at the Figeurel, treating myself to a dozen pages of Le Carré while the Fat Family argued with the waiter: something to do with the quality of their crisps.

I went to bed quite early – there wasn't a great deal else to do – but I couldn't sleep. The bed was fantastically uncomfortable, the mattress thin and stiff and somehow ridged so that I might as well have been trying to kip on a sheet of corrugated iron. Then there was the yelling and screaming from the street, most of it joyful but some more ambiguous, and the infrequent but none the less alarming screeches that seemed to come from inside the hotel, disquietingly close to my room.

Eventually I dropped off, only to be awoken within a few

minutes by the unmistakable sensation that something was crawling up my right leg, heading north from the ankle.

I lay quite still, or as still as it is possible to be with a heart pounding like a pneumatic drill. I ran through the list of candidate creatures.

Do they have cockroaches in Brazil? Unquestionably.

Scorpions? Probably.

Large, poisonous spiders? For sure.

This thing didn't feel all that large, but it was definitely moving, and I was going to have to do something if it was to be dislodged before it got to anything more precious than my knee. Very slowly, almost imperceptibly, I began lifting the single sheet with my left leg, while inching my left hand towards the light switch. The creeping little legs had reached the top of my shin. Time for action.

I swept the sheet away, simultaneously sitting up and switching on the light. Gotcha.

It wasn't a spider. Or a scorpion. But it was green, and that was bad enough for me. I twitched my right leg once, twice, but the creature was still attached, clinging on to the hairs. I picked up the two shot-glasses that had come with the half bottle of lemon vodka from duty free. I would have preferred pint mugs, given the scale of the insect, but these would have to do. By nudging with the lip of one and shoving with the lip of the other, I managed to dislodge the interloper and dump him on the smeary glass top of the desk. He seemed disinclined to move, but I popped a shot-glass over him anyway.

Why not, you might have been wondering, mash him to a paste with the sole of my shoe? Because I have a sort of wishy-washy sub-Buddhist namby-pamby attitude to squashing things that aren't actually doing me any harm. Besides which, he might have had a much bigger mummy, and she might have been watching.

I peered through the shot-glass at my captive. He peered back. Hard to say which of us was the more disgusted.

Now I had to make sure that there weren't any more where he came from. I switched on every available light, to no great effect, and got down on my hands and knees for a thorough safari of my room.

I'll remember that moment if ever I'm tempted to apply for a place in the *Big Brother* house. Any cameras present would have recorded a pale, flabby figure dressed only in boxer shorts, crawling every inch of the room with his nose pressed to the floor, muttering from time to time: 'Come on out, you little bastards, I know you're in here.'

I had no alternative. I wanted to sleep. I would probably be working at midnight the following night. I *needed* to sleep. And I would not be able to sleep without knowing that my personal space was free from creepy-crawlies.

I caught two more: a smaller green one, and a brown item of altogether more robust construction. Soon these had joined the original trespasser under glasses on the desk top. A zoo of my own: who needs a nightclub?

The next morning I liberated the insects out of the window and rang Ellen's team co-ordinator, who was staying in a hotel on the other side of the city which sounded much nicer than mine. There was bad news: something had broken on Ellen's boat, and while neither she nor Gautier had been hurt, they had lost the lead of the race and looked unlikely to get it back.

There was worse news: her estimated time of arrival into Salvador harbour was two o'clock the next morning. What was I going to do with myself?

I decided to go on holiday for the day. I was going to forget about cultural exploration and ocean racing and veg out from dawn until dusk. I established myself on a sun lounger beside the pool, shut my eyes and waited for the sounds of Salvador on a Sunday to fade from my consciousness. Which they did so completely that I can recall very little about the rest of the day. I moved my lounger once

216

or twice, from sun to shade and back again. I lunched on bread filched from the restaurant, washed down with Diet Coke; I read rationed snippets of paperback; I watched wonderful butterflies and hummingbirds flutter in and out from the big city outside. I thought: I really must do this more often.

By mid-afternoon, though, my sense of responsibility had unfortunately returned, and I supposed that in the interest of research (and in order to avoid unnecessary travel by nightfall) I should head on down to the port.

'The port?' the copper-tanned hotel receptionist asked when I requested a taxi. 'Are you sure you want to go to the port?'

'No,' I said. 'I am not at all sure that I want to go to the port.'

'Good,' she said. 'Sometimes it is not a safe place.'

'I believe you,' I said. 'I don't want to go there. But unfortunately I have to. For my work.'

'Ah,' she said, and tapped her nose. 'I understand.'

Whatever had she meant? I wondered, as the taxi hurtled past the spot where I'd been mugged and on down the hill towards the harbour. Did she suppose I was a drug smuggler? Or an Interpol officer? Or something altogether less glamorous?

The driver was trying to tell me something as we drove past a series of shuttered and bleak warehouses, bumping over potholes. This is the port, seemed to be the gist of what he was saying. Where would you like me to drop you?

Normal communication being clearly impossible, I leant forward and waggled my fingers around to indicate as clearly as possible: 'I don't know exactly where I'm going. I'm sure I'll know it when I see it. Please don't drop me off here because knife-wielding thugs lurk in every shadow.'

That did the trick for a while, but eventually the driver ran out of patience and pulled up at a dilapidated petrol station. Probably just filling up, I thought. But then he turned grumpily in his seat and indicated that I should pay him and leave.

'Go, go,' he seemed to be saying. 'That way.'

Oh dear. That way was a ferry terminal, seething with passengers, meeters and greeters and – to my febrile senses – ne'er-do-wells. I don't like this, I thought. And then I saw a poster on the terminal wall next to the ticket office. It had a picture of a trimaran cresting a great wave, and the magic words 'Transat Jacques Vabre'.

I stood by the poster until a port official wandered by. I grabbed his arm, showed him the poster, mimed geographical confusion.

'Salvador,' he said, frowning.

'No, no, I know that,' I said. 'But where in Salvador?'

He smiled, gestured 'follow me'. He took me out of the ferry port entrance and pointed at a fenced-in compound next door.

'Oh,' I said, sheepishly.

There was a large security man on the gate of the TJV compound, who wouldn't let me in without ID. 'Don't you understand?' I protested. 'My ID was nicked by the people out here.' I may have been becoming slightly hysterical by this point. 'If you don't let me in they'll steal something else.'

Just then, before I could further slander the good citizens of Salvador, a nice lady appeared with a clipboard and rudimentary English, and I was in. Hooray. Safe at last.

The TJV compound was a combination of civic reception and trade show, not a particularly alluring prospect but better than vegetating by the hotel pool. There were half a dozen stands in a fenced enclosure erected in what seemed to be the car park of a smart yacht club. The club building housed the race headquarters, a press-conference room, and a roof terrace with a bar and restaurant overlooking the harbour. No wonder people were so keen to get past the security man.

The stands were promoting local brands – soft drinks, hotels, doughnuts – and were staffed by very pretty, very bored Brazilian girls. Since the vast majority of the people present were from Salvador, they knew all about Bahian goodies – which is why they were in the restaurant upstairs and not at the doughnut stand.

I joined them. The sun was setting, and Salvador was changing its appearance: by day, brooding, ugly, industrial port; by night, twinkling harbour. I had some supper – bread and butter and fruit from a buffet – and, mindful of the need to stay awake, declined the offered beers and *caipirinhas* in favour of water. Then I tried to find someone who knew where Ellen was.

There had to be Kingfisher people there somewhere. By a process of elimination, discarding those speaking Portuguese or French, I identified a likely table at the end of the terrace closest to the harbour, and one of the people sitting there was Lou Newlands, Ellen's shore manager.

Lou was festooned with equipment – walkie-talkie, mobile phone, pager – with which she was being updated on the progress of Ellen's boat and the one narrowly leading it. She and the others around the table, who, it turned out, would be sailing the boat back to Europe after the race, were hoping that some minor misfortune would befall the leaders and allow *Foncia* ('*Kingfisher-Foncia*,' I heard Justin's ghost insist) back into the lead.

There was a lot of talk about going out to meet the incoming craft. Lou had secured some kind of speedboat, which everyone was terribly keen to hop into and head out to cheer *Foncia* home. I was absolutely terrified that I would be asked along for the ride.

I hate small boats. They are uncomfortable and move about in disconcerting ways, and you can't get off them when you've had enough without getting wet and making people cross. For some reason – I'm not ruling out sadism – the Sports Editor kept making me write about them, which so far I had managed to do from dry land. But this was looking bad. Lou kept stalking a few paces away to gabble alternately into her mobile phone and her walkie-talkie, discussing the logistics of small-craft hire in Salvador harbour. I felt sick at the very notion of bobbing out into the Atlantic in pitch darkness. Worse still, I felt sick at the notion of being sick. What would MacArthur think?

There was a precedent here. A distinguished sports writer had recently, after much effort, persuaded MacArthur to allow him to accompany her on a cross-Channel voyage in *Kingfisher*. Not long after the start of the journey the journalist had disappeared below, looking green. His problem was that on a racing boat there is nothing so convenient as a toilet or a bucket. After a short while, MacArthur called out to him, asking if everything was OK. 'Fine,' came the muffled response, 'except that my boots are full.'

I really did not want to undergo anything similar that evening, but when Lou holstered her phone and returned to the table I was expecting the worst.

'It's bad news, I'm afraid,' she said.

'Not Ellen?' I asked. 'Not another problem?'

'No, no, she's fine. The problem is that I can't get a boat big enough to take you out to meet her.'

'Oh, no,' I sighed. 'That is – that's a real shame.' Restraining the ecstatic smile that was trying to break out on my face was about to cost me a torn cheek muscle. 'Still, never mind, eh? Mustn't grumble. There'll be another time for all that boaty stuff.'

In a far corner of the roof terrace people suddenly started whooping and waving binoculars around. They were pointing out to sea, but at what I had no idea. Then Lou pointed too, and I got a fix on a triangle of little lights moving remarkably fast across the inky sea. *Groupama*. The winners.

Everyone stampeded for the stairs, leaving me alone on the terrace, surrounded by half-finished beers. This was it, the climax of the big race, the moment of victory, the story the assembled media had come for, and to me it was irrelevant. It wasn't my story. I was waiting for Ellen.

Fireworks exploded, followed by champagne corks, as the trimaran nudged up to the dock. The walkways swarmed with people, television cameramen doing their usual best to use their cameras as battering rams. The crew were carried ashore for more champagne and a press conference; I lingered soberly among the beer bottles, wishing I had a crossword to do.

Some three hours later, at two in the morning, the lights of *Foncia* twinkled over the dark horizon, and Ellen and Alain Gautier were cheered into the harbour. They, like the winners, were mobbed by the media, and rushed into a press conference, which was conducted entirely in French.

Afterwards, Ellen showed me over the boat once more. 'This is the bit that broke,' she said, indicating a nine-foot carbon-fibre pole that apparently helped to keep the mast standing up. 'We had to swap it with one from the other side,' she said. 'Tricky, though, when the deck's covered in oil and the waves are breaking over you. How was your trip?'

How was my trip? 'Oh, not bad. Got mugged. A dog weed on my sandcastle. A chef came at me with a big knife and my room was full of insects, but otherwise . . . not bad.'

'It sounds to me,' Ellen said, 'as if you would have been safer on the boat.'

Conclusion: Next time, take a bucket and spade.

Chapter Nine

Disney on Ice, with Guns

Objectives: describe the Salt Lake City Winter Olympics and interview British medal-winners, should there be any. Try to get a drink. Time allocated: eighteen days.

I woke in absolute blackness and swiped at the screeching alarm. In the silence the luminous green numbers on the clock swam in to view. Five in the morning.

'Where am I?'

Salt Lake City. The Winter Olympics. Oh God. It's coming back to me now.

'Who's winning?'

They haven't started yet, numbskull. They start this morning, up a distant mountain, and you had better be there.

Every cell in my jet-lagged body longed to remain in the big, comfortable, warm bed. But if I slept again I'd over-sleep, miss the ski-jumping, miss my deadline and, sooner or later, start to miss my salary.

I got up, yanked back the thick curtains. Snow fell from a black sky and was squashed into slush by the juggernauts on the I-95 highway. It was going to be very cold out there.

I clambered into my gear – so *much* gear – and stumbled downstairs and on to a shuttle bus. At the vast press centre in downtown Salt Lake City I collected my accreditation ('Sir, would you mind opening your eyes for the camera?') and – eventually – found the shuttle that would take me to Utah Olympic Park. As we trundled up through the dawn into the mountains the local radio station was running through the back catalogue of The Eagles. I dozed off. The vast Finn next to me sneezed, pebble-dashing my trouser leg.

The bus pulled into a white car park and its groggy cargo stumbled out into a blizzard. Snowflakes the size of golf-balls were blown horizontally on an angry gale. The wind brought instant pain to any exposed area, and quickly penetrated several layers of clothing. In the distance, the dawn light revealed thousands of people queuing in front of a line of marquees. Security.

The line for the media was the longest and the slowest moving: the public were not carrying laptops, television cameras or Dictaphones, every one of which had to be switched on for the benefit of the inspecting soldiers. After fifteen minutes I had lost all feeling in my feet and my fingers. After half an hour the numbness had reached my knees, and my fingers had started to throb. Every now and then an American journalist would spot a friend close to the front of the queue, and brazenly join him there. And once, after I had been in line for forty minutes, an Indian gentleman in a long, beautiful, shiny green coat sauntered straight to the front of the queue and was surprised to find that he had to be inspected as well. As he passed quickly through the search, I saw the Olympic rings on the back of his coat.

'International Olympic Committee,' said David Walsh of the *Sunday Times*, who was standing with me. 'An impenetrable aura of entitlement.'

Close to the front of the line, the volunteers manning the security gates started their spiel.

'How are you today?'

'Where are y'all from?'

'Cold enough for ya?'

'Have a nice day . . .'

The pain in my fingers was abominable, the volunteers' banter unbearable, and there was no escape: to do my job I had to get through that gate. I started to hum an Eagles medley.

I hummed on while a National Guardsman patted my thighs – yessir, that's frozen Finnish snot – and a local dotard fiddled with my laptop, then I climbed on to another bus to take me to the top of the mountain. In the media centre at the foot of the ski-jump ramp, 150 journalists were crowded around a noticeboard. A photocopied statement announced that the morning's ski-jump qualification competition, the reason I was up the mountain, had been postponed for an hour due to high winds.

And then another hour.

And another, by which time my deadline loomed.

It was funny, only I didn't feel like laughing. The people of Salt Lake City had done everything they could to make their Games a success: they had bribed Olympic officials in order to become a host city, then grovelled to the IOC to hang on to their prize. They had built splendid stadiums, recruited an army of volunteers, brought fleets of buses from all over America, welcomed the armed forces and made ready to receive the President. All was set for the biggest extravaganza in the history of the state, and then what?

It snows. And the wind howls, and the ski-jumpers at the top of their ramp can't see the bottom, and don't fancy being blown off course into the trees, and clearly there is not going to be any sport on this mountain today.

The one thing these Winter Olympics couldn't cope with was too much in the way of winter.

The whole point of getting up at 5 a.m. and schlepping up the mountain had been to write about the one event at the Games that was to take place before the opening

ceremony. Now the opening ceremony, which I had no inten-
tion of attending, would actually open the Games.
Organisational symmetry had been achieved, but I still did
not have anything to write about.

I scuttled around in the persistent blizzard. Snowflakes
smudged my notebook. I obtained a quote from the young
Canadian whose distant ancestry qualified him as the sole
British ski-jumper ('It's pretty windy today'), grilled various
volunteers ('Sure is windy') and officials ('Well, our biggest
problem today is the wind'), then composed and filed an
article contrasting neatly with the local conditions, in that
it comprised for the most part hot air.

*'The first thing you learn about rhino-training is: the rhino
has got to want to do it.'*

From KUTV

Early on my second evening in Salt Lake City I finished off
a long introductory piece to the Games in the Main Press
Centre and set out in search of a bar. Somewhere with beer
and a television set, where I could watch the opening ceremony among the locals. In almost any other city in the United
States, this would have been an easy task. But Salt Lake City
is in Utah, and Utah is run by Mormons, and Mormons do
not drink alcohol, or coffee; neither do they smoke, or swear.

So there are no bars, as such, in Salt Lake City.

The previous night, in my featureless hotel on the airport
perimeter, I had asked the lady behind the reception desk,
a little blonde called Marise with braces on her teeth, if I
could get a drink.

'Why, surely,' she said. 'Follow me.'

She unlocked a glass door and led me into a nasty lounge.
Under a fake-mahogany mantelpiece, a gas fire flickered
behind a glass screen. A giant television set was tuned to NBC.

'Take a seat,' Marise said, 'and I'll bring you some goldfish.'

I thought this over as she fiddled with the lock on a cupboard in the corner of the room.

'Did I hear you correctly?' I asked. 'You're going to bring me some goldfish?'

'Surely right,' she emerged from the walk-in closet with a metallic smile and a plate of orange fish-shaped crackers. 'Can't get you a drink 'less you have something to eat, and these goldfish here are the cheapest thing on the menu. They'll be seventy-five cents. Now, what else were you wanting?'

'Um . . . white wine?'

'Sure. Ya like Chardonnay?'

'Well, yes, or . . .'

'That's good. Chardonnay's what we got. I'll be with you momentarily.'

It was sweet, nasty, Californian, and served in a glass the size of a mosquito's crash helmet.

Marise locked the cupboard behind her. 'When you've finished that, just holler if you want some more,' she said, closing the glass door behind her.

So it was just me, the goldfish and a muted advertisement for Chevrolet sports utility vehicles. Conviviality, Utah style.

That was the prospect facing me as I left the press centre and trudged towards the shuttle bus that would take me back to the hotel. Two and a half weeks of the disapproving Marise, her shiny braces, the goldfish and Chardonnay in an insect's skid-lid.

There had to be a better way, and I found it blinking at me from across the street opposite my bus stop. The battered sign's sputtering neon was a beacon of hope in the chilly dusk. It said 'Dead Goat Saloon', and a glowing red arrow pointed down a dark alley like an invitation to perdition.

I'd catch another bus.

The alley was deserted, treacherous with frozen slush and lined with spindly fire escapes and corroded drain-pipes. Fifty yards down, another neon arrow pointed diag-onally down some black iron steps to a solid wooden basement door. I reminded myself that this was Salt Lake City in the friendly state of Utah, not the south Bronx in New York, gulped all the same, and tiptoed down the steps.

The door opened on to a reception area plastered with posters for blues bands. A young man with several earrings and a wild goatee beard looked up, unsmiling, from behind his desk.

'You a member?' he asked.

'Er . . . no,' I said, and started to turn and leave.

'We'd best make you a member, then, right?' He cracked a yellow-toothed grin. 'You in town for the Olympics? OK, temp will do. Ten dollars gets you three weeks, thank you, sign here and here, keep this card with you when you come along and you can sign in up to five guests. Bar's right through there. Enjoy!'

It was very dark, and there were dead goats everywhere. Stuffed, mounted, skeletal, sketched: in fact there were more deceased *Bovidae* in the saloon than there were live humans, of whom I could identify two behind the monumental oak bar, one propped against it and two more playing a desul-tory game of pool. Also playing: acoustic-era Bob Dylan and a silenced television showing NBC's coverage of the Olympics.

It seemed like home to me.

'Welcome,' boomed the barman, a chunky chap with thin-ning hair dragged into a long pony-tail, 'to the world-famous Dead Goat Saloon. What will be your pleasure, sir?'

'A beer, I suppose.'

'A beer.' The barman put his hands on his hips, mock perplexed. He had black eyes under twitchy brows, and a good line in ironic intimidation. 'I suppose we can run to that.' He ticked off the contents of the fridge behind him. 'Rolling Rock, Molson, Coors, Coors Lite, Bud, Michelob, some Spanish stuff, some New Zealand stuff, Foster's and your very own Boddington's. And on draft, the local specialities: Moab Amber, Park City Steamer, Dead Horse Ale – that's horse, not goat, you'll notice – Ogden Pale, Wasatch 2002 Amber Ale, unofficial beer of the Olympics . . .'

I stopped him there. 'Amber 2002 it is.'

It was. Several times.

Almost every day of the Games, when the sun set over the mountains and the last deadline passed back home in Blighty, a rag-tag gaggle of British journalists would trudge into the Dead Goat, shedding cares and layers of insulated clothing to gossip and drink in the finest traditions of their profession.

Certain local ways had to be observed, the most important of which concerned tipping. Bar staff in Utah are not only rare, they are also poorly paid, and it is considered proper to donate twenty per cent on top of the cost of your beer to the person who served it. If this was Leesa, she of the cascading purple hair and multiple piercings, your tip would earn in return an almost-sincere smile and a generous glimpse of the splendid dragon tattooed on to her cleavage. If it was the pony-tailed Michael, he would acknowledge the gift with a sonorous ritual announcement: 'Thank you, kind sir. For the poor, the needy and the wayward girls. We are particularly concerned for the welfare of the wayward girls . . .'

It was also important to contribute to the accumulated wisdom inscribed on the wooden walls of the bar's booths. Most of this was either unintelligible or unintelligent, but there were one or two gems, and the whole had a certain appeal as folk history: 'Challenge yourself daily.' 'H_2O – got to go.' 'Coach Buffery has NO system.' 'Live to learn, not to burn.' That last had a certain Mormon ring to it.

All too erudite for the Brit Pack. We drank our Dead Horses and our Amber Ales, munched on Goat Burgers, swapped idle slanders about whichever of the group were absent, played poor pool and every now and then glanced at the silent action from the Games, in case anything exciting was happening. Which it usually wasn't.

Then on again with the layers, out on to the icy streets to loiter for a shuttle bus or taxi and the return to the world's least exciting hotel, where Marise grinned through the railway junction in her mouth and trilled 'Y'all have a good night, now!'

But the nights never lasted long enough.

5 a.m.: Alarm goes off. Fumble, switch. Squint at luminous clock-face, adjust alarm hand minimally.

5.14 a.m.: Alarm goes off again. Switch it off. Switch on bedside light. Wince. Swear. Self-interrogate.

'Where am I?'

'Salt Lake City.'

'Who's winning?'

'NBC.'

'What do I do next?'

'Call the office.'

Where it is shortly after noon, and the day's sports pages are being designed.

'It's Baker. What am I doing?'

'Dunno. You tell us.'

'Erm, it's . . . Monday, right? Snowboarding, then. Park City. How many words?'

'Dunno. We going to win a medal?'

'Probably not.'

'Say eight hundred, then. By . . . noon your time?'

'Argh.'

Then the kit marathon: socks, tights, long johns, vest, trousers, fleece, boots, jumper, jacket. Hat, sunglasses, mobile, laptop, notebook and event guide, undergloves, gloves. Then steal a can of grapefruit juice and two slices of cardboard-style bread from the breakfast room, and flop on to the shuttle bus, where the air temperature was always hovering around ninety degrees. Grunt at Winter Olympics correspondent of *Sun, Star, Mirror, News of the World, Sunday People,* etc. etc., i.e. Steve Bunce, who is asleep.

5.45: Bus arrives at press centre. Run around like headless but well-insulated chicken looking for bus stop for Park City.

5.50: Find it as bus departs, chock full of Germans.

5.58: Wonder if circulation will ever return to toes.

5.59: Catch next Park City shuttle. It is full of Swedes, so full that cannot reach bread in pockets.

6.40: Arrive Park City. Enter queue for security checks.

Ah, yes. Getting out of bed and on to the buses was a breeze compared to gaining entry to an Olympic venue.

In the build-up to the Games the American media speculated constantly on the scale and nature of the terrorist threat to Salt Lake City. There seemed no question in the minds of security pundits that the Games would be one giant target, and the organisers, the military and the Secret Service responded accordingly.

On the way to Salt Lake City, the security started in New Jersey. All passengers flying to the Olympic venue were subject to vetting that was rigorous even by recent American standards: undo your trousers, take off your shoes – that kind of rigorous. Approaching Salt Lake City, all air passengers were instructed to remain belted into their seats for the last thirty minutes of the flight, and were inspected by armed marshals on disembarkation.

All Olympic areas had their own airport-style security

checks, although their ferocity seemed to vary according to the status of the site and which VIPs might be visiting. At best, you would be patted down by a National Guardsman and have your laptop prodded by a volunteer Mormon housewife. At worst you would have to remove certain items of clothing, walk through an X-ray machine, demonstrate any technology about your person and submit your wallet to violation by a crew-cut conscript.

These processes took time. A lot of time.

'I tried to file my own tax return. And look what it did to my hair!'

From KSLTV

Argh.

'Where am I?'

'Salt Lake City.'

'Who's winning?'

'The Utah State National Guard.'

Tuesday. The women's downhill at Snowbasin. My mission – eagerly accepted – to intercept and interview Chemmy Alcott, the pneumatic, charming and brave young blonde who was most of the British women's ski team.

Snowbasin was one of the more distant venues at the Games, a good hour's bus ride from the Main Press Centre. For twenty minutes we ran alongside the perimeter of Hill Air Base, whence came the F16 fighters that were protecting the skies above the Games. The base was the size of an English county, and, or so a local had told me, was the place where the planes of the world's mightiest air force came when they needed their wheels overhauled: a giant military Kwik-Fit.

At last the bus turned away from the runways and up into the mountains, passing through a layer of thin, brownish mist, courtesy of Salt Lake Valley's heavy industries. We parked on a sea of asphalt evidently laid down specially for the Games, then transferred to an ancient yellow school bus which chugged us up a switchback road between towering banks of snow to the arena halfway up the mountain.

The sky was blue, the sun powerful, the snow blinding. Red flags and orange fencing zigzagged up the mountain away from the grandstands at the finish, marking the route the women would take. It looked terrifyingly steep. When Alcott first saw the course, I recalled one of her team-mates remarking, 'She was bricking herself.'

To reach the press centre, I had to cross the road via a tall scaffold bridge. I got to the top of the bridge and had to stop for a rest, feeling suddenly elderly and light-headed: climbing stairs at 10,000 feet really can take your breath away.

The press were housed in a giant marquee with a sloping floor, and here there was bad news. Up at the top of the mountain, the winds were gusty: dangerously so. Like the ski-jumpers before them, the downhillers did not fancy being deflected into the upper reaches of a pine tree. The event was delayed; then delayed again. The Sports Editor was keen to know what I proposed to do if, as seemed likely, Chemmy stood me up. He pointed out, politely, that there was a 900-word hole in the newspaper that needed to be filled in precisely one hour's time.

'Hackl,' I said.

'I beg your pardon?'

'Georg Hackl. Iron man of the luge. Seeking, as we speak, to win his fourth consecutive Olympic gold medal by travelling down an ice chute at 80 miles an hour wearing a suit like a giant condom.'

'Great,' the Sports Editor said. 'Can you get there?'

No. Hackl was competing at the Utah Olympic Park, and the only way of getting there would be to take a bus down the mountain, a bus to the press centre in Salt Lake City, a bus to the UOP, and another bus up *that* mountain, by which time the lugers would be not only done and dusted but boozed and bedded too.

'No, I can't. But I can probably rustle something up for you. Just find a picture of Hackl. He's got a big moustache, wears lederhosen and drinks frothy beer from a stein.'

'Where's he from?'

'Berchtesgarten.' Well, where do you think? Brentford? Busy, busy, busy.

I tuned a nearby television set to the satellite-feed coverage of the luge. There was no commentary – the various national broadcasters add their own – and I found myself muttering my own description of the action.

'Bloke in a big condom. Not Hackl. Bugger. Bloke in a big condom. Not Hackl. Bugger . . .'

At a PC in the centre of the press room I ransacked Info, the Games' computerised reference system, for any mention of luge and Hackl. While the files printed out, I scanned the local and national papers for any preview pieces.

With one eye on the television, I started to type. Thirty minutes to deadline.

The next time I looked up, there were no lugers on the course, just men with brooms. They were still there five minutes later. What was going on?

'Guess they've finished the first runs, taking a break before the second runs,' suggested the languid official at the Snowbasin information desk. 'But I can't say for sure, being as how I'm a ski guy and they're luge guys.'

Spend your life in these mountains and it's easy to lose your sense of urgency.

I sighed, smiled. 'Could you possibly, as a great favour, ring up the luge guys and find out when they plan to start their second runs? It's really rather important to me.'

The ski guy said he would, but then became embroiled

in a lengthy dispute about a ski pass with an Italian photographer. I went back to my laptop. I needed a plan. Here it was: write 900 words vaguely concerned with the topic of luging, and increase their relevance as the opportunity arose. So by deadline there was plenty about jolly Georg, the lager-loving luger, and a paragraph of my interpretation of the silent events at the UOP. I would wait until the office was howling for copy, and perhaps something would show up.

It did: the lugers had finished their coffee and biscuits and were once more hurling themselves down the ice chute. Every passing minute brought us one competitor closer to Hackl's final run. I suggested that the sports desk stop asking when they were going to get my copy and let me get on with writing it, and tapped out two versions of an introduction to the piece, one for a Hackl win and one for a loss.

As he swept across the line – to win only silver – I pressed the button to send the relevant article. For once, the mobile phone plugged into the back of the laptop connected faultlessly with London, and within a minute the email was through. My work here was done.

Michael the barman placed an Amber Ale carefully in front of me, then tucked his tip into the glass jug on the bar, which sprouted dollar bills like a flower arrangement. 'For the wayward girls,' he intoned. 'We must always remember the wayward girls.'

'Amen,' I said.

Michael lit a Marlboro Light. 'I have a concern about these Winter Olympic Games,' he said. 'And my concern is this. I do not believe that they are catering adequately to the afternoon bar audience of America.' He gestured at the television screen, which displayed NBC's coverage of cross-country skiing from Soldier Hollow. The Finns, so far as one could tell, were winning. Then he gestured at his customers. 'Observe such an audience,' Michael suggested.

Three men were seated at the bar with me. Eric, who in theory looked after the Dead Goat's computer system but in fact specialised in beer consumption, was squinting at the *Salt Lake City Tribune*. Jason, a snowboarder from the Salt Lake suburbs, had his eyes screwed shut and was singing along with Bob Dylan on *Highway 61 Revisited*. The unidentified old man in the battered blazer and tie was staring at the ranks of bottles behind the bar and repeating the whispered mantra 'I lost the darn car! Goddam!' as he had since taking up his position forty minutes ago.

'Would you say,' Michael continued, 'that any of these gentlemen were gripped by the action at Soldier Hollow?'

'I would not,' I said. Michael had a way of provoking solemnity. In a former life, one of his colleagues had told me, he had been an attorney-at-law.

'What these Games need,' Michael declared, 'is some competitive aerobics. Aerobics is what the American male expects to see on his afternoon television. Break out the leotards! Make with the high-heeled boots! March the girls to Soldier Hollow! Let them strut their stuff in the snow!'

''Robics,' mumbled Eric through his beard. 'Way to go.'

'One moment high, one moment low? Call 565-MOOD, and let Utah State Hospital help you out.'

From KSL Radio

With the Games half over, and not a sniff of a British medal, the massed hacks – the dirty dozen – descended on the Olympic Village to meet Simon Clegg, the chief executive of the British Olympic Association, and Alex Coomber, the skeleton bobsledder widely reckoned to be our best (our only?) chance of exporting decorative metalwear from Utah.

The Village, in normal times the campus of the University

of Utah, now resembled an army camp, encircled with razor wire, every entrance manned by armed troops. Our bus entered a kind of canvas tunnel, within which a squad of soldiers swarmed all over it, inside and out, with sniffer dogs, mirrors to examine the vehicle's underside and ladders to check the roof. Despite all the precautions, we were not actually being allowed inside the Village itself, which was a press-free zone. We met Clegg and Coomber in a cramped press-conference room in a student boarding house just outside the Village gates.

Clegg is a former army officer who can be extremely good company when he knows that the tape recorders are switched off and the notebooks put away. On duty, he is guarded, defensive, occasionally defiant. Coomber is a serving RAF intelligence officer, when she is not piloting an oversized tea tray face-first down a mountain at 80 mph. She, too, is unlikely to win any awards for loquacity. Her husband, Eric, a Royal Navy officer, looked on, completing the resemblance to GCHQ.

No front pages would be held to accommodate the quotes from Coomber, who was rightly focused on her competition the following weekend rather than our newspapers the next day. Clegg had predicted that these Winter Games would be the most successful for a British team since the Second World War – the target was hardly awesome, anything better than two medals would do – and he was sticking to his guns.

'It can still be done,' Clegg said, back straight, chin out. 'It won't be easy, but it can still be done.'

On the bus back to the press centre, one or two of the journalists were incredulous at Clegg's attitude. One Sunday-tabloid writer, a man never lacking confidence in his own opinions, declared that he had had enough, and would be heading back to London in mid-week. 'Why hang around until next weekend? We're not going to win anything.'

We had certainly had little to celebrate so far. I'd travelled to Park City, a beautiful and trendy resort much favoured by America's lawyers and media executives, to watch Lesley McKenna, a nasally pierced Scot tipped for a medal in the half-pipe snowboarding event. She fell on her bottom and finished seventeenth.

I returned to Snowbasin to watch the lovely Chemmy complete the downhill course – which she did, to her credit, but only in thirty-second position. In the combined event (downhill and slalom) she finished a fine fourteenth, in the giant slalom she was thirtieth, and in the super giant slalom she was twenty-eighth. Why Olympic skiers had to try so many different ways of getting from the top of the mountain to the bottom remained beyond me.

Our ski-jumper failed to qualify. (But he was Canadian, anyway.)

Mark Hatton, the brave luger I'd met in Norway, didn't rattle Hackl.

We didn't have an ice-hockey team.

Hammy McMillan, the curling hotelier from Stranraer, had been one of the British banker bets. Out at the Ice Sheet in Ogden, he had started confidently, but his form faded away, and so did any hope of qualifying for the semifinals. Rhona Martin and her team of female curlers had lost four matches in the opening rounds, and seemed doomed.

Good news was harder to find than a Mormon bartender. I went in search of divine inspiration.

It had been widely assumed, when the Winter Olympics were awarded to Salt Lake City, that the Mormon Church would exploit the occasion with a massive recruiting drive. More than half the population of Utah are Mormons, and only slightly less than half of the population of Salt Lake City. The Church is the dominant landowner in the state and the city, and its influence on the region's business and political communities is immense. Utah's Governor, two US senators and three US congressmen are Mormons. The chief executive of the Games, Mitt Romney, personified Mormon excellence: white, neat, rich and married with lots of children.

Mormons are members of the Church of Jesus Christ of Latter-Day Saints, or the LDS Church, to give it a snappier title. But what do they believe, exactly? I consulted the copy of the Book of Mormon kindly left in my hotel room by the Church. The texts in the book, originally inscribed on golden plates, were supposedly discovered by the church's founder, Joseph E. Smith, with some help from an angel called Moroni (I am holding out against the cheap gag here), on a mountain in New York State in 1827. They tell the story of America in biblical times, and pretty heavy going it is too. Traditional Mormon teaching relied on these texts and the recorded wisdom of Smith as God's latter-day prophet. The early Mormons were chased from state to state for a quarter of a century before finally arriving in what was to become Utah and establishing Salt Lake City in 1847.

Mormons have a reputation for being anti-fun, but polygamy – one lucky man taking multiple wives – used to be a central tenet of the religion. It was formally abandoned in 1890 (though there are said to be 50,000 members of polygamist families currently resident in the state), and partly as a result Utah was granted full US statehood in 1896.

The priesthood was opened to blacks as recently as 1978, and other aspects of the faith reflect conservative values: dress and act soberly, be courteous at all times. Male missionaries are called Elders, females Sisters, which tells you something about the hierarchy of the sexes. The Church claims eleven million members worldwide, a little less than half of them in the US, and also says that it is growing fast, mainly because Mormons have lots and lots of children. By the end of the twenty-first century, they reckon, theirs will be the world's second largest religion after Catholicism.

The current prophet, a sprightly nonagenerian called Gordon B. Hinckley, spoke of the Winter Games as a confirmation of a prophecy by his predecessor, Brigham Young, that 'kings and emperors and the noble and wise of the earth' would one day come to the Salt Lake Valley. Young had not specified that the world's media would also be in attendance, but they were, and the modern Church was not about to miss the chance of some valuable PR work.

But they would operate, Prophet Hinckley had decreed, by stealth. Visitors would arrive expecting to be ambushed by missionaries – young Mormons are expected to spend two years abroad spreading the faith – only to find the lips of the faithful sealed. During the Winter Olympics, Salt Lake City was the only place on the planet where you could guarantee that no Mormon would come knocking on your door. This was certainly frustrating for the faithful, who could sense needy souls all around them, and a little frustrating for the visitors, too, who if they were anything like me had been hoping for a healthy dose of Mormon weirdness while in town.

Was it true that good Mormons stored a year's worth of food in their kitchens in expectation of the end of the world? That you could convert to Mormonism after you were dead? That Mormon men wear underwear of a peculiar design?*

Eventually – in line, I suspect, with the expectations of the cunning Prophet Hinckley – I went to try to find out.

Temple Square is the geographical centre of Salt Lake City and the spiritual centre of the Mormon Church. The temple itself, built by pioneering church members between 1853 and 1893, is a great grey oblong topped with Disneyland

* Yes; yes; don't know. I couldn't bear to ask the Sisters in Temple Square (I am pretty sure that the concept of men in underwear had never occured to them) and I never found a garrulous Elder. They don't drink, you see.

finial spires, on one of which perches a golden statue of the Angel Moroni. (I can't resist it any more: in Salt Lake City, it's a compliment to call someone Moronic). Strikingly floodlit at night, the temple was the symbol of the city and the Games, and was the only building in Salt Lake City that visitors were desperate to see. Unfortunately, non-Mormons are not allowed inside.

'It is not a matter of secrecy,' said Sister Finkels, one of my guides. 'Soon after a Mormon temple is finished, visitors are welcome to look around. But then it is dedicated, and after that it is for the use of Church members only.' And she smiled, and my objections faded away.

I am sure that such a worthy body would never stoop to such cynical tactics, but one could not help but notice that most of the Mormon guides operating in Temple Square at Games time were young women, and that a high proportion of them were startlingly attractive. Sister Finkels was from Belgium, and, like her German colleague Sister Kleine, was thrilled to be serving her two years as a missionary at Church headquarters. Sister Finkels had long, jet-black hair, eyes as blue as the Snowbasin sky and a delicate, pale complexion. It is the kind of look that heathen women spend hundreds of pounds to achieve with cosmetics, but the Belgian Mormon was au naturel.

The Sisters and their half-dozen visitors – myself and five elderly, silent Americans – walked first to the Seagull Monument, a statue that commemorates a Mormon miracle. According to Sister Finkels, the Mormon pioneers were pioneering away in the Salt Lake Valley when a swarm of locusts descended and started to eat all their crops. No sooner had the locusts tucked in than a flock of seagulls arrived and ate all the locusts. The Mormons, Sister Finkels said, were full of joy and raised a statue to their beaky deliverers.

As a miracle, this seemed to me somewhat low-key. Seagulls are, after all, indigenous to the United States, and very partial to a nice plump insect. If, on a miraculous scale, the parting of the Red Sea scored a perfect ten, I would rate the intervention of the seagulls at about 0.5, close to the area where miracles stop being miracles and start to become jolly good luck. Of course, I was thinking, had the seagulls instead been puffins, say, or ostriches, we would be pushing in to the high sevens. I was about to point this out to Sister Finkels when I realised that the group had walked on without me.

I caught up with them in the Assembly Hall, an un-assuming little building that had been the first church in all of Utah when it opened in 1877. Sister Finkels was com-menting on the quality of the woodwork while I boggled at the sheer youth of Utah's ancient monuments. The next Mormon missionaries to ring my doorbell in London can expect a tour of my house, which is fifty years older than their Hall.

Next we moved to the Tabernacle, home to the famous Mormon Tabernacle Choir and the world's finest acoustic. 'If you stand at the back of the hall,' Sister Kleine said, 'you can hear a pin drop.' We stood at the back of the hall. On the stage, 170 feet away, Sister Finkels dropped three pins, quite audibly, and a small nail for comparison. Very literal people, Mormons.

We saw the Family History Center, a world-leading genealogy institute whose computers hold the family trees of millions of people: very convenient for locating suitable ancestors for conversion, I suggested, but Sister Finkels would not be drawn.

The tour concluded in a kind of Mormon-Christian art gallery, with huge kitschy canvases of Old Testament scenes and a model of ancient Jerusalem. We were herded up a long spiral ramp to a sort of planetarium where a giant white statue of Christ, called the Christus, stood beneath a starry dome. A Sister stepped forward and, in the manner of an air hostess, requested that there should be no flash photography or talking during the following narration.

This was a tape recording, and emphasised heavily the central role of Jesus in the Mormon faith, as if the statue were somehow too subtle for most visitors. Then Sister Finkels and Sister Kleine ushered us out of the chamber towards a flight of stairs. As we went I noticed that another gallery – not one we had seen – led away from the Christus chamber. The paintings on the walls were more naturalistic than those downstairs and showed contemporary people, doing . . . what? There was another statue, too, of someone in modern dress . . .

'This way please,' said Sister Kleine, quite firmly.

Outside, Sister Finkels handed me a card to commemorate my visit. It had the Church's website address under a picture of the Temple.

'I don't suppose you'd care for a beer in the Dead Goat Saloon?' I asked.

'I don't suppose I would,' said Sister Finkels.

Cisco was the regular bus driver on the shuttle from the hotel to the Main Press Centre. Silver-haired and mahogany-skinned, he was from New York, and a kind of one-man antidote to Mormon conformity. 'Me, I'm a veteran,' he would say, guiding his vehicle up the on-ramp to the freeway. 'I done two tours. One in 'Nam, one in the funny farm.'

Which was tougher, Cisco?

'The funny farm. No contest. See, in 'Nam you knew who the enemy were.'

Where's home, Cisco?

'I was brought up in New York, in the Bowery. Know the Bowery? Chief export industry there is bums. I remember one time when I was a kid sitting up on a fire escape in Alphabet City with a bum named Jake. Jake, he liked to bomb rats with bottles. Wait till the little guy crept out far enough, then let go with three bottles. You didn't have to hit them, see, the flying glass would do it. State he was in. Man, that rat was killed good . . .'

It was advisable to breakfast lightly before boarding Cisco's bus.

Connie, who drove us up to the UOP for the skeleton event, ensured a more wholesome journey. She was a native Utahn, born and raised a Mormon, and no more likely to bottle a rat than she was to break the speed limit or vote Democrat. I marvelled at her self-control as her Jeep-driving compatriots cut us up on the freeway, then barged into our line as we edged into the snowy parking lot.

'Don't you ever get cross?' I asked, as the other journalists disembarked.

'Sure,' she said. 'But it doesn't do to get riled when you're driving a bus.'

'What do you say when you get annoyed? Is it true that you're not allowed to swear?'

'Oh, well,' she giggled. 'We can swear in our own way. When I'm off-duty, now, I might go talk to some of the other drivers and say, like "Out on that freeway, there's folk don't know what the H.E. double hockey-sticks they're doing".'

It took me a moment to work it out. 'Gosh,' I said, hoping that was not offensive.

'If I really disagree with someone, I might say they're full of manure,' Connie admitted. 'But I'd have to be real riled.'

'I bet you would. But what if the worst happened, what if . . .' I was lost for a scenario.

'What if I dropped a bowl of soup?'

'Yes.' Of course. The worst that could happen to a Mormon mom.

'Well, if there were none but family around I guess I

might come out with . . .' She leant close, and whispered: 'Oh fudge!'

'Mindy, do you regard yourself as a living miracle?' 'Why yes, Bob, I do. How about you?'

From KBYUTV

A gentle blizzard enveloped the Olympic mountain, but skeleton bobbers are hardy souls and there was no danger of abandonment. This was it: the big day for British hopes. Plucky little Alex Coomber, the RAF's own blonde bomb-shell, favourite for gold in the first ever Olympic women's skeleton event. Hold the front page!

Or at least a portion of page twelve of the sports section, if you please. Skeleton is obscure, let's be honest, even in Winter Olympic terms. My experience of the sport was limited to watching Philip Pope descend half the course in Lillehammer; but even that gave me an edge over most of the journalists present. We are essentially talking about riding a tea tray face-first down a mountain, something that has always appealed to the British sense of sporting lunacy (think of those daffy toffs on the Cresta Run) but has never been a huge draw in terms of television coverage or casual spectators.

To give the sliders their due, it is certainly spectacular. The tea trays, which are actually carbon-fibre platforms a yard long and a body's width, sit on narrow steel runners and the sliders, prone, nose two inches above the ice, steer by subtly shifting their weight. At the bottom of the steep, sinuous course, they're doing 8o mph. As in bobsled and luge, the knack is to avoid contact with the walls of the ice chute: every scrape costs time. The skeleton sliders have an added incentive: if a bobsled driver makes a mistake, it is his craft that clouts the ice. A skeleton slider, riding the bare bones of a bobsled, whacks the wall with a shoulder or, if they get it really wrong, with their head.

No such dramas from Coomber on her first run, which put her in third place. There was a pause between rounds to allow the course workers to clear fresh snow from the track. Up in the press room, the British corps, with deadlines looming, hammered at their laptops, writing ninety per cent of their articles but leaving space for an introductory paragraph and a conclusion to be added as the last slider crossed the line.

Turning over in my mind alternative descriptions for Coomber (flying spy, pocket rocketeer, Captain Plummet, etc.), I glanced up and out of the window. On a hillock just outside the Olympic compound stood what looked like a rickety garden shed sporting a large brown television aerial. Then the shed moved, shambling through the snow.

I grabbed the arm of a passing Mormon matron, who was distributing result sheets.

'Excuse me. Am I hallucinating, or is that shed moving?'

She followed the line of my pointing finger, and burst out laughing.

'That shed,' she said, 'is a moose. Three of them live just around here.'

The moose looked up, ruminatively working on a mouthful of frozen grass. His lifestyle seemed unaffected by the sudden appearance on his doorstep of 10,000 people and the world's media. But then he hadn't had to go through security screening. I wondered if al-Qaeda had considered the concept of a suicide moose.

Coomber was her usual fast, consistent self, and as she hopped off the sled at the bottom of the second run, husband Eric ran across to hug and congratulate her. The leader board showed her in first position, with only two Americans left to race. She was guaranteed bronze, and had every chance of gold.

But what was this? The Americans' runs were delayed, while track workers once again swept the course clear of fresh snow. This was patently unfair. Snow builds up under the runners of a skeleton, making it more difficult to steer with accuracy: Coomber's main rivals were going to have a clear advantage.

Which they exploited. First Lee Ann Parsley (the curly-topped variety, I noted) went faster, then Tristan Gale breezed down the mountain quicker still. There were mutterings of discontent from the British corner of the press room while the Americans, for the umpteenth time at the Games, hollered and whooped and high-fived.

But Coomber looked happy enough on the podium, and as we tapped out our intros and payoffs, the Brit Pack cheered up too. A medal!

The moose munched on, seemingly unaware of the scale of this magnificent British achievement.

Coomber was presented to the press later that afternoon at the Main Press Centre, where she stubbornly but good-naturedly refused to accuse the Americans of bare-faced cheating, much to the disgruntlement of our small tabloid contingent. They cheered up when a trip across the road to the Dead Goat was proposed, and by artful jockeying for position I became the first man in the saloon's thirty-five-year history to sign an Olympic medal-winner into its crepuscular premises.

'Hail!' boomed Michael from behind the bar, brandishing a bottle of champagne. 'Hail to the all-conquering British lugette!'

One of the hacks whispered to him.

'Skeletonette!' he corrected himself. 'Whatever.'

Soon everyone was having a jolly time, with the exception, it seemed to me, of the reason for the celebrations.

'Are you OK?' I asked Coomber.

'Not really.' She put down her half-empty glass. 'I haven't had a drink for eighteen months, I don't smoke and this place . . . does. I don't feel very well.'

Husband Eric appeared instantly to chaperone her outside for some fresh air, while the journalists attacked another bottle. We'd been training for a medal-winning session for nearly a fortnight.

Back at the hotel that evening, I nibbled goldfish and watched NBC. The women's skeleton did not feature massively in their Games coverage. Instead they were talking about the story that had taken the Winter Olympics from the back pages of American newspapers to the front, and tripled the television viewing figures. In an ideal world, this story would have concerned a multiple gold medallist or teenage sensation, a plucky comeback from illness or injury, or at the very least a snowboarding Mormon minister.

But this was America, where interest in the Winter Olympics is traditionally stirred by just one phenomenon: sleaze on ice.

In the run-up to the 1994 Games, wholesome, pretty, all-American ice skater Nancy Kerrigan was whacked in the knee by a hired thug. Her nasty-looking blonde compatriot and competitor, Tonya Harding, denied that she had commissioned the assault but confessed to helping to cover it up. Justice prevailed. Kerrigan recovered to win a silver medal in Lillehammer and made every American front page, while Harding was banned from the sport for life, and earned further notoriety when her ex-husband released an explicit videotape of the couple's wedding night. Viewing figures for the Lillehammer skating events were, predictably, stratospheric.

The Salt Lake City Games needed something similar to ignite the interest of the average American household, and the pairs ice-dance competition provided it. This is the discipline – I find the word preferable to sport in this context – at which Jayne Torvill and Christopher Dean excelled. A discipline in which fashion sense, musical taste and cosmetic aesthetics became stuck in the mid-1970s, and in which bitchiness and skullduggery are never far from the slippery surface.

The heroes and villains of the Salt Lake City drama fitted a time-warp Cold War scenario. The good guys were a wholesome Canadian couple, clean-cut David Pelletier and his winsome companion, Jamie Sale (a girl, or so we were reliably informed). The bogeymen were the Russians, Anton Sikharulidze and Elena Berezhnaya. The catalyst, the *femme fatale*, was the French member of the judging panel, a fur-festooned lady *d'un certain age* named Marie-Reine Le Gougne.

Here's what happened:

The Canadians – diminutive, sweet brunette and hunky lumberjack – skated a charming routine that seemed to the audience and the expert commentators well-nigh perfect. The Russians – bottle blonde and lounge lizard – performed a routine notable for blatant wobbles and at least one bottom-on-the-ice blunder. The judges, by a margin of 5–4, awarded the gold medal to the Russians. Pandemonium. At the medal ceremony, the Russians looked relieved, the Canadians peeved. The crowd booed and whistled relentlessly, delighted to have such a blatant injustice to condemn.

'Someone has nobbled the judges!' was the popular cry, and Le Gougne was identified as the nobbliest of the lot. From the sanctuary of her hotel suite, she admitted that she had favoured the Russians, under pressure from the French Skating Federation boss, who was expecting subsequent favours from the Russian judges.

The networks piled in, and shortly an anchor-man had coined the inevitable: 'Skategate'. Accusations and counter-accusations flew across the airwaves. The Russians had gone to ground. Le Gougne was filmed emerging into her hotel lobby, thinking better of it and scuttling back into the lift. Sale and Pelletier were shuttled from studio to studio, and for a queue of chat-show hosts reprised their virtuous-sadness routine.

Proof that the Games of Salt Lake City had arrived in the national consciousness: Jay Leno, host of the nationally celebrated *Tonight Show*, was doing Skategate gags.

The shabby scandal raised the profile of the Games in a way that no success story ever could, and while the IOC president, the latter-day-saintly Jacques Rogge, quickly orchestrated a satisfactory solution (duplicate gold medals for the Canadians, bans for the conniving French) and expressed his dismay at the affair, secretly he must have looked at the viewing figures and smirked.

'Break out from the diet of doom and get yourself a snack of good news!'

From KANN Radio

More rumblings from the ice – this time positive vibrations – were emanating from the rink at Ogden, where the British women's curling team (entirely comprising Scots) had redis-covered their best form, won three matches on the trot and a place in the final. Another medal was guaranteed. Could we dream of gold for Rhona Martin and her team of broom-wielding housewives?

Back home, apparently, millions had sat up into the wee hours watching the semi-final. The final, against the mighty Swiss, would not start until 10 p.m., British time. Taking my place in the press seats at one end of the rink, I imagined the nation gathering in front of their television sets, Horlicks in hand. Improbably – unprecedentedly – a place on the front page was being held for my impressions of the final, to be transmitted the moment the last stone had come to rest.

I had arrived at a professional pinnacle – albeit a pretty bizarre one – and might have felt quite proud, were it not for the fact that I knew next to nothing about the subject in front of me. The nation at home had watched a semi with the benefit of expert television commentary. I had never seen a curling contest, and I had no commentary at all.

I saw ladies with spherical boulders into which handles had been inserted; others with brooms, all moving in a seemingly choreographed manner towards targets painted on the ice. I knew where I was – at a suburban ice rink on the fringes of a desert, 5,000 feet up in the heart of the American Midwest – but who was winning? And how could you tell?

I spotted a gap on the press benches next to a familiar figure in a scarlet Team GB anorak and, stooping so as not to distract the curlers, dived into it. Philip Pope had not only ridden a skeleton bobsled halfway down a Norwegian mountain. He had also, I happened to know, watched a fair bit of curling, and had, himself, curled. I shamelessly grilled him, nodding wisely as if each revelation merely confirmed what I had long suspected. By the time the scores were tied at three apiece, I had picked up enough to understand that the situation had become critical. The British skipper, Martin, a determined-looking Glaswegian blonde, had one 'stone' left, and needed to knock a Swiss stone out of the way before settling her stone close to the centre of the 'house', or target. This would decide the destiny of the gold medal. As she consulted with her sweepers and squinted down the ice to line up her shot, the crowd ceased their speculative murmuring and the rink fell quiet.

My mobile phone thrummed silently in my jacket pocket.

'Hello?' I whispered.

'Hello,' said my friend Eliza, sitting at home in Shepherd's Bush, 5,000 miles away. 'You just picked your nose.'

I looked up, and saw the television camera's red light wink at me.

'How very observant of you,' I said. 'Could we talk later?'

'Bye,' said Eliza. 'Don't do it again.'

Martin's stone was on its way down the ice, chaperoned by the Scottish sweepers. The hush built gradually into a roar from the British fans as the two stones kissed, and . . .

Jubilation. The victorious curlers leapt into the air, waving their brooms like extras in a Harry Potter film, then scampered across the ice to embrace their Team GB colleagues in the grandstand.

A gold medal, I scribbled, resisting the urge to add an exclamation mark. Britain's first at a Winter Olympics since Torvill and Dean in 1984. I counted up my words and rang the newspaper's copytakers, who sit and take dictation in a call centre somewhere near Leeds.

'It's Andrew Baker in Salt Lake City. I've got three hundred and fifty words on the curling.'

'Smashing, chook. We've all been watching on the telly.'

'Copy starts . . .'

It was a marvellous climax to the Games for the British contingent, all the more satisfying because the curlers proved to be as charming as they had been cool. We asked them how they would enjoy or exploit their new-found fame: they just wanted to talk about their families back at home. Families, I thought. I've got one of those. I need some presents.

The first thing I watch out for on arrival in any foreign city is a toy shop, and I had noticed a branch of Toys 'Я' Us close to one of the designated media hotels on the outskirts of the city. The next morning, I hopped on an Olympic shuttle bus. En route, at eleven o'clock – 6 p.m. in the UK – I called home for my daily fix of that most bittersweet of indulgences, the voices of distant children.

'Daddy,' said Lucy, who was now four and three-quarters.

'Yes, Lucy.'

'Daddy.'

'Yes, Lucy.'

'Daddy. Um, where are you?'

'I'm in America. Do you know where that is?'

'America.' She thought for a moment. 'Big hole in the ground? Smoke coming out of it?'

'Ah. No. That's a different bit of America. I'm in Salt Lake City.'

'Have you swum in it? Does it taste nasty?'

'No, you can't swim in it. It's not deep enough. It's just lots of dry salt.'

'Good for crisps, though.'

'Good for crisps. Lucy, could I say goodnight to Emily?'

'Yup. Emily? Do you want to say goodnight to Daddy?'

Emily (three and a quarter): 'Noooooh!'

At Toys 'Я' Us I spent an hour searching fruitlessly for Thomas the Tank Engine among the Transblasters, Battlezoids and Hammernukes that shape the junior American character. Thomas is such an innocent, trusting engine, with his apple cheeks, guileless smile and cheery whistle. Ten minutes among the local toys here and he'd be a pile of bullet-riddled scrap.

It was a Saturday, the only day of the week on which I knew I wouldn't have anything to write. But such is the dearth of entertainment in SLC that I soon found myself back in the Main Press Centre, wandering the streets of that strange indoor town. The MPC was constructed inside a convention centre, the Salt Palace, which occupied three blocks of Salt Lake City a snowball's throw from Temple Square. During the Games it hosted 9,000 journalists and the 1,000 support staff needed to keep them fed, informed and secure. It had a Main Street half a mile long where you could eat burgers, bagels and burritos, drink shakes, smoothies and sodas and buy anything from toothpaste to a facsimile edition of my newspaper. Branching off Main Street were highways with names like Attitude Avenue, which led to vast barns partitioned to house the offices of the *Yomuiri Shimbun*, the *Corriere della Serra* and the *Cleveland Plain Dealer*.

Many journalists – especially those attempting to cover a number of sports at one time – arrived at the MPC before dawn and left after dark, never seeing Salt Lake City in daylight, still less the magnificent mountains around it. One or two overly cost-conscious types made the MPC their home, sleeping on benches, shaving in the toilets and scavenging by day for blank hotel receipts. Dave would have been proud of them.

I didn't like the place: the conditioned air, the atmosphere of tacky impermanence, the absence of weather, the unsmiling, crew-cut, machine-gun-wielding soldiers. I was fortunate in rarely having to write about more than one sport every day, and I felt sorry for those who had come to see the Winter Olympics and found themselves sentenced to hard labour in the Salt Palace. But I had to concede that the Bullpen – in a corner of which the British contingent based themselves – was a useful place in which to write. Six hundred journalists shared a room the size of two football pitches, equipped with giant television screens, information system computers and ranks of pigeon-holes for official results.

Having nothing better to do, I took a seat in the Bullpen to watch the men's slalom skiing event, in which there was one last, slim chance of a British medal. It was just as well that I decided to hang around: an extraordinary story was beginning, a tale of joy and despair that would run on through the summer and conclude only when the snows returned again to Utah in the autumn.

The course at Deer Valley was abominable, a sheet of ridged and treacherous ice, and one by one the form-book favourites for the event were tumbling off their skis and out of contention. Some of the less experienced skiers, spooked by what was happening to their elders and betters, became overcautious and slow. But these are not character traits applicable to Alain Baxter, the motorbiking maverick from Aviemore.

Baxter is known among the skiing fraternity as The Highlander, and it is a measure of his fearlessness that he has been known to ski through thick powder snow in a kilt. Unable to wear his national dress in Olympic competition, Baxter had instead had a cross of St Andrew dyed on to his close-cropped hair.

Hold on a moment, BOA Chef de Mission Simon Clegg had said. This is the British Olympic team, not the Scottish. The cross goes.

But it wouldn't. All manner of shampoos, conditioners, detergents and bleaches were applied but still the stubborn hairy flag remained.

Right, Clegg decreed. Fill in the white stripes.

So it was that Britain's third medal of the Winter Olympics was won by a tearaway tough with a blue rinse of which Maggie Thatcher would have been proud. Baxter flung himself down the course with frightening commitment, scattering a hail of ice chips in his wake, and recorded the fastest time of the day. Two others would later go a smidgen quicker, but The Highlander had his medal.

There was more champagne in the Dead Goat that night, a venue that suited Baxter rather better than it had Coomber. As the massed Brits drank his health, none of us, including, I am convinced, Baxter himself, could have known that the samples he had given before climbing on to the medal podium would test positive for a banned substance.

Amphetamines, said the IOC. A nasal spray to clear my breathing, said Baxter. Tough, said the IOC. A positive test is all the proof we need.

They took away his medal, gave it to his friend, Benny Raich, the Austrian who had finished fourth. The saga continued through the summer as Baxter appealed unsuccessfully to the IOC and then to the Court of Arbitration in Sport. He never did get his medal back.

That was my last night in the Dead Goat Saloon, and Michael the barman and I had a little unfinished business. It seemed he had seen on the Internet an article I had written about Coomber's visit to the bar, in which I had, perhaps unwisely, emphasised his physical presence.

I was playing pool very badly in the upstairs saloon when Michael loomed in the doorway. He held up a large fist and advanced towards me. The other players stood back.

'This,' he said, bringing up his bunched knuckles to within an inch of my nose, 'is "a ham", right?'

'Erm. I may have described it as such. Inaccurately.'

The fist stayed put.

'And this "beefy" stuff, huh? Masculinity, huh? Power, huh? Everything but intellect, right?'

'I . . . did not mean to convey that impression.'

He lowered the fist, revealing his black eyes beneath deeply ironic brows. I almost preferred the fist.

'You did not mean to convey that impression.'

I shook my head.

'Let me tell you something,' Michael said, and leaned in closer. 'Brightly though the laurel blooms, it withers quickly on the vine.'

I couldn't think how to reply to that. So I didn't.

'Know what?' Michael said. 'I hope the next championships they send you to is in Bogota.' But then he grinned. 'What time do you fly in the morning, Andrew?'

'Five-thirty. Pretty early.'

'Well, I'd love to come and see you off,' Michael said.

'Let's say, if I'm not at the gate five minutes before take-off, I won't be coming. You can let the plane go.'

He never showed.

Conclusion: There's life in the Dead Goat yet.

Epilogue

In the summer of 2002 the Commonwealth Games came home, which meant that I could as well. It was a pleasant change to be covering a major international sporting event in my native clime. Manchester is distant from London in many ways – communication with taxi drivers would be no easier than it had been in Malaysia – but the weather is just as lousy, and at least I could ring home without setting my alarm clock. Location aside, there were other differences between Kuala Lumpur and Manchester: there was not a whiff of tear gas to be scented outside my hotel, there were no tropical downpours (just dreary drizzle), and as far as I could ascertain the Deputy Prime Minister was not in jail on sodomy charges.

Manchester's population had already contracted Games Fever when I arrived the afternoon before the opening ceremony. Stilt-walkers, fire-eaters, a Punjabi dance troupe and assorted *Coronation Street* starlets attempted to attract the attention of passers-by in Albert Square. The local evening paper dedicated its first four pages to the coming spectacular, relegating a minor news story ('Giant meteorite on collision course with Earth') to page five.

I managed to curb my enthusiasm as I scuttled from venue to venue. The Sports Editor was in town, so conspicuous conscientiousness was in order. 'I've been to the velodrome,'

I would puff into the phone, 'and I've done the pole-vaulter and the Aussie swimmers. Where next?' Good boy, I kept expecting the Sports Editor to say. You see that rhythmic gymnast? Fetch!

I was pursuing a taciturn Scottish sprinter through the interview zone at the athletics stadium one evening when it suddenly struck me that I had yet to pay a visit to the city's most celebrated sporting venue. Over the previous four years I had seen some impressive arenas: the Stade de France, Kuala Lumpur's Bukit Jalil edifice, Osaka's Nagai, Stadium Australia and the pool room at the Dead Goat Saloon. But with Wembley now so much demolition dust, Manchester was home to the daddy of all sports stadiums: Old Trafford.

So the next time I had a spare couple of hours I caught a cab to the Theatre of Dreams to see if I could sneak a peek backstage. I had a pint of foamy John Smith's in The Trafford, the huge and surprisingly civilised pub over the road from the stadium. I had expected the place to be a shrine to the United heroes of the past, but instead of pictures of Bryan Robson and Eric Cantona and Duncan Edwards there were sepia photographs of 'Handicap Day at the Old Trafford Golf Club, 1903' and a 'Donkey auctioned for £350 in aid of the Farmers' Red Cross, 1904'. Three hundred and fifty quid? In 1904? You could have bought United's squad for that, and still had enough left over for a carrot for the donkey.

I walked over the road to Matt Busby Way, past a red-and-white off licence, fish-and-chip shop, newsagent and a burger joint which among other delights offered a 'foot-long hot dog', for people who can't afford a stretch limo but can just about run to a stretch sausage.

There used to be a huge official souvenir shop next to the South Stand, but it had closed down. Times must be hard, I was thinking, when I noticed that the former shop had been adapted into offices. 'Manchester United Merchandising' said the sign on the door, and through the window I could see marketeers hunched over laptops, tweaking designs for Roy Keane door-stops, Ryan Giggs bibs ('for little dribblers') and comedy Fergie red noses. But where was the shop?

Behind me. And it wasn't a shop any more: it was a superstore.

An entire grandstand underpinned by aisles of replica shirts. Here were the true foundations of Old Trafford: not concrete, but cotton. And not just shirts: socks, shoes, knickers, nighties, hats; romper suits, swimsuits . . . It was like M&S after an outbreak of scarlet fever. Fans wandered the corridors of cloth in careless rapture, piling their baskets high: Japanese fans, American fans, German fans – a veritable United Nations of football consumers all contributing to the music that most characterises this stadium. Not the chanting of supporters, the ringing of tills.

On exiting the superstore I found that I had accidentally attached myself to a train of people in suits walking away from the shop and towards the South Stand. I shook off my feelings of retail rage and noticed that the group were sporting Commonwealth Games accreditation badges. I had one of those, too. I tagged along.

Up some stairs at the back of the South Stand was a large conference room called the Europa Suite, decorated with pictures of United triumphs in European matches, and crammed with people in suits drinking cups of coffee. Not my sort of scene at all. But not a bad pretext for some more exploration. I edged across the room, bumping and apologising and smiling sweetly at anyone who seemed puzzled by my presence, and finally escaped through a door on the far side. There was a door to a Gents' toilet here (a good excuse if I were to be apprehended) and a corridor running the length of the stand. The brightly lit white walls were lined with photographs of United players enjoying moments of exultation. Some of the captions were misspelled, I couldn't help noticing: Dwight Yorke and Lee Sharpe, for instance, were both missing their terminal letters. Imagine the horrified headlines: 'Madchester United: Players Drop E's in Corridor at Old Trafford'.

Keeping a pedantic eye on the picture captions, I made my way down the passage, through another door and then had a choice: stairs going down, or door straight on. I went through the door straight on, and found more stairs going down, into a kind of deserted reception area: flowers on a table, more pictures on the walls. All the doors leading off the reception were marked with forbidding notices: 'Staff'; 'No Unauthorised Admittance'; 'Private'; 'Vituperative Scotsmen Only'. Never mind, I thought, they are probably all locked anyway. I leaned curiously against a double set of white doors and, to my surprise, they gave way.

I was in a bar: plainly furnished, grille down over the counter. Not a public bar, I thought: too smart. Nor yet a corporate entertaining venue: too intimate. Then I thought again about the geography of Old Trafford, the location of the tunnel, the benches and therefore the dressing rooms, in the South Stand . . . my goodness. This must be the Players' Bar.

What tales these walls could tell. What sweat, tears and lager must have fallen on this carpet. Surprisingly – given that I don't come from Manchester – I am not a Manchester United supporter, but I could feel the power of mythic forces gathering around me, whiffing slightly of stale beer and embrocation. How many sports writers had dreamed of standing in this spot, trading insights and grievances with the stars in a mood of post-match euphoria? How my colleagues would envy me now, I thought, if only the room was not completely deserted.

There was one more door I had to try. It opened on to

a bare concrete hallway, from which a coarsely carpeted corridor sloped down, and then up . . . on to the pitch. In the footsteps of giants, where buttocks mightier than mine have clenched in fear, I emerged into the daylight, to the stupefying roar of tens of thousands of fans.

Ranks of scarlet seats stared blankly down at me from the mountainous stands. I turned full circle with a broad grin, acknowledging the cacophonous cheers that only I could hear, then turned right, right again and up a short flight of steps. I chose Sir Alex Ferguson's regular seat. It was comfortable. I had arrived.

Never mind the hours in departure lounges, the synthetic hotels, the dreary press conferences: this was what sports writing was about. The chance to empathise with greatness, to perch upon the throne, share the view from the top. I started to compose the opening sentences of a triumphal autobiography, charting my progress from clueless football hack to the manager's seat at Old Trafford. I knew where I was now, and who was winning. I felt the power, felt a flush of righteous indignation, felt a surge of pure adrenalin in my veins . . .

Felt the groundsman's hand on my shoulder.

Acknowledgements

Many thanks to David Welch, the Sports Editor of the *Daily Telegraph*, for giving me a fantastic job and the resources with which to pursue it.

Thanks also to Martin Smith, my commissioning editor at the *Telegraph*, not only for his patience with my whinges when on assignment, but his generous help in reading and considerably improving this book. The remaining mistakes are all my own work.

To Beatrix Miller CBE, a cherished family friend, a wise mentor and a laser-eyed editor, for her encouragement and invaluable assistance.

To my agent, David Smith, who coaxed the book into being, and to Tristan Jones, my editor at Yellow Jersey, for his limitless advice and enthusiasm. And to Sarah Edworthy snd Robert Philip, for well-timed empathy.

To Simon Kelner, Neil Morton, Ben Clissitt, Richard Askwith, Hugh Bateson and Richard Williams for all their help in attempting to turn me into a sports writer.

To the many colleagues at the *Telegraph* who have helped me to travel and write, and rescued me from horrible hotels, factual errors and grammatical howlers. They know who they are (they also know what the mistakes were): I thank them all.

I thank my brother James, and my parents, Richard and Margaret, for their love and support; and my brother- and sister-in-law, Stuart and Kathryn Sanders, for being there for my family when I was so often abroad.

Most importantly of all, I thank my wife and daughters. Travelling the world writing about sport is a wonderful and privileged existence. But nothing beats coming home.